Seeing

moir of
Truth and Courage
from China's Most
Influential Television
Journalist Chai Jing

Translated by Yan Yan and Jack Hargreaves

Astra House ⋀ New York

Interior Photo Credits:
Associated Press: chapter 8
CCTV: chapters 2, 3, 6, 10
Courtesy of author: chapters 5, 11
Wang Jin: chapter 9
Ming Xi: back cover, chapter 4
Wei Chen: chapter 7
Wang Yishu: chapter 1

For information about permission to reproduce selections from this book, please
contact permissions@astrahouse.com.

Astra House
A Division of Astra Publishing House
astrahouse.com
Printed in Canada

Publisher's Cataloging-in-Publication Data:
Names: Chai, Jing, 1976–, author. | Yan, Yan, translator. | Hargreaves,
    Jack, translator.
Title: Seeing : a memoir of truth and courage from China's most influential
    television journalist / Chai Jing ; translated by Yan Yan and Jack Hargreaves.
Description: Includes bibliographical references. | New York, NY: Astra House, 2023.
Identifiers: LCCN: 2021909565 | ISBN: 9781662600678 (hardcover) |
    9781662600685 (ebook)
Subjects: LCSH Chai, Jing, 1976–. | Television journalists—China—Biography. |
    Television personalities—China—Biography. | Journalism—Political aspects—
    China. | Investigative reporting—China. | Freedom of the press—China. |
    Government and the press—China. | Women—China—Biography. | BISAC
    BIOGRAPHY & AUTOBIOGRAPHY / Editors, Journalists, Publishers |
    BIOGRAPHY & AUTOBIOGRAPHY / Cultural, Ethnic & Regional /
    Asian & Asian American | BIOGRAPHY & AUTOBIOGRAPHY / Women
Classification: LCC PN5366.C427 2021 | DDC 079/.51092—dc23

First edition
10 9 8 7 6 5 4 3 2 1

Design by Richard Oriolo
The text is set in Sabon Roman.
The titles are set in Spezia Medium.

To my daughter, who always wants me to tell her a story.

Contents

Seeing

Introduction

When I was four, I always begged my dad to tell me a story before bed.

In 1980, like most families in China, we couldn't afford a TV. The power always went out at night anyway, so I kept a small red candle beside my bed. The blue flame flickered, and there were many dark shadows on the wall. The five of us lived in a room less than twelve meters square, because all my relatives with the surname Chai had been living in this house for three hundred years, dividing it smaller and smaller. The north wind beat the paper windows in the winter. I always begged my dad to tell me a story.

My dad was a nice man. He would say, "Once upon a time, there was a mountain. On the mountain there was a temple. In the temple there was an old monk and a little monk. The little one asked the old one to tell him a story. The old monk said, 'Once upon a time, there was a mountain. On the mountain there was a temple . . .'"

The story circled again and again until it bored me enough to put me asleep. It was the only story my dad knew. I was born in 1976, the year the Cultural Revolution ended, and there wasn't much culture left for people. There were few books in my home, so the only story my dad could offer to his little girl was a fake one with a hollow shell, and a big hole inside.

My mom bought a radio for me when I was sixteen. I found out I could hear broadcasts from Taiwan. Listening to "enemy radio" had been illegal for a long time. One of my father's colleagues had been tortured as a spy in the 1960s, when there was hostility between Taiwan and mainland China, for breaking this law. He ended up cutting his own throat with a razor.

The way the hosts spoke surprised me. They didn't read from a script or talk like official spokespeople. They shared literature, music, plays, and jokes. One time one of them even went out to her balcony and described how beautiful the sunset was. I'd never experienced such a thing in any media before. I learned to make my own tape, telling stories to myself, in my lonely girlhood.

In 1994, while studying at a railway college[1] in Hunan Province, I took one of those tapes to Hunan People's Broadcasting Station to look for a summer job. I was too naïve to know that there was no possibility for a student like me to work at a state-controlled media network. The state allocated jobs to everyone. My role was decided already, as an accountant working at the 17th Railway Bureau. The head of the station told me to leave. However, after listening to my tape, the radio host Shang Neng offered me a half hour in his program. He was famous enough to be able to fight against his boss's disapproval. All state-controlled stations needed money to survive after the 1992 economic reforms—when China set the goal of establishing a socialist market system, opening the gate to the outside world—and Shang Neng attracted a lot of commercials for them.

One year later, in 1995, I signed a contract with the radio station by winning an open competition. It was the first time the station had selected staff through an open market and fair competition. Thinking that a contract meant a job that was only temporary, my mother wrote a harsh letter to warn me of what I might lose if I gave up my

---

[1] Under the centralized economy, all universities were state controlled. Railway colleges were among these universities, designed to train qualified workers who would exclusively work in railway stations after graduation, as opposed to students at broadcasting universities, who would have the chance to become radio hosts.

state-allocated railway job: my house, hukou,[2] social benefits, safety. In short, all she had had to struggle for her entire life. I didn't write back to her. Living in a society with a long history of collectivism, we rarely talk about our personal feelings at home, and this was especially true after a period of excessive politicization where the idea of individual humanity was seen as "spiritual pollution." It was hard to tell my mom that, for me, a job was a spiritual human bond. People wrote to me and I read their letters on the radio; it was a human bond. There were long-suppressed voices that wanted to be heard, and I was there. I did nothing but listen, yet the hole in my life was filled by strangers. More than making a living, I was alive.

In 1999, in order to survive, all the stations—radio and television alike—had to produce programs that spoke to people's needs. *New Youth*, a program on Hunan TV, invited me to be their host, and my job was to interview young people who brought sharp ideas to different fields. This was during China's explosive economic growth, and I realized these people had one thing in common: instead of destroying the old, they built the new where creativity was most unfettered. Life itself has to grow, and where there is a gap, there is a way out.

I ended up writing their story as well, including the parts that the station cut, to provide a fuller picture for the magazines. The media market was expanding quickly and competitively around 2000, so it had been to my advantage to work freely, and not sign a contract with the TV station. As one of the first generation media freelancers, I got a

---

[2] On January 9, 1958, the Hukou Registration Regulation was signed into law in China. It was an instrument of the centralized economy, helping the government implement its plan to industrialize the nation. The system divided the populace into an agricultural hukou and a nonagricultural hukou—state welfare programs were tied to hukou status, and heavily favored urban residents. Over 85 percent of the population were agricultural hukou holders, who could not access these benefits. Transfer of hukou status was highly restricted—official quotas were 0.15–0.2 percent per year. My parents struggled for many years to get urban hukou status so that they could pass it on to me. They dreamed of me getting a "big city urban hukou" by accepting the job that the state assigned to me, since hukou limited migration to big cities, and all citizens were grouped by district.

taste of what it was like to be independent. Like the rock-and-roll star Cui Jian sang, "As long as I have a pen, no one can stop me."

Even still, I never wanted to be a news reporter. Journalism remained a monopoly when I began building my career. For a long time all Chinese people watched the same program, *Joint News*, on CCTV, which contained countless political meetings and aired every night at seven P.M. For me, all it meant was the start of dinnertime. The only CCTV program I watched was *Oriental Horizon*. What impressed me was the candid state of people's lives on screen, full of struggles in a rapidly changing society, conflicting desires that led to inevitable consequences. I watched it as a work of art, not just as news. The slogan of these stories was "Telling the ordinary people's own story." After being ignored for a long time, ordinary people in a fast-rising society became protagonists on a national television station. Chen Meng, a man who had never been trained by any official news school, created a slogan in 1993 to express the goal of China's journalism reform at the time: "Turning propaganda into communication." In the beginning, CCTV asked the program to "serve people" by teaching them how to cook. But when Chen Meng became a producer, he said, "If we serve people, we serve their spiritual life." He put life in a shell.

Chen Meng invited me to join CCTV in 2000. Since I was a young girl who hadn't studied any news textbooks, he asked me to learn the principles of journalism from life: from the pain, joy, struggle, and bloody lessons of people in general and myself in particular.

Fourteen years later, I quit my job, went back to freelancing. I used what I had learned, and used some royalties from the book I'd published (which you're now holding in your hands) to make a nonprofit documentary about air pollution in China. On February 28, 2015, I put it online. It got over three hundred million views before being removed seven days later. I left China then, and have been living in Europe ever since.

For those fourteen years, working at CCTV gave me the opportunity to travel to different places over a hundred and fifty days a year, to see my country, which was changing dramatically, and understand the trajectory of that change. What I saw showed me that China's development depends on its ability to free people's creativity from unnecessary shackles. It can explain the country's stagnation, and it can also explain the country's success; it can explain the past, and it will explain the future.

Chen Meng never told me why he chose me until he became seriously ill. The last time we talked in the hospital, he told me that eight years prior he had seen a young girl talking on TV. He didn't remember what she had said and didn't check her background, but he thought, "This girl has many flaws, but there is one thing about her I value—she doesn't follow blindly."

That was when he called me.

Arrival at CCTV.

One
Chen Meng Calls
2000

The year was 2000. One fall afternoon, I received a phone call from a stranger.

"I'm Chen Meng."

Then came a long, meaningful pause, as if he was waiting for me to shriek in amazement.

"Who?"

"It's me, Chen Meng . . . you never took my class?"

"Who on earth are you?"

"Argh . . . China Central Television. Our news commentary department wants to work with you."

We met at a hotel behind the CCTV building.

I looked at him. He had medium-length hair, an old leather jacket with the collar turned up. He didn't exactly look like a boss. He crossed one leg over the other, so I did too.

The first words that came out of his mouth were, "How ready are you for fame?"

Oh. Did everyone at CCTV speak with so much bravado? At twenty-four years of age, I didn't care about hierarchies, so I said, "If fame is something one feels, then I already experienced it when I was twenty."

"I'm talking about the household-name kind of fame."

"I know how high I can reach."

He was so angry, he laughed. "Come again?"

"I know how high I can reach."

He was silent for a moment. Then he asked, "If you did news, what would you care about?"

"I care about the people I report on in the news."

He sat there squinting at me for a while through the cigarette smoke and said, "Come on board."

"I'm not interested."

I had my show on Hunan Satellite TV, *New Youth*. There was no contract involved. I lived in Beijing and took a trip out once a month. The station paid me in cash. So I said, "I'm not cut out for work inside the institution."

After putting out his cigarette, he stood up and said, "How about this? Come to the news commentary department's annual gala and just hang out for a bit."

The annual gala began with an award ceremony honoring the top ten employees in the news commentary department. These ten were something. The first one was Sun Jie. He wobbled onto the stage with a roll of toilet paper in his hand. "Got a cold so I didn't have time to prepare. I wrote a few basic principles down on this paper . . ." It was a parody of a popular political slogan at the time. When he finished, he ripped up the toilet paper and sniffled his way offstage.

Cui Yongyuan was the host. He was full of innuendos, mocking the bigwigs, roasting the bosses. He said, "Director Chen, please stand up."

They forced Chen Meng to dress like a Japanese hipster, with a topknot shooting out of his head and layers upon layers of flannel. He leaned on his katana and stood up. The crowd roared. Young Cui quickly pointed to a row of squiggly writing on the big screen. There was only one Chinese character in the line: *Money*.

He asked, "What do these words say, Director Chen?"

Chen Meng hesitated for a long time before mumbling, "I can't read that."

"Oh, Director Chen can't even read the word *money*."

Everyone laughed.

"I'll give you one more shot," he said. "Of these words, which do you recognize?"

Chen Meng answered more quickly this time: "Money."

"Oh, so Director Chen only recognizes money."

The crowd whistled and screamed. With his ridiculous katana in hand, Chen Meng was as in on the joke as the rest of us.

This was around the time the program *Oriental Horizon* was planning to break off from the news commentary department. So next they played a video parody by Cui Yongyuan called "The October Divorce." A voice was dubbed over the film *Lenin in October*: "*Revolution comes only once every seven or eight years . . . Brothers, grab the money and female producers, and the disposable paper cups and napkins too . . .*" He was mocking the internal power struggle between the bosses. The bosses sitting in the front row all got a fair roasting. Among them was the head of the news commentary department, who was pantomimed being robbed by the masses. Money was tossed into the air as everyone laughed. One of the red hundred-yuan bills drifted and drifted until it landed in my hand.

Hmm, maybe this place isn't so bad.

Chen Meng grabbed a piece of crumpled paper and told me to sign my name on it.

"And you'll officially be a part of CCTV," he said.

I glared at him dubiously. It wasn't a contract, or a press pass, or proof of employment, or a salary card. It wasn't even an entry pass into the building.

"We've had our eyes on you, isn't that enough?"

The look on his face.

He took me on a tour of the news commentary department. I studied my surroundings as I walked. The sign outside the department door read: "To be truthful, fair, balanced, and avant-garde." Avant-garde . . . a newsroom wanted to be avant-garde?

He didn't turn to look at me as he walked, trying to bring me down a notch. "You are a tennis ball. I am a tennis racket. No matter how high you reach . . ."

Oh—he was a keeper of grudges.

He turned and stared into my eyes. ". . . I will still be a centimeter above you."

You wish.

As soon as we entered the office, there was a chair in the middle of the room. With practiced hands, a makeup artist wrapped a towel around me and said, "It's time to cut your hair." The hair that had always covered half of my face fell to the floor. I was like a bald little duckling.

"You can fly even higher now," Chen Meng said.

My male colleagues sat in a circle looking at me with uncertain smiles. "Go, fetch us some water, Ms. Anchor—we'll be serving you all year, you can do a little something for us as well."

I had never been the witty type, and besides, I was used to the more feminist culture of the South. I didn't know how to react to this type of humor, so I ended up pouring water for them one by one.

They continued to tease me. "Chai Jing, who's more powerful, a director or a bureau chief?"

I honestly had no idea. I didn't know about politics and wasn't interested.

Chen Meng handed me off to Sun Jie, the guy who'd had the toilet paper on stage and said, "Drill her."

Sun Jie seemed different from how he'd been at the gala. With a stern gaze, he said, "Write me a narration for the eightieth anniversary of the founding of the Party."

I wasn't afraid. Each of us has received this writing training since elementary school. Words flowed out like an ocean.

When I handed the piece to him, he was so kind, he didn't even let out a sigh before saying, "Go home and get some rest."

I was to appear on a show called *Connecting Horizons*, a daily sixteen-minute news commentary segment bringing together experts from various fields. I had never done news before.

The first episode was a disaster. The topic we covered was Caesarean sections. I contacted doctors, mothers, and sociologists, and after scheduling the recording studio, I had my makeup done and began. A few senior directors from the station passed by and watched me through the glass panel. We recorded thirty minutes of a live interview, talked about how Caesarean sections weren't good, and promptly finished. Back then, I didn't pay much attention to video recordings. After editing the transcript on paper, I asked a colleague to cut the clip and submit it for review before setting off for a vacation.

When I came back from vacation, I hung up a large framed photo that I'd taken in Tibet, and on my desk, I put out a vase filled with flowers and grasses.

From the looks on my colleagues' faces, I could tell that the review process hadn't gone well. At first, they left out the harshest critics and told me that with the way things stood, I should just redo the ending.

But at the office meeting, Chen Meng criticized me in front of everyone.

"You tell the audience that Caesarean sections are a mistake, and how much better natural births are, but that's only one side of the story. Did you bother to dig deeper? Who has the right to decide whether or not to perform a C-section? The doctor and the family. How do they decide? This is a question of medical practice. Is there a deeper angle behind the story? If you think that it's a mistake for so many people to choose C-sections, how did this popular attitude come about? Why do people believe it? The facts behind a news story can be seen from at least three different angles: scientific knowledge, institutional practice, and social norms. The deeper you delve, the more people you can speak to. How many angles did you explore?"

I changed the ending again and again, but it was useless.

During the end-of-year party, a colleague acted out one of my interviews on the stage. With a shawl over her shoulders, wearing high heels and a pencil skirt, she sat with her legs twisted, and flicked her bangs out of her eyes with one hand while caressing the hand of a male interviewee with the other. She asked, "Does it hurt? Does it really hurt? Does it really, really hurt?" The audience broke out in laughter, affirming the caricature of me.

Bai Yansong, the producer, was under more pressure than anyone else to deal with me, but he couldn't make my tree grow just by pulling on the sprout. When our colleagues laughed at me, he probably felt more frustrated than anyone else in the room. Once I wore an embroidered satin skirt into the office. He called me over and said, "Get changed."

My old artsy routine wasn't cutting it. But I didn't want to talk in the same old way I had heard on TV.

It was no use. Repeatedly, I failed to pass the test. Once, out of desperation, Bai Yansong handed me a note. He had written me a script.

Whenever I had to re-record something, I called the crew back into the station in the middle of the night. The gaffer and cameraman no longer complained or asked why. They put up with it in silence. After recording, I didn't take a taxi; I walked. With every step, I carried a heavy load of guilt, for what I was putting others through.

The department arranged for all the anchors to take a group photo together. I was the unknown girl, so naturally, I stood in the back row. When Cui Yongyuan turned and saw me, he held my elbow and brought me down to the first row where he was standing. He didn't even know my name. That's the kind of person he was. At dinner, when everyone else was daring one another to empty their shot glasses, he entered the room, sat down at the table without a word, and everyone stopped drinking.

Young Cui was like the sun at noon. He was the most well-known host in China and ran a famous talk show called *Tell It Like It Is*. People loved him. But he revealed to everyone at the dinner table he was depressed, and whenever he was about to record, he felt so nervous that he had to clench his fists at the wall.

I was used to tough guys, which really made me appreciate his vulnerability.

I didn't make many new friends at the station, but Snoopy was one of them. We were the only ones who were still single, so our colleagues tried to set us up. He didn't seem old, but the way he looked . . . Once, in the subway, he stared at a girl for a long time, until the girl reluctantly stood up to offer him her seat. He said to me in all seriousness, "I've looked like this ever since I was a kid. But when I hit forty, I'll still look like this, and then you'll see my advantage."

I call him Snoopy because I was like the unlucky Charlie Brown. He was my naïve friend, and we were both teased all the time. He published a piece in the news commentary department's internal newsletter titled "My Dream: A Meal in the Pot, a Woman in the Bed," which elicited plenty of sneers from the news folks—the dream seemed too small to them. They were concerned with interviewing officials and making news headlines. Snoopy, however, always covered people who were not in the limelight. He said, "The ignored person has the right to make his voice heard."

During editorial meetings, whenever he opened his mouth, the entire room would shake their heads and mock him, calling him "humanist."[3] He never tried to argue, and I never saw him raise his voice at anyone. Once, at a banquet, when everyone had been drinking a little too much, someone smashed a bottle on the ground. Snoopy was pretty drunk himself, and he stumbled to the ground to pick up the broken pieces. When I went to help, I heard him grumble, "What is a humanist? A humanist is someone who doesn't smash bottles on the ground."

He was living hand-to-mouth. Every day, he carried a company-issued paper bag with a pair of swim trunks and a stack of pirated movie discs in it. After finishing his complimentary swim, and having eaten his three free meals in CCTV, he went home and watched movies. Though he was a thrifty person, he still bought a pot of flowers for me once because he knew that I was unhappy. On his way to work, he'd seen people crowded around the subway stop. Thinking that it must be something good, he'd squeezed his way in. They were selling pots of chrysanthemum taken from Tiananmen Square after the National Day celebration, a buck each.

Later, when he carefully placed the cheap little yellow flowers on my desk, he leaned in for a deep sniff, and nearly fainted from the odor.

Yet, during the midday meeting when everyone was critiquing my segment, he defended me. "Everyone says, 'I will skip the compliments and go straight to the critique.' Why skip the compliments? The good parts need to be mentioned too. Let me start . . ."

---

[3] The word "humanist" had a bad reputation for a long time, as it was considered detrimental to the political needs of the "class struggle." Until the 1980s, the word was still used as a symbol of bourgeois liberalization, a "spiritual pollution" that needed to be "cleaned up"; twenty years later, it no longer evoked strong hostility, but still represented a sense of weakness and sentimentality, and had become an object of ridicule.

In private, though, he liked to lecture me. "You live a life too plastic to be real."

I rolled my eyes at him. "What about it?"

He said I looked exhausted, spending forty minutes a day on the phone before each interview, writing over a hundred questions on my notepad for each segment.

He had a point. In the makeup room, as the makeup artist would do my eyeliner, I always kept writing out of the corner of my eye. The makeup artist would sigh and say, "I see all the other anchors reading a Louis Cha novel right about now. Why are you so nervous?"

I didn't have an answer. When I interviewed, I went through the questions on my notepad, hardly even paying attention to the interviewees' answers, desperate to go on to the next question.

Snoopy said, "It's like firing a gun. First aim like you mean it, then pull the trigger like it was an accident. You need that nonchalance."

My program was piloting a three-way interview format for news events, seeking to create an atmosphere of debate. The technology was only in its nascent stage, not yet able to show all three guests on screen at the same time. We had to conduct the interviews over the phone while cameramen recorded the guests separately, to be combined in post-production. In the studio, I stared into space while listening to the voices of the guests in my earpiece.

"Look over here." The cameraman oriented me in the dark, trying to make me appear engaged with the three guests. I tried to ask questions with a little more expression, putting my body into it, pretending to be in a conversation, or at least creating the sense of one. The body language alone was enough to break me.

"Cut," said the cameraman. "There's nothing in your eyes."

I replied, "That's right, the interviewees won't be visible until post-production. Of course I can't see them."

The cameraman shook his head.

Later, when everyone was eating in CCTV's canteen in the southern courtyard, *Connecting Horizons* came on TV. Chen Meng quickly finished his meal and called me on the phone. "Everyone is talking about how you were recruited by me! Don't make me lose face." With that, he hung up.

"The way Chen criticizes people," Snoopy explained, "makes people want to kill themselves." After reviewing someone's clip, for example, he'd ask how old the editor was. When the person felt confused and asked why, he'd say, "I want to know if it's too late for you to change careers."

One time, he commented on my schoolgirl style of reporting by saying, "Your style is unbearably pretentious."

My eyes were full of tears. He then added, "You shouldn't be afraid of my criticism. Be afraid when I give up on you."

It wasn't until he saw that I had lost all confidence that he warmed up to me.

"You need to find your desire," he said.

"But my desire is strong," I retorted.

"Your desires are only about yourself. You need to forget yourself."

Yet there were so many things I had to consider during every segment. I had to focus on my body. Turn it thirty-five degrees, forty degrees, or sixty degrees. I needed to think about my expression, word choice, makeup, and outfit. "How do I forget myself?" I said obstinately.

"Go home and ask your ma, your sister, what they desire from the news. Don't forget to be human just because you're a host," he said.

I ended up asking my mother and sister about every show. It helped, leading me to structure my questions with a more common-sense approach. But as soon as I was on stage baking under the spotlights, and the director's voice blared in my earpiece, "Three, two, one, *go*," my body tensed, my voice pitched, and I was stilted once more.

Chen Meng said, "When you ask a question, what's the answer that you expect? If you don't know what to expect, then don't bother asking the question."

I was getting wound up tighter and tighter. When a cameraman named Yang took me home in the snow one time, he said, "Girl, you've got to up your game. The bosses say, 'If we can't lift her up, just let her fall.'"

Slowly, I was forgetting how to write. I stared at a blank page, unable to scrawl a word. Soon after, I forgot how to speak. When I ran into Zhang Jie from *News Probe* at a restaurant, he said he knew how I felt. He had reported on a form of treatment for patients with advanced disease in which all the blood drawn was to be replaced with fresh blood. He thought it was similar to the situation I was facing. I wanted to say something to him, but I was out of old blood and without a drop of new blood, I had lost all ability to express myself and could only give him a pale, fake smile.

I only went downhill from there. Back when I was in the audience, I used to sneer at all the platitudes on the news. Now that I was an anchor, I used them more liberally than anyone else. At the end of every segment, I would say, "Let us hope that one day soon, the democratic rule of law will bind our society."

Afterward, I could shed my makeup and be done with work.

One day, a girl took a two-hour-long bus ride to come to my office. She introduced herself as a listener of my old radio show. She skipped the small talk and asked me pointedly, "Do you feel like what you're doing is worthwhile? Can you still feel that sense of trust you once had with your listeners?"

Before I could think of a reply, she walked out the door.

I had hosted a weekend nightly radio show for three years, starting in 1995. When I'd taken the job, my boss had told me there was no pay for it.

I said, "Okay."

"And no overtime pay, no travel reimbursement."

I said, "Okay."

I had tried to hide my glee—was this for real? I could do something I loved and not have to pay for it?

Listeners sent in letters telling their own stories. I read them out word for word, including dates. All details were as precious as gold to me. I didn't reply, didn't comment, just read. As time went on, listeners would say, "You've become my second self." When I finished, I would press the play button, and from the soft, moist leather headphones would come the sonic embodiment of the mountains and the seas. I would lean back in the thick leather chair. Deep in the night, a tiny light bulb hovered above. The soundboard and leather trim emitted a burnt, musky scent. The glass in front of me reflected the tiny ball of light, as if this was the only place left in the world. From the first moment I'd sat down, I was no longer fired up, no longer distressed. I'd settled my heart—*this is it.*

Years later, doing news at CCTV, I knew I was slaving away for the producers, for the bonuses, for vainglory, and out of fear. But my heart was nowhere.

One day, with my hair permed high and makeup on, ready for recording, I ran into an old friend on the street. The person looked at me for a while and said, "You should be careful. Don't become one of those people you used to hate."

I dreamed I was back in fourth grade.

The eight-year-old me was standing in an aisle in a classroom with one hand over my left eye as a room full of students buried their heads in their books. The teacher pointed to the eye chart's bottom row.

It was the most terrifying scene from my childhood. Even now, whenever I see an eye chart, I feel revulsion, a conditioned reflex.

I had been nearsighted for some time. But no one could tell.

Standing in the aisle, I was calm. My index finger swung up and down, left and right. I had already memorized the bottom row. The teacher put down her pointer and lowered her head to write the result while shouting, "Perfect, next."

I had become just like everyone else. No one noticed me as I quietly made my way back to my seat.

One day, as I was passing through my living room, I noticed a program on TV called *The Economy in Thirty Minutes*, where a journalist was interviewing a comedian who had just become a county mayor. The journalist's name was Chen Dahui, and he was a real shark: quick, brutal, precise. With a flash of the teeth, heads rolled. I stood there holding my bowl until the show ended.

His methods were controversial within the industry, but everyone agreed he worked hard. "He's the first interview journalist to have systematically studied foreign programs," people would say. "He dissects shows like he's cleaning out a snail; he studies and imitates every framing, every question, even expressions and gestures."

So I printed out his interviews, and those of Oriana Fallaci, Larry King, and anyone else that I could get my hands on, and filed them away in a folder. I copied out their questions and used them directly.

I ran into Chen Dahui once, and he told me that when interviewing multiple guests, one must be single-minded. Don't worry about the purpose of the show, don't worry about the mood or things like a conversational feel. Don't worry about neglecting any one guest.

"Remember this," he said, "the news itself is what is important. If one of them can get at the heart of the story, then just talk to that person. The other two can sit there and be quiet, it doesn't matter."

I was skeptical. "Wouldn't the guests feel uncomfortable?"

"It's not important how comfortable they feel, a journalist's only goal is to reveal the truth."

I learned from Chen Dahui, but trying to teach myself something so arcane was like a teenager without any experience trying to fight from a martial arts manual. You could easily go astray, imagining yourself to be a powerful journalist while in reality doing nothing more than shaming people.

I came upon a story about two young cyclists from the Shaanxi Youth Team cycling across the Great Wall. One of them lost his life. I planned a segment called "The Limit of Crossing," where I interviewed the deceased's teammate and coach. During the show, the teammate recited an impassioned patriotic poem. So I asked, "Is that the special thrill you were looking for at the risk of losing your life? Some sort of publicity stunt?"

After recording the segment, my colleagues looked at me differently. "Wow," they said, "that was sharp." I was even pleased with myself.

Li Lun, who was the lead editor at *Living Space*, sent me a quick text message soon after the show aired: *Missing the point?* Before I had time to digest his meaning, I saw an article in the press that criticized my segment: "A TV journalist speaks with sarcasm—a relentless onslaught." In the author's opinion, I should have directed my pointed questioning at the department in charge of safety inspections. There was no need to make fun of the cyclist. After watching the segment, audiences left online comments too, calling me cruel.

One of my few remaining fans said, "I used to think you were at least sympathetic. Now I really don't like you anymore."

• • •

I asked my doctor friend, "Why am I having trouble breathing?"

He said, "Stressful emotions can slow down your breathing, causing carbon dioxide to build up in your system."

"Is there something I can do about it?"

"Sure, take deep breaths."

Walking up the stairs, I took deep breaths; walking down the stairs, I took deep breaths. I looked at the elevator attendant. She sat relaxed, with nothing to do, staring at the wall forever and ever. How I envied her. At work, it was only in the bathroom where I could let loose for two minutes. I washed my hands for as long as I could, keeping the faucet running, taking deep breaths, while looking at myself in the mirror. I knew I was already on the edge of failure. Soon, everyone would smell it—in the animal kingdom, as soon as you give off that sort of scent, you're basically done for. Soon, very soon, predators will have their eyes on you, and before you know it, they'll mercilessly pounce on you and take you down. Your herd will scatter without so much as a glance back at you.

During that period, I was reading *Silence of the Lambs* before going to bed. I don't even know where my pirated copy came from; it was full of typos and the cover was falling off. A few years later, after I read the sequel, I wrote an angry letter to the author in my diary. I wrote, "Your insipid, bullshit backstory has ruined my image of Starling. She's nothing at all like the woman who eats Italian food, appreciates fine paintings, and talks to a cannibal doctor about childhood traumas."

In my mind, she would always be that twenty-four-year-old intern at the Federal Bureau of Investigation who spoke with a bit of a twang, sprinkled in a few profanities, wore a pair of bargain shoes, and set out to investigate a murder all on her own. The insane inmates in prison flicked sperm into her face. A senator accused her of stealing her daughter's jewelry. She knew what it felt like to be belittled, how it felt to be a failure. But she could fire seventy-four rounds in one minute with her left hand. The veins in her arm bulged like gold-plated wires.

When she rolled up her sleeve to inspect a decaying corpse, she said to the men who thought she was only there because of her looks, "Now please, go on out . . . go on now."

At first, she wanted to find a corner she could call her own within the institutional machinery of the FBI, but in the end, she no longer worked for a career. "To hell with the special agents," she said. When she stopped caring about her own career, only focusing on the victims, she found the clues.

Before the cameras started rolling, I often thought to myself, "No, a plastic bubble like this would not intimidate Starling. That girl is never scared."

I did my planning and editing to figure out what my desire was, as Chen Meng had instructed. Every day, I called many institutions in search of a topic. When old Yang, the cameraman, saw me calling the Foreign Ministry about a diplomat who was robbed, he laughed. "How ignorant would you have to be to be so fearless?" But later, when we were shooting the interview, Yang gave me a quiet nod from behind the camera. It gave me a warm feeling.

Every day, I submitted three topics. In the afternoon, I reached out to contact people. At night, I recorded. At midnight, I edited the clip and submitted it for review.

I was hanging on by a thread. One winter day at two in the morning, everyone had left the office. There was no one left to work the editing machine, and I didn't know how to use it myself. *That's it*, I thought to myself, *first thing in the morning I will call Chen Meng and tell him to shove it, he can find someone else.* I sat at the desk sulking until seven. When I made the call, the first thing that came out of Chen Meng's mouth was, "Can you turn in the clip today?"

"Sure," I said, like I was possessed. I couldn't quit like that. This man had no sympathy for me, but he treated me like a responsible adult.

I lugged the tapes to another editing room and edited until four o'clock the next morning. Then I locked my coat in the editing room by accident, so I ended up walking to the TV station in a sweater, dragging my left foot that was injured in the accident a few days ago. I was still a temporary worker, not yet in possession of an entrance pass. An associate producer kindly came downstairs and took the tape from me through a slit in the gate. When I got home, the elevator wasn't working. I climbed up eighteen flights of stairs, stressing my left leg along the way, and jumped into bed. Then I got a call. There was something wrong with the tape and I needed to offer a new one. I dragged my injured leg along as I limped my way back downstairs.

There were already people out on the street, though it was still the break of dawn. Two teenagers pointed at me with smiles. I thought they recognized me.

"Gimp," they said, and laughed.

In the blue-gray dawn, the wind had cleaned out the heavens. Only a few silver little stars and a moon like a silver scimitar were nailed in the sky.

One time, Bai Yansong tried to console me: "What people call the best days of their lives are also usually the hardest. It's only when you look back that you recognize happiness."

I kept on going. The program continued to air, season after season. Some segments were syndicated, some even won awards. Life started getting easier. But the reason I did my job at all was because I wanted to be accepted by my bosses and colleagues. I wanted to find stories that could become tomorrow's headlines. But in my heart, these weren't the stories that I desired.

There were some stories that did tug at my heart. I tried to pitch one about a thirteen-year-old girl teaching a class of HIV-positive orphans. But at the editorial meeting, everyone said, "That's not our beat." Another time, I noticed a lawyers' association report saying that, in Yunnan Province's female prisons, 60 percent of the violent offenders were there for murdering their husbands. I was astonished. But again at the editorial meeting, I was shot down. "Who cares about those rural women?" one of my colleagues said. "You should care about how my wife emotionally abuses me." They all laughed.

It reminded me of when I'd first arrived in Beijing and taken an internship at a magazine. The editor had asked me to pick a cover story related to the theme of biodiversity. So I went and interviewed botanists from the Chinese Academy of Sciences and wrote about the challenges they faced in their research. The editor looked at my draft and said, "This is not what I'm looking for. Get some cutting-edge foreign research and translate it."

I said, "But I feel that the state of research in our country should be exposed too."

"What good would that do?"

"I don't know, but if we don't talk about it, it definitely won't do any good."

"It's not what our magazine is looking for—change it."

"But . . ."

"Change it."

I went silent.

"Are you going to change it or not?" the editor pressed.

"No."

We both hung up the phone at the same time. That was my first job in Beijing, and I lost it.

In February 2003, Bai Yansong suddenly called me into the office to tell me that there was an earthquake in Xinjiang and that I would head out on location in half an hour.

"Time to get your hands dirty," he said.

I took an Il-76 military cargo plane to Kashgar, with three large trucks and over a dozen cages containing rescue dogs. I found an old tire to sit on. There were no windows, and the noise was so loud that I couldn't hear someone talking in front of me. On the five-hour flight, several of the male comrades from the Earthquake Administration vomited.

We arrived in Kashgar at three in the morning. The enormous moon illuminated the vast fields of the Northwest in snowy white. I shivered in the light of such a moon. Large military trucks drove out of the plane. Then we got in. It was a bumpy four-hour ride to Jiashi County. The road was in shambles. At one point, when there was a sudden jolt, I fell, along with a big German shepherd. The dog and I rolled all the way back to the tailgate. But without a sound, the dog crawled out from under me and pulled its long tail free. It slapped its tail against the tailgate and stared at me through its amber eyes. When I finally got up, it turned its gaze off to the distance with its ears perked.

When it was finally time to get out of the truck, I stepped onto the ground and thought something was wrong with my legs. They felt like they had turned rubbery. I was standing on the thatched roof of what used to be a hut. It had been flattened. Grass sprouted up through the straw.

I walked in a daze. The 6.8 earthquake had led to over two hundred dead. I looked around and saw that pretty much all the mud and wooden structures were destroyed. The grassland was empty as far as the eye could see. Farther up, hundreds of men stood in a circle. An imam stood in the middle, reading the Koran over bodies draped in white. Farther still, women were gathering rocks in a clearing to build a fire pit for cooking. Dawn was just beginning. The enormous plain was dark. Crimson embers licked the bottom of the pot.

Had I been in the news studio, such a disaster would have been just another assignment. I would have only cared about whether I had the relevant stats fully memorized. But here I saw an old man with one foot bare and the other in a canvas army shoe, limping a kilometer to the trucks, rummaging through the supplies until he found a tattered leather shoe, which he studied and then put on before walking away. And that was when I understood what an earthquake disaster meant.

Chen Meng had said, "Go, feel the news with your skin."

Farther ahead, I passed by a half-collapsed wall. When I touched what remained of the wall, it crumbled. The people who'd built it had made it out of dirt and a bit of concrete; now it turned to dust with a pinch. There was an old Uyghur woman wearing a yellow turban next to me. Before I even spoke, she hugged me and cried on my shoulder. I instinctively held her and her cheek pressed against mine. Her wrinkles were icy cold.

The next day, we shot footage of the raising of the national flag at a tent school. The journalists crowded the place. School children pulled out red and green backpacks from their desks under the rubble. After dusting them off, they raised the flag and recited the essay, "My Beautiful Campus." When the clip aired, someone complimented me: "Not bad, nice details."

While the video equipment was being put away, there were two twin sisters playing nearby. I asked them where they lived. The kids led me to some debris. The house had collapsed. Two rolls of blankets salvaged from the rubble lay on the ground, without even a mat to put them on. I reached in and felt wet grains of sand. That night it was minus twenty degrees Celsius.

"How do you get water?" I asked.

Their slightly older brother grabbed a metal bucket and led me down half a kilometer to a pothole that had been collecting rainwater. After brushing away the dead grass on the surface, he filled up the bucket. Back at the debris field, he gathered up a few rocks and boiled the water in a tin kettle on the fire.

That was their life. And just before, I had told the entire country that they were already happily going to school with their backpacks on.

I was at a loss for words. I could only squat down to help a little girl tie her shoelaces.

• • •

On my last day in Xinjiang, Sai Na, the producer from *One on One*, called to ask me to interview someone.

"Interview whom?" I asked.

"I don't know, you pick someone."

I found a person called Dawuti Aximu, a village chief. He wore the black leather skullcap that older Uyghurs wear. His face was ruddy and wide, covered with a graying blond beard. Sitting on a broken chair outside a ramshackle house, his face was covered in dust, as was mine. His hair was creased from wearing a safety hat for so long. This time, I didn't have questions prepared. I looked around and asked, "Now that your house is gone, where will you sleep at night?"

"On the ground."

"Can you fall asleep?"

"Five people in my family have died, I cannot sleep."

"What do you think about when you can't fall asleep?"

"I think about life before, about how the one thousand four hundred people in my village will live now."

Had I been in the news studio, I would have been thinking about the structure of this interview and how to build up a conclusion. But out on the open earth, everything fell away. There were no lights, no reflectors, and no director in my earpiece. The person I interviewed couldn't speak Mandarin, and the interpreter was a local, so I could only follow my instinct to ask the simplest questions.

"How did the earthquake play out?"

"I thought I heard gunshots. Twice, the earth shook and shook. I squatted where I was. The wall next to me collapsed. I rolled into a ditch. In the ditch, I grabbed onto a mulberry branch. Dust blotted out the sky."

"What happened after you got out of the ditch?"

"Ran home. Climbed onto the roof. There was debris everywhere. I began digging out the roof. It took a long time to dig out an opening."

"What did you use to dig?"

"Couldn't find any tools, just used my hands. At first, when I saw a hand, I wasn't sure if it was my wife's or my daughter-in-law's. When I saw the sleeve, I knew it was the mother of my child. And then I stopped. Other people dug her out."

Tears left streaks of dark and light lines. When the interpreter said, "And then I stopped," my heart lurched.

Later, back in Beijing, a program director who had always ignored me, Chen Yao Wen, sat down across from me in the canteen with a tray of food. He said, "I can finally talk to you now. The show is human. You can see people now."

On April 7, 2003, I got notice to leave *Oriental Horizons* to go work on *News Probe*, a forty-five-minute investigative news segment. This meant I would go on-site to a real news scene.

I packed my things. Snoopy helped me take down the picture frame hanging on the office wall. It was big and heavy. He carried it by the wire and painfully juggled it from one hand to the other as he carried it downstairs.

I turned to him and said, "You can go back now."

He said, "I'll walk you over."

In the new office, he studied the room with a look of satisfaction, like some country dad, and even nodded at my new coworkers with a pleasing smile, as if to say, "Take good care of my girl. Knock her on the head if you must, yell at her if she needs it." The only thing that was missing was someone handing him a cigarette for him to wedge behind his ear. He found my desk. He took a few steps back and looked around.

"Where should I hang the picture?"

He looked around, holding the photo of Tibet.

"Don't bother," I said, "I'm not hanging it up anymore."

Interviewing with Wang Jishan, Vice President of Peking University People's Hospital, the place where the SARS infection and transmission was the most concentrated, which was still unknown at that time. April 22, 2003.

Two
The Mystery of the Courtyard
2003

On April 19, at nine P.M., I got a call from Zhang Jie, the producer of *News Probe*. "Do you want to cover SARS?"

I said, "Count me in."

After ending the call, I dropped the cell phone on the sofa. Right away, I picked it up again and sent him a text message: *Can we meet now?* Before waiting for a reply, I called him and said, "Be in the office in ten minutes."

I had been waiting for a long time. For several months, Severe Acute Respiratory Syndrome was already being widely discussed, but shallowly. We only knew it was a very severe disease, transmitted through droplet infection. It sounded like the flu, but it caused death in around 10 percent of patients on average. In the fatal cases, patients would suffocate to death. There was no effective medicine to treat it. Chinese doctors didn't even have a name for it. They just called it "atypical pneumonia."

Yet all official indications were that everything was fine, and it was just a regional issue. The first case showed up in Guangdong Province in November 2002. On April 3, the head of China's Ministry of Public Health, Zhang Wenkang, announced on CCTV that the epidemic was effectively under control—there were only twelve cases in Beijing, and it was safe to go about daily life with or without a mask.

However, there were a lot of rumors. The plump lady selling fried bread downstairs was growing anxious. With a plastic bag full of herbal medicine for the flu hanging from her tricycle, she asked me, "Don't you work at CCTV? What exactly is going on?"

I did not know. All the information I had also came from government releases. A painful thought crossed my mind: if in the future I had a child and he asked me what I was doing during SARS, I'd have to say, "Ma saw it on TV." That wouldn't be something I could bring myself to say.

I ran up to the third floor to the office of *News Probe* and opened the door to a hot and steamy conference room crowded with people. I jumped straight to the point. "What exactly is the situation right now?"

"Don't know."

"What do we do?"

"Go out there and find out."

The slogan of the program was on the wall: "Hunting the truth."

During the meeting, we decided to interview Health Minister Zhang Wenkang, as well as Meng Xuenong, the mayor of Beijing. The two men would be giving a press conference the following day, April 20. But shortly after the press conference—which ended up being led by the executive vice minister of health, Gao Qiang—the health minister and the mayor were dismissed. And there was more shocking news: the official number of cases in Beijing the day before was thirty-seven, but Gao Qiang said that there were 393 confirmed cases on that day, with 402 potential infections on top of that. That was a huge spike.

Panic spread like the buzzing of a hornet's nest. The day was chaotic. We couldn't reach any officials. I felt like we were going through a systemic collapse. CCTV also stopped running, because an employee was confirmed to have SARS. To prevent the spread, managers whittled down the production and broadcast personnel to a minimum. The official editorial process was closed; *News Probe* would show reruns for safety's sake.

But we weren't entirely out of commission. We built a five-person filming team, and decided we had to go investigate, even if we couldn't get permission. We would visit a hospital, the only real source of information. Back then, it wasn't standard for journalists to be issued hazmat suits. CCTV didn't have any of these suits. The secretary in our office gave each of us a plastic jacket. It was slippery, like maybe she thought the germs wouldn't stick to it. I remember mine was pale yellow.

We went to the Beijing Center for Disease Prevention and Control and asked them to let us accompany one of their teams to a hospital.

A representative looked at the boom mic and said, "This furry thing can't go in."

"Fine," I said, "the sound guy won't come."

He then looked at the camera. "This thing can't be disinfected—not acceptable."

"Then let me go alone, you can disinfect me," I said. "Give me a lapel mic. I can clip it inside my clothes."

"Is it really worth it?"

"Yes."

We followed an infectious disease researcher into the Capital Medical University's pulmonary hospital and were relieved to put on the hazmat suits they provided for us. The sick ward wasn't in the hospital building, but inside a row of single-story buildings, with a tightly closed glass door. The researcher walked ahead of me and pushed the door open just wide enough for one person to enter. Later, the executive producer said she watched the clip over and over in slow motion as I turned to wave at my coworkers and smiled before slipping in the door. She must have taken the moment as my eternal goodbye. In the moment, I didn't even have time to think about it.

When the door opened, there was darkness. The sunless corridor was long, like a hallway at a school. I felt a sudden chill, like having just jumped into water. The corridor was full of open windows. But there were no UV disinfection lights, no smell of peracetic acid or even Lysol. Airflow, it seemed, was the only means of disinfection.

The door to the patients' room was dark green, and the paint was peeling. It opened with a loud creak, and nearly touched the end of a hospital bed. An old man lay there with what looked like a high fever. His face was burning bright; his neck was thick and swollen. The flesh on his face seemed to pile up and there were dark purple half-moons under his eyes. He breathed with a sort of gurgling sound.

"Where are you from?" the researcher asked.

"Harbin." His accent was acutely Northeastern.

"Any family members?"

"Spouse."

"Her phone number?"

"She caught it too, passed away yesterday." At this point the old man began coughing violently. His entire upper body shook. Phlegm rattled deep in his throat.

I stood over a meter away; I wanted to hold my breath. But I breathed in sharply. The mask rubbed up and down against my nose. I felt out of breath. The door was right behind me. It was the first time in my life when I felt unable to control my body. I shrank back a step, desperate to flee.

The researcher, who was in his thirties, stood by the bed, unperturbed. He wasn't tall; his face was only a few dozen centimeters away from the old man's face. He wrote notes with a steady hand. He had his goggles pulled to the side, wearing only his glasses so he could see the words on the paper. After the old man's cough subsided, the researcher continued to ask questions, not a hint of fear in his voice.

I stared at the researcher for a few minutes to gather up enough courage to stand still.

Before leaving, I glanced over at a young man in another hospital bed. There was a towel for collecting phlegm wrapped around his neck, covered in stains. His calf poked out of the blanket, full of bulging veins. When we passed by him, he didn't even look at us. I studied him for a moment. He was conscious; his eyes were open, but there was no expression on his face. In the following days, when I saw the same expression on several faces, I understood it was desperation. I wanted to say something to him, but the researcher stopped me.

It was then that I realized why the whole place felt so eerie—in the sick ward, there were only patients. No doctors, no nurses, no sounds of shoes rubbing against concrete or the hum of machines, or metallic trays clanging against this or that. There was only utter silence. I had the sense that the system had stopped working.

The pulmonary hospital didn't have separate sterile and quarantine zones. After exiting, there was nowhere to sit, so we undressed standing up. I hopped on one foot as I pulled off a shoe cover, nearly tripping in the act. When I looked up and saw a cameraman pointing his machine at me, with the red recording light on, I realized I should say something. I stammered as I tried to organize into words what I had just seen. No one minded my stutter, or the red streaks left by the mask straps along my face.

When a machine suddenly starts after a long pause, it often does so with difficulty, issuing loud noises and shaking. This was how things seemed to me as I watched the government try to take action against the worsening crisis.

All potential cases of infection were to be quarantined immediately, the residences of each patient disinfected by a team of specialists from the Beijing CDC with the help of doctors. There was a feeling of chaos. I remember watching a doctor at the Haidian District Hospital as she put on a hazmat suit for the first time. Halfway through dressing, she went to get a bucket, perhaps for disinfectant. With the red bucket in hand, she seemed to have forgotten what she wanted to do next as she circled in place. I asked her what was wrong. She mumbled, "My child is only one, my baby is only one year old."

Eventually, she and a few other doctors ran to a CDC van that would take them to a disinfection site. We ran with them. The footage was shaky, like in a disaster movie. "While there's still daylight, quick!" the doctors shouted. Inside the van, they didn't speak. They nervously tied on their masks. Then they untied the masks and re-bound them more tightly.

The van arrived at the dormitory of China Agricultural University, where a student had been diagnosed with SARS after going to the Peking University People's Hospital for treatment of a cold. Two attendants were stationed there in dark blue suits. A doctor stuffed masks into the attendants' hands and said, "Put 'em on." Dumbfounded, the attendants put on the masks in complete obedience; each wore two blue masks layered one on top of the other. The chubbier of the two somehow also got a white nurse's cap, and wore it to eerily comic effect.

The patient had lived on the second floor. The disinfection specialists led the way. When they reached the student's room, they didn't knock, just began spraying disinfectant, making a lot of noise. The girls inside opened the door and saw a group of masked men dressed all in white spraying liquid at them. They screamed and slammed the door. After a few knocks and chatting for a bit, the door cracked open slightly. The sprayer entered first, aiming his nozzle at the checkered blanket, the poster of Maggie Cheung on the wall, the pink stuffed bunny . . . a fog of peracetic acid slowly settled, landing in a still-steaming bowl of instant noodles.

I noticed that in situations like these, people's natural reaction wasn't actually to cry or resist. Sitting at the table, a young girl who lived in the room anxiously handed me a train ticket.

"This is my ticket home this afternoon . . . Can you return it for me?" she asked. I didn't know what to do. After taking the ticket, I put it down on the table.

As we were leaving, the girls in the dormitory wanted to follow us. But they had to be quarantined, as close contacts of people infected with the virus. As the door slowly closed behind us, I saw their mouths pulling downward. They were about to cry. The doctor with the one-year-old baby went back in to comfort them. When she came out, she already knew what I was about to ask. She said, "I'm a mother."

At that moment, I could answer Chen Meng's question about how to forget myself.

Only when you care about someone else can you forget yourself.

Then we arrived at Hospital-721. This time, doctors and nurses charged toward the van, a mobile disinfection clinic. But they weren't wearing hazmat suits. A doctor in his forties with gold-rimmed glasses slapped the hood of the van heavily. His face was covered in tears. "Where has the government gone?" he cried. "Why is there no one helping us?"

The person responsible for disinfection was a young man who had just graduated from school and joined the Center for Disease Prevention and Control. He patted the doctor on the shoulder and said, "Bring me a bucket of water." He carefully poured a bottle of peracetic acid into the bucket. After filling the sprayer, he turned it on. Gears hummed into motion. He said, "Please step aside." Colorless liquid reached the nozzle and exploded into a million tiny droplets of mist, to be carried away by the wind.

"You can operate the sprayer later, when you need it again," he said. The doctor nodded, calm at last.

Since it had not yet been disinfected, the condition of the ward promised to be terrible. The young man in charge of the team of specialists asked the rest of us not to accompany him inside; he would go in alone. I tugged on the wristbands of his pale yellow latex gloves so that they would go under his sleeves—his gloves were too small, always slipping down, exposing his wrists. He looked at me. I didn't even know what his name was. We were both wearing hazmat suits, so we could only see each other's eyes.

He said, "Be careful. The real peak will come after the May 1st holiday."

Alone, wearing a sprayer on his back, he turned a corner and disappeared.

Before May, anyone with the means left the city. Everyone thought Beijing would be under full lockdown by then. Some even thought that planes would spray disinfectant from the air. Beijing was like a boiling pot about to have a lid put on it. I couldn't go home, so my younger sister was there alone. She jostled her way through the supermarket, unsure of what to buy, eventually carrying home a case of eggs.

Then, as if with a loud crash, everything collapsed. All work stopped, schools closed, stores closed, and entertainment venues closed. The rug was pulled out from under daily life. My crew and I were posted at the emergency center. The number of calls coming in there on any given day used to be around three hundred. Now it was over seven thousand.

On April 22, the emergency center received an order to transport patients out of Peking University People's Hospital. It was rumored that this hospital was the source of the most SARS patient infections, and it was where the girl from the Chinese Agricultural University had been diagnosed. Six ambulances left, and we tailed them. Even the drive was eerie. Chang'an Avenue, one of the widest streets in the world, was completely empty, not a single traffic cop in sight. We were in a Jinbei van, chasing the ambulances with speed and fury. Spring had come late that year, but when it did arrive, it seemed to do so in a rush. The winter jasmine lining the streets had grown restless. Golden branches of new growth shot out everywhere, framing the drab, empty road. The old Jinbei van reached a hundred and twenty kilometers an hour on the road. With the windows down and no one outside, the wind blasted our faces savagely. I used to think that my entire life would consist only of asking the right questions every day, putting my clothes on the right way, and walking down those familiar, tiresome streets. I had never imagined there would be a day like this.

When our van came to a stop at the hospital, I saw two doctors pushing something covered in white cloth, running down the bumpy pavement.

For a moment, I was terrified.

It wasn't until they hoisted the thing into an ambulance that I realized it was a wheelchair. It carried an old lady draped from head to toe in white cloth, which was so long it dragged on the ground. She was a SARS patient, though she wasn't wearing a hazmat suit or a mask, and she'd come down the regular visitor elevator. The white cloth covering her body was only a bedsheet, ripped off of a hospital bed as a make-shift layer of isolation.

Other patients followed her, one by one, into the ambulance, many of them carrying their own IV drips. I counted twenty-nine of them.

None of the doctors transporting these patients was wearing hazmat suits, goggles, or even gloves—for protection, they only had the usual blue surgical gowns and a thin mask of the same color. I waved down someone who looked like an authority figure. In a rush, he said something about a "courtyard problem." He was the vice president of Peking University People's Hospital, Wang Jishan. A week later, he too would be infected.

When we returned to the hotel at night, everyone was quiet.

The editor Tian He smoked his pipe tobacco for a while and said, "Feels like being in *The Cassandra Crossing*. The train is heading toward danger, the passengers hear a loud noise—and the people outside are nailing the windows shut."

We stayed at a small hotel. It was brave of them to accept us under such circumstances. Inside the front door were two thin ropes tracing out a path to an elevator just for us. Inside the elevator, only the third-floor button lit up. They boarded over all the other buttons in case we even thought about wandering. There were no other guests on the third floor. The empty corridor was lined with UV lights, giving the space a fluorescent glow. The floor attendant called our rooms to say she was leaving. We would have to take care of ourselves. She left us each a thermometer. The courtyard outside the window where boys usually played with balls was empty. It was full of clothes drying on steel wires, swaying beneath a pale sun.

We didn't bring our footage directly to the office, but left it in a bag at the gate to our office building. Someone would pick it up and steril- ize it before editing.

The concierge of the building complex where I lived knew that I had been to the hospitals. He called me. "Are you okay? Everyone is worried about you . . . you won't be coming back soon, right?" Of course, I understood. My little sister came to the hotel to deliver some clothes and a small stereo. The street was empty at night. When she was about four meters away, I told her to stop right there.

"Put it down and go," I said. I waved at her. "Just go."

Little Sis stood in the dim streetlight and looked at me. Before I left for the hospital, we talked about our parents. I asked her, "Do you think I should go to the hospital?" She said, "You can decide to not be a journalist, but once you are a journalist, you no longer have the right to not go."

In the mornings, when my eyes were still closed, I felt around for the thermometer under the pillow and stuck it in my armpit as I snoozed for five minutes longer. Whether or not I had a temperature, I had to go to the hospital anyway. But one day, the air exiting my nose felt hot. The heat traveled all the way to my temples. I was sure I was infected. Eyes closed, I tried to imagine how to sneak a camcorder into the sick ward—I wouldn't die for nothing. After opening my eyes to look at the thermometer, it only read thirty-six and a half degrees Celsius.

I once spoke to a police officer who took the portraits of inmates on death row. She said it never scared her, except for when she was showering at night, as she was lathering shampoo into her hair and soap bubbles formed. Suddenly, those faces appeared.

During SARS, I seldom felt fear. There were much more powerful feelings in command. But that night, under the showerhead with water running down my skin, when I closed my eyes and rubbed the foam on my face, I felt something touching my cheeks. My eyes opened wide, my heart hit my chest. I reached to touch the vein in my neck out of some primal instinct, to make sure that I was still alive. Later, I learned that the rest of the team had also thought they had been infected. We all took long hot showers, as if it would clean off the invisible virus covering our bodies, irritating our noses and mouths.

The station allotted the five of us antibody shots, which were treated like life-saving injections and in short supply. Since our driver, Zhou, wasn't an employee of the station, they did not give him one.

"Either all six of us go or none of us will go," we declared. We made phone calls requesting an extra allotment, but it didn't work. The five shots were scheduled to be administered at eight P.M., after which the offer would expire. The sound mixer, Liu Chang, said, "Forget your damn offer." At seven-thirty P.M., he locked his door and refused to come out no matter how much we knocked. One of the cameramen, Chen Wei, who was his old friend, nudged me and said, "Let's go, he won't come out."

When the rest of us returned, Liu had just finished his tea. With a cigarette dangling from the corner of his mouth, he "sterilized" his boom mic the old-fashioned way—wrapping a women's black silk stocking over the windscreen. Squinting from the smoke, he said, "If I'm going to die, I'm going to die with my cock high."

The next day at the hospital, we ran into a female patient holding her own IV drip. When she saw Chen Wei's camera pointing at her, she turned to the nearest doctor and said, "Film some more and I'll rip my mask off and kiss the son of a bitch." We all laughed.

As long as people can still laugh, they won't easily be defeated.

In the emergency ward, our other cameraman, Xiao Peng, looked for pretty nurses to sterilize him. His favorite was the one he called "Wire Eyes." The girl wore a mask, so all he could see were her big bright eyes and long lashes like a row of steel wires. He stared at her from a distance, never daring to go close. Wire Eyes screamed at him, "Get over here! Sterilize!"

He said, "I'm not afraid to die."

Wire Eyes sneered. "Plenty more of your type around. Yesterday, I dragged out two that were even less afraid of death than you. They're both dead now."

He quickly approached her. "Then give me a little extra."

Wire Eyes rolled her eyes at him and poured a bottle of disinfectant onto him.

"Should I get some on my head too?" He pointed at his bald head jokingly.

The girl poured the rest of the bottle on his head. He was humbled.

Hanging with the guys brought out my rougher side. As the van cruised down the empty streets, they handed me a cheap cigarette, assuring me that smoking it would prevent SARS. After work, we looked for somewhere to eat. All the restaurants were closed except one Hunan restaurant that was still open in spite of the lockdown. Bored, with no customers, a couple of servers dressed in red coats and green pants stood outside swinging a workout rope. When they saw our van approach, they put away the rope with smiles on their faces. They served us their spiciest stir-fried donkey meat on a hot wok, enough to pile up into a precarious pyramid. I don't know who said that chili can "disinfect," but the guys asked for extra bowls of garlic slices, chili pepper slices, and bright green garlic scapes, which were all thrown into the bubbling red broth. They poured the meat and broth over bowls of rice, soaked it with ice water, then buried their faces in the food. Big droplets of sweat covered their bald heads. Someone said to a server, "We need ten thousand napkins."

After finishing the whole wok, they poured me a shot glass of baijiu and began reminiscing about the time they shot a solar eclipse in Xinjiang. They said the entire world had gone black except for a tiny red dot at the center of the sun, as bright as a diamond. Xiao Peng said he threw his equipment down on the sands of the Gobi Desert and cried with his face up. That's the kind of person he was. When he shot interviews, he often used extreme close-ups. Sometimes there would be nothing but a pair of eyes in the frame. "Look into someone's eyes and you'll know if they're for real."

Some of the patients we had seen being transported out from People's Hospital went to the Capital Medical University's You An Hospital, where doctors had experience in treating infectious diseases. We were granted permission to interview these patients. When a middle-aged woman sitting up in her bed saw me come in masked, she heaved as she said, "So CCTV sent over a little doll?"

I smiled back. "I do look young with my face covered up."

She talked about having trouble breathing and being delirious four or five days prior. Then she pointed to a doctor. "She pulled me back from death." I asked the patient what she thought about the most. Looking outside, she said, "If I get better, I'd really like to fly a kite."

Xiao Peng's camera panned, following her gaze through the window. It was spring; the city had grown thick with weeds.

Exiting the room, I spoke with a doctor. "How is her condition?"

The doctor, whose name was Dr. Meng, looked to be around forty years old. She wore a smile like a spring breeze, and didn't answer me directly. "After the patient arrived, she didn't sleep at night. She was always sitting with her eyes open, afraid that she might never wake up again. If it goes on any longer, she'll collapse. I said to her, 'Give me three days, I promise you'll be well.'"

When heaven collapses and the earth shatters, people can only depend on people—those people that you don't see, don't notice in your day-to-day. Everyone in this sick ward looked at Dr. Meng's expression with a sort of childlike neediness. Before leaving her, I said, "When a doctor wants others to live, she must be prepared for her own sacrifice. Are you?"

"I am." She opened the glass door for us.

While we sorted out our gear in an open area, Tian He asked me with a camcorder in his hand, "Are you afraid of SARS?"

"I'm not afraid of it, I detest it." I turned and walked away.

We came out of the hospital to a rosy May sunset and a grove of slick black Siberian elms. Why were the trees so pretty? At night, I listened to piano music on the small stereo. Why did it sound so darn good? On the streets, even the run-down buildings elicited a few extra glances.

After work there was nowhere to go, so we sat around in Beihai Park. The bird keepers, the fishermen, the feather ball players, the people who gorged on street food . . . they were all gone. The park was empty. It was an exceedingly rare occasion when you could smell the wet scent of nature in this bustling public venue. An old man in a blue cotton shirt sat in a faded red gazebo. A gray cloth covered his knees as he sat playing a Chinese fiddle to the lake. His music had a tone of calm that no disaster could destroy. We listened for a long time until dusk folded into night.

•   •   •

The episode titled "The War on SARS" aired on April 26, 2003. The crew and I watched it from our hotel rooms, along with over seventy million people. That really brought home the power of television for me. Ten minutes into the broadcast, we buried our heads in our phones, answering calls and responding to texts. Before that moment, I really had not realized how many people I had known in this world. I received a text from an unknown number saying, "If you are infected, can I marry you?"

Xiao Peng studied his cell phone for a while but couldn't understand why the public's reaction was so overwhelming. He looked up and said, "Aren't we just doing our jobs?"

Chen Meng called me as well. He didn't compliment me or criticize me. He said, "I want to give you a couplet—till the land for its own sake, without expectation of harvest."

My parents, who lived in Shanxi province, didn't know about me going to the hospital. The school where my mother worked was temporarily closed. When she saw the broadcast, she was playing mahjong at a neighbor's house. Her hands froze. The neighbor later said that my mother cried. But she said nothing to me about it. She wasn't the sentimental type. All she asked me was, "What do you plan to do next?"

Next, I wanted to go back to People's Hospital, because I couldn't stop thinking about the "courtyard problem." By then, it'd become the site of one of the biggest and most difficult battles against SARS. Starting on April 5, about 222 people had been infected at the hospital, including ninety-three hospital staff across nearly half the departments. The emergency ward north of the outpatient wing was the most severely affected; that was where the courtyard was. On April 22, I had seen patients covered in white cloth being rolled out of there. Two days later, when our van passed by once more, the eighty-five-year-old hospital had just announced a full quarantine. Beyond the yellow quarantine tape, three nurses sat on the empty steps, holding their blue nurse's caps. Their long wet hair was drying in the sun. As they sat in silence, one would occasionally comb her fingers through the hair hanging in front of her chest. Our van parked in front of the hospital for over ten minutes. Xiao Peng pointed his camcorder at them from a distance.

I felt that there must be a correlation between the twenty-nine patients I'd witnessed being transferred without proper protection and the high rate of infection now sweeping the hospital. I wanted to know more about what had happened. No one asked me to work on the story. I wasn't even sure if I could make it at all, let alone get it on the air, but my team was willing to work with me. No matter what, I needed to know, I had to know—that was when I finally understood what Chen Meng had meant by "desire."

I ended up getting an interview with Zhu Jihong, the director of the emergency ward. He confessed to me that, at the time of transfer, the twenty-nine patients I'd counted were all in fact infected with SARS. In fact, the emergency ward had already been battling known cases since April 5. But rather than report the cases, the real numbers were hidden from the World Health Organization when they came to inspect the hospital. The patients had been transferred to ambulances that drove around Beijing in circles until the inspectors left.

I'd spent a long time convincing Zhu Jihong to accept the interview. I said, "You don't need to make any judgments or draw any conclusions, just describe what you saw, heard, and felt, that's all."

After a long pause on the phone, he said, "The memory is too painful."

"Of course," I said, "but pain can be cathartic, consolation for one's sacrifices."

· · ·

Zhu Jihong led me through the emergency ward corridor. He leaned over, undid the heavy chain lock, and pushed the door open. He reached for the wall with his left hand and after some flickering the lights turned on. In the ashen light, the classroom-sized space was filled with blue IV chairs tagged with white labels that read: *April 17, Thursday; April 17, Thursday* . . .

The beds were littered with rumpled blankets, some of which had fallen to the ground. Chairs were upturned, four feet in the air, left there by people fleeing for their lives.

This was the courtyard I had been hearing so much about. It was a space wedged between four buildings. With the addition of a roof, it had become an indoor space, sealed off from traffic in the rest of the hospital. They'd used it as the IV room, where all the patients with fevers came to receive their drips. Twenty-seven beds sat shoulder to shoulder with only the space of a fist between them. Every day, almost sixty people had sat tightly together on the beds and among a few chairs. Even during the daytime, the room completely depended on artificial lighting. There was no airflow, no windows, only a ventilation panel connected to the central air conditioning system, which spread the germs across the whole hospital.

The patient files that piled up in a mound on a desk were yellowing with age. I hesitated for a second. Zhu Xuhong said with a dismal smile, "Allow me." He opened the files, which said *pneumonia*. He pointed toward a blackboard. Next to the twenty-two names written in white chalk, nineteen read: *pneumonia, pneumonia, pneumonia* . . .

"In fact, it was SARS," he said.

Even the patients had not known. It was like a taboo. No one in the hospital had even called SARS by its name. They'd called it "that thing."

The first patient had come in on April 5. The doctors suspected she was a SARS patient after seeing her chest radiograph. But the government announced that all cases were from outside Beijing. All public hospitals are managed by the government. And according to the standards for diagnosis and treatment in Beijing, the doctors could only diagnose someone who had a history of direct contact with a confirmed infected person.

The patient denied this possibility, because she was afraid of being expelled by the hospital, and so for two days, she stayed in a room with other patients until the CDC confirmed she had a relative who'd died from SARS. The nurses and the patients who had been in contact with her were never quarantined. The hospital had no infectious diseases department, no isolation ward, and no one had received practical training on how to handle SARS even though it had started two months prior. Two patients who stayed in the same room with the first case went on to infect fourteen doctors and nurses after being transferred to general wards. Six nurses in the emergency ward developed symptoms a week later, then more. The courtyard was still open. A public hospital couldn't close its clinics or issue warnings to patients without a government order.

"What about the patients who needed to be on an IV for other reasons?" I asked.

"Tough. They were stuck in here."

Had I been sitting in the recording studio, I would have said, "How can you guys be so irresponsible?" But standing there, watching Zhu Xuhong speak with a numb look of despair, I felt like my heart was being squeezed, like I was unable to draw another breath. When all the cleaners in the hospital fled, he and his colleagues were stuck in here as well. Of the sixty-two people working in the emergency ward, twenty-four were infected, and two doctors had died. One of them was another director of the emergency ward. When the young nurses looked through the glass window at a colleague who was on a ventilator, they cried because they all knew what it meant. Zhu said, "We were ready to sacrifice all."

I nervously donned a full-body gown and went back into the pulmonary hospital ward, then spent forty minutes at the emergency center, sterilizing. I soaked my hands with sweat from my rubber gloves. These doctors and nurses didn't even have the most basic protective equipment, yet they were caring for over twenty SARS patients in the courtyard, alone. Niu Xiaoxiu, the emergency ward nurse, said with tears streaming down her cheeks, "I made requests every day but I couldn't even get a mask, so I just boiled them in a pot and made everyone reuse them . . . I don't know if it was my fault or whose fault it was . . ."

I asked Zhu what it was like to be there. He said, "I didn't look in the mirror for days. Later, I saw my beard was all white."

On April 18, the hospital finally transformed a boiler room into a SARS sick ward for twenty-seven people—the room was full in one day. Zhu Jihong led me to the ward, but I only saw ordinary rooms. Skeptical, I asked him, "Where are your sanitized zone and quarantine zone?"

He pointed to the ground and said, "Just draw a line on the ground."

I couldn't believe what I was hearing, so I followed up: "How do you separate your sanitized zone from your contamination zone?"

After a long pause, Zhu Xuhong raised his hand and pointed to his heart. "With this."

I asked, "What did you use for protection?"

Expressionless, he said, "We protected ourselves with our spirits, our bare hands."

The doctors' families were so distressed; they called the head of the hospital, Lyu Houshan, and yelled at him. "Did the dog eat your heart?" He had no reply. He had begged and begged his superior to allow the hospital to stop accepting new patients. The answer was no. He had asked to transfer the SARS patient, but there was no place to receive them. He had asked for protective clothes, but there were none. He had tried to buy white cloth to make some, but the market was out of stock because of panic hoarding. He could only cry in despair. "What am I still living for?" he asked in front of the camera. "I am worthless . . ."

The courtyard was finally quarantined, but the emergency ward had to stay open, and it was impossible to isolate others from SARS patients. New patients continued to flood in, then left the hospital carrying the danger with them. The hospital had become the center of the outbreak. The emergency ward ended up seeing 8,363 new patients by April 22. There wasn't even enough space to hold all the IV stands, so patients took their drips outside to the clearing.

Zhu took me over to see. There were still some chairs left, and bottles hanging on IV stands and on the side-view mirrors of cars. When there hadn't been enough chairs, they'd made do with stools. An official from the medical establishment had been infected here, and when he'd went home, he'd infected his wife and child. He did everything he could to get a hospital bed, but there was only one left, so they put their son in it. The couple was soaking wet from their fever and couldn't stand upright. They shivered as they received drips, sitting on tiny stools. By the time the child recovered, his parents had already passed.

The chairs scattered outside had stayed exactly where they were from April to the end of May. No one touched them. Though they'd started out blue, they became faded in the sun and turned green. They seemed like a crowd of invisible mutes facing the hospital's wide-open front door, just opposite China's Ministry of Public Health.

On April 22, Zeng Guang, the chief scientist at the Chinese Center for Disease Control and Prevention examined this hospital. He said, "When buildings are about to collapse, escaping is the only choice." Two days later, People's Hospital quarantined. Zhang Wenkang, the minister of health, was fired, and within one week, the army built the biggest field medical hospital in Beijing. There were 686 SARS cases there, almost one-tenth of all global cases.

• • •

On May 27, Wang Jing, a nurse from the emergency ward, passed away. At thirty-two years old, she had hooked up the first SARS patient to a ventilator on April 5, having worked from that day to the day when the courtyard closed. She fell there, in the line of duty.

Her husband read me her text messages at their home.

The first said, *The flowers outside the window are blooming; I'll be better soon.*

He couldn't visit his wife, so he stood outside the hospital every day. Unable to enter, he guarded her from the closest position he could.

She wrote, *Go home. Stay strong. You're the only person in this world I can depend on.*

After that, when she realized she would not get better, she texted him the password to her savings account. In her final text, she told him to put on a red waist strap. *It's your zodiac year, it'll keep you safe.*

He wailed as he read. My tears followed. Xiao Peng gave me a look as if to say, "How can a journalist act like that?" But I couldn't help myself.

He hadn't yet told his daughter, Da Bao, who was six years old with soft short hair and sharp eyes, sitting on her bed folding lucky stars. On her bedroom door was a note that read, *Mama loves me, I love mama.*

I said, "You want your mama to see it as soon as she comes home, right?" She nodded. Once she filled up a whole jar of lucky stars, her mother would return. I watched her fold those origami stars. The wide-mouthed glass jar was already one-third full. She folded slowly. When she finished a star, she didn't throw it in the jar, but ever so carefully placed it at the top of the pile.

After I left, as the van drove down Beijing's second ring, black clouds weighed oppressively upon the city—an impending storm. In our van full of people, no one spoke.

Nine years later, people would often say, "This is the journalist who went into SARS sick wards," which left me feeling embarrassed. When the courtyard was full of SARS patients, the information provided by the media still told citizens that they could walk on the street without masks.

In the beginning, I was just watching TV, a tiny cog in a giant machine, not doubting the official story. By the time I reported it, it was too late. I beat myself up for this. I only hoped that our coverage would prevent it from happening again. That it would be a future remedy.

In the episode, the last question I asked Zhu Jihong was, "After being through such a tragic war, do you think your hospital could win if a similar crisis happened again?"

He said, "If the layout and conditions remain the same, we would still fail."

After our segment aired, a colleague said to me, "You guys are just creating panic." Sitting next to me was Hu Shuli, the editor-in-chief of *Caijin* magazine. She said, "What's worse than panic is carelessness."

The episode "SARS Attacks People's Hospital" aired on June 2; the same day, there were zero new confirmed cases in Beijing. We would go back home if the results of our tests were negative.

We sat in the van and waited outside Beijing Union Medical College Hospital for half an hour. At first we cracked some jokes and laughed, but before long, everyone was quiet. Tian He's phone rang. He answered. "That's right . . . The results are out? . . . Oh, really? Who? . . . Yes, there's a girl . . ."

I sat in the front row, motionless, cursing silently to myself.

He poked me with his phone. "Hey, the doctor says your Immuno-globulin A count is low, your immune system's not great."

Our Jinbei van cruised aimlessly down the streets. No one wanted to break up the band. We wanted to keep going. The producer Zhang Jie called. "Where do you want to go next?" he asked.

I said, "I'll go anywhere."

Back at the hotel, while packing my bag, the band Skinny Puppy was playing on the small stereo. From the upper floors of the hotel, I could see the vast city that would come alive from the ruins. After staring outside for a while, I turned around, put on a pair of headphones, tied a bandana around my head, and maxed out the volume. Had someone seen me, they would have thought that I was crazy, because those movements were not a dance, only the hapless twitching of a body under extreme stress, and the music was like someone standing on a precipice screaming into a storm.

Eyes closed, limbs flailing, I twitched and gyrated until my left ankle, the one with an old wound, crashed into the leg of a table. The pain was like being stabbed with a knife. Such a combination of pleasure and pain could make a person's hair stand on end. The synthetic voice behind the electro-industrial pop sounded like metal scraping brutally against metal. Chains shattered, eyes opened, like a critter that had just been freed, I stared longingly at a new world.

Months later, I received a letter. It was short. "Do you still remember Hospital-721?"

I quickly skimmed my way down the page.

"Ever since, I have been searching for your eyes on every street."

I sat up. It was the young man whose glove I had stretched under his sleeve in the hospital. We had never seen each other's faces or known each other's names.

"Once, when I thought I recognized you, I grabbed a girl and asked, 'Is it you?' It mortified her. It wasn't until I saw you on TV that I finally knew who you were. So you're a famous journalist."

He finished by saying, "Do you find it funny too? That I once thought you might be my other half?"

Interview with a little boy who lost his sister, the central figure in the mass suicide of elementary school students. Shuangcheng, Gansu, 2005.

Three
The Wounded Twin Cities
2003

On my first day at *News Probe*, a young intern came in to talk to me. She wore a crooked hair clip and several sets of dangling earrings. She sang wherever she was, and a pair of headphone wires descended from her ears. Short shorts, long legs, and for every word you said, she'd chirp back with a hundred. At twenty-three years old, she resented her youthfulness and always covered her red lips up with white lipstick. "It adds a little je ne sais quoi." Well, since this little girl wanted to look older, I told her, "I'll call you Old Fan, then." After struggling a few times, she accepted it.

Fresh out of college, Old Fan had applied for a job, and every time the boss opened his mouth to ask her a question, she'd beat him to the punch with a "Listen . . ." It was probably out of some sort of fatherly compassion that the producer, Zhang Jie, let her stay.

"I have three *-less* qualities," she said to me once. "Brainless, fearless, shameless."

You really haven't suffered yet, young lady, I thought to myself.

One of the leads she'd come up with seemed to attest to this. The gist was, in May 2003, several students from a sixth-grade class committed suicide by ingesting poison. No one knew why. The kids who'd survived had kept silent. The media thought it had something to do with a cult. She took this lead everywhere, but nobody was interested, so finally she came to me. I wasn't into this kind of sensational story, but the silence touched me.

Zhang Jie looked at the two of us in a meeting we called to discuss Old Fan's lead, knowing full well that it would be a waste of money to report this story. Usually, we needed to be at least 80 percent certain before taking on a story, or else the cost to travel to the site was too high. But he said, "Fine. But go easy on the budget, forget about two cameras, don't bother taking the sound mixer. A camcorder will do."

Outside the Wuwei airport, in Gansu province, we hailed a cab. The driver's name was Mao, and he had a stoic Northwestern face. There was a Teresa Teng disc in the car that he must have listened to for years. Old Fan and I swayed our bodies as we sang along to "Repay:" *"Silent lips, rolling tears, but it isn't the rouge . . ."* He peeked at us in the rearview mirror, then peeked at us again, smiling.

In the wide open Northwest, golden rapeseed blossomed like an endless river. Behind one sage-colored hill was another. During the drive, I mentioned how much I loved *Friends*; it had been a formative part of my youth. Old Fan cackled and pounced on me, shaking me until my hair became disheveled.

The journalist who'd come to Twin City before us had said that the local government hadn't been kind. Undaunted, under the cover of a windy, moonless night, we searched for the home of Little Yang, the last child to have survived.

Twin City was an economically underdeveloped satellite town in the west, with a population of just over thirty thousand. After ten o'clock at night, only a few houses kept their lights on. One of them was Little Yang's. We knocked even though it was late, and a man, Little Yang's father, let us in. In the courtyard was a vegetable garden soaked in chemical fertilizers. Nearby, a row of shoes dried on a concrete pipe. The father had just returned home drunk, red in the face; neck swollen, chest out; he couldn't speak clearly. The mother sat in complete silence. I asked her if we could talk to her son; she said nothing, just stood up and led us to his room. The moment we sat down, the door crashed open. Five local brutes who refused to reveal their identities tried to scare us off so that we couldn't report news that would negatively impact the city's image. Old Fan argued with them about human rights and freedom of the press, like a donkey debating a horse. It was enough to buy me some time.

I seized the moment and asked Little Yang, "Would you be willing to come back to our hotel in Wuwei tomorrow for an interview?" The boy had been sitting with his thin neck bent, head bowed in silence. All I could see were his two thick eyebrows. I expected little, but he said, "I'm willing."

I couldn't help but ask, "Why?"

He said, "Because I saw your report on SARS."

All the compliments I had received for months about my SARS report couldn't compare to this.

On the way back to the hotel, Mao, our driver, made a fuss. "We're being followed."

We looked behind us. There was only a black Santana with a lone driver and no one in the backseat. We got out of the car at the hotel. The next day, when Mao came to pick us up, he told us that two people had stepped out of the Santana the night before and gotten in his car. "Those journalists who were in here before," they said, "who are they with?"

Mao drove to the police station and dropped the two guys off there before going home to sleep.

We learned that the two guys were the town mayor and his colleague. We went to talk to them. "What's up with the clandestine operation? This story has nothing to do with you."

The middle-aged mayor let out a sigh of relief and removed the aviators that obscured half of his face.

I said, "How come we couldn't see you guys in the car?"

Pleased with himself, he said, "When you looked back, the two of us instantly crouched down. Quick reflexes, right?"

Little Yang agreed to see me, but wouldn't talk about what had happened. I didn't want to push him and said, "I want to see where it happened. Tomorrow, we're going to your school."

He abruptly asked, "Can you take me with you?"

The next day, we went to school together. The principal came out to open the gate for us. He was middle-aged, graying. Combing his fingers through his hair reflexively, he sheepishly smiled.

"These couple of months," he said in a hoarse voice, "there's been a lot on my mind. Too much stress. I'm about to have a breakdown." When he strained to put on a smile, his face practically twitched.

We arrived at the tile-roofed sixth-grade classroom. Studying the desks, I saw that some had the numbers *519* carved into them, leaving deep, crooked grooves. Even the thick coat of red paint that had been slathered on afterward couldn't hide them. Little Yang stopped in front of a desk, head bowed in silence. He touched the numbers.

The desk had belonged to the first girl to take poison, Miao Miao, who'd died on May 19. She was also the first one to have carved the number. Another girl, Little Cai, who took poison with her, was in stable condition after immediate treatment. Around noon two days later, on May 21, their classmate Little Sun took poison; on May 23, Little Ni took poison. The night of the twenty-third, Little Yang also took poison, and these three boys were all rescued after treatment.

All their desks had *519* carved into them.

As the people in town rolled their cigarettes, their eyes glimmered; it was hard to tell if they were excited or horrified. "I'll tell you what," some of them said, "it's definitely some sort of cult. I hear they even have skin-bound books." Their eyes would roam to a nearby stone building. "And that thing, probably cursed."

The building was the Dipper Temple. Apparently there was a statue of the Deity of Fate in there. They said the kids often hung around there; they even carved something in places.

My eyes met Old Fan's. We felt chilled.

Little Yang wouldn't say much. He told us to go ask Miao Miao's friend Little Chen. She knew everything.

We found the girl's home. Twelve years old with thick black hair, a pale face, and a sharp chin, she was wearing a white blouse with tiny floral prints, sweeping the ground with a broom. When she saw us approach, she calmly waved her broom and said, "Wait 'til I finish." She swept slowly, row by row, leaving fine streaks on the earthen floor. When she finished, she hung the broom on a hook against the wall. After telling her mother to bring us some chairs, she went into the room to make a call, then brushed the bamboo fringe to the side and sat down in front of us.

No matter what question I asked, she would calmly answer, "I don't know, I'm not sure."

I said, "Wasn't Miao Miao a good friend of yours?"

She said, "There are lots of people in our class. They're all my friends."

"Don't you care about what happened?"

She said coolly, "Too busy with schoolwork; no time to care."

She looked at me, politely waiting for the next question. There was nothing in those bright black eyes, only my reflection. At a certain point I ran out of questions. That was when footsteps rustled outside. Several adults entered.

"Do you have a press pass?" they asked me.

They wore dark blue jackets and black leather boots. These weren't townsfolk; from the looks of it, they were from the city's propaganda department. The little girl had called them, as she had been told. They didn't want us hanging around the town, so they put us in their cars and drove us to a scenic area called the Leitai Han Tomb, a local tourist attraction.

"Now this is something interesting to report on," they said.

Tour guides followed us the entire way, explaining everything. This was Old Fan's first time in the countryside. When she saw a real live frog on the ground, she hopped along with it, laughing and screaming. The comrades from the propaganda department had never seen such a childish journalist. Old Fan was awestruck by the majestic Northwestern sky, screaming at me as she pointed, "Cloud!"

There was a guy in his thirties who was in charge of the propaganda department walking in front of us. The last character in his name was "Cloud." He blushed as he turned to us in surprise: "Yes?"

Everyone laughed. After that, it became too awkward to keep up the serious act.

I said, "I know it's a difficult situation for everyone, but if we don't let the real story out, everyone will continue to think there's some sort of cult. That's not good for anyone. The more we can find out, the more you will have to work with. Agreed?"

Cloud sighed. "We've been investigating this incident for a long time now. At first, we thought it was a cult. Now we're sure it's nothing of the sort. But beyond that, we can't figure it out. Go ahead and try if you want."

We went to the Dipper Temple, where local people believed the cults gathered. The door had long been barred with steel wire. There were signs that people, perhaps children, had climbed over a sloped wall on their hands and feet. Their passage had worn a gray brick smooth. I found someone to open the door and walked up the stairs.

The statue of the Deity of Fate had been missing since before anyone could remember. Its pedestal was like an empty stage. There was a stone screen wall that had, until recently, been covered in engravings.

After the incident, the government had tried to plaster it over with lime. The wall wasn't large. I didn't have any tools with me, so I began rubbing it with my hands. The plaster was thin and dry; the engravings quickly revealed themselves. The squiggly characters, carved with razor blades, read, "Love at first sight" or "Master of the universe," nothing more. I grew up in a small town, so it wasn't surprising to me that kids would hang out at a place like this; it was perhaps the only thing of any cultural significance in the entire town, the only place that could offer a small nook for one's imagination to flourish inside of.

The government officials told me that all they had found in terms of possible evidence was a teen magazine on Miao Miao's desk. One page was dog-eared. It was a story about a girl who died for love. They thought these stories had influenced her. So they had arranged a sudden search of all the students' bags to see who else owned these magazines. Some students threw the contraband on the roof to avoid being found out.

I asked Little Yang if the magazine was the reason for Miao's suicide. The boy was impatient and dismissive. "How would that even make sense? We all read it."

The small town had no Internet café, no bookstores, and the only entertainment at school was a ping pong table where two rows of bricks passed for a net. The street vendors were still selling Zheng Zhihua's cassette tapes from the nineties, and there were no posters of any stars for sale. The only thing Little Yang had put on the wall of his bedroom was a big square sheet of white paper, on which was handwritten the lyrics to a love song, with squiggly musical notation written above. Kids in the countryside started school late, and Twin City Elementary had six grades. So at age thirteen, Miao Miao was still in elementary school; when I was thirteen, I had almost finished middle school. At that age, I remembered, all the girls in my class were copying out romance stories by hand, obsessed with the drama and the sentimentality. The magazine clipping Miao Miao had glued onto her book jacket was the same I would've picked at her age—a picture of Barbara Yung, a popular TV star who had killed herself over a love affair.

When Miao Miao committed suicide by eating rat poison, another girl, Little Cai, had attempted to join her.

When we went to speak to Little Cai at her home, her mother blocked the door. "No filming, my daughter has already recovered. She was just under evil influence."

I asked her, "Do you know why she took poison?"

No answer.

"How long has she kept her silence?"

"Over ten days."

"Are you worried?"

She stayed silent.

"May I try to talk to her?"

At that, her mother cleared the way.

Little Cai sat on a small chair outside the door. The crew and I hated blurring out the faces of our subjects with mosaic tiles, finding it hideous and disrespectful, so the cameraman, Hai Nan, shot her in silhouette against the backdrop of a deep blue sky and the lush green pumpkin leaves growing in her garden. She had thin eyebrows and wore a single, crooked braid that cast a shadow on the ground. I asked a question; she said nothing. I handed her a bottle of water and she hugged it like a doll.

I saw her elbow. Cut into her thin wrist was a tiny character that meant "bear it," filled in with ink.

I asked, "What are you bearing?"

She didn't speak.

"Can you sleep?"

The child shook her head.

Face-to-face, we sat in silence. I said to her, "When I was your age, I had a friend named Gao Rong. She was my best friend, but suddenly, one day, she stopped coming to school. For the first time, I had to walk home alone, and it made me so sad. Later, as I got older, I understood. It's just like the line from that poem in our textbook: 'We are separated by this world forever, but our hearts are always together.'"

Tears streamed down her face. She turned and went into the house, retrieving a slip of paper from a booklet. On the paper were squiggly words written in colorful markers: "We, six sisters, are the best of friends, rich or poor, 'til death do us part." Below were six signatures. They included Little Cai's, Miao Miao's, and Little Chen's.

Little Cai told me that, a few months back, a boy touched Miao Miao's breasts at a party. A few students saw it and gossiped about it. "They made it sound awful." That was when Miao Miao began contemplating suicide.

I asked, "What pained her the most?"

"After the party, many classmates criticized her . . ." She didn't go on.

When I talked about the event with Little Yang, he handed me his notebook, in which he'd written about Miao Miao: "She had no way out, but she still had self-esteem. I understand her, which is why I'm also heartbroken." He refused to go into any details, so I asked him, "From what you understand of Miao Miao, what do you think troubled her the most?"

He whispered, "The way other people shamed her, I guess."

Little Cai told me that Miao Miao had tried to commit suicide more than once. On April 29, she'd spent fifty cents at a small shop to buy a bag of pellet-shaped rat poison called Sniff 'N' Die. During a weekly class meeting, she pulled the bag out of her desk drawer. Her classmates noticed. They said, "If you eat it, we all have to eat it."

Over a dozen students tried to stop her. They each took two pellets. The teacher was correcting homework and never noticed the poison-taking. Shocked, I asked Little Cai, "And then?" It was the first time I saw a child crack a bitter smile.

"The drug was fake," she said.

On May 19, during afternoon recess, Miao Miao was sitting alone on the blacktop reading a book. A male classmate tried to strangle her from behind with the leather strap on his slingshot, then let her go. She grabbed anything she could find on the ground and tried to hit him with it, but missed. Two other boys appeared. One of them shouted, "He touched Miao Miao's boob!"

After that, Miao Miao talked about wanting to die again. Little Cai said, Then we'll die together.

"Is friendship more important than life?" I asked her.

Her voice was barely audible. "Maybe it is."

After school, they stopped at a shop to buy a jar of powdered Sniff 'N' Die. The shopkeeper gave them a buy-one-get-one-free deal. The two girls played a few rounds of badminton. It appeared that they chose to play this game as the last activity they would enjoy in this world. Then they borrowed a glass from a nearby shop, filled it with some tap water, dissolved the rat poison, and sat down on a chair, back to back, hand in hand.

Little Cai said, "We both laughed."

"Why did you laugh?" I asked.

"We laughed about leaving this world."

"Weren't you afraid of death?"

"Nah. It's just another world."

"What world?"

"A world without troubles."

"Who told you that?"

"I figured it out on my own."

Miao Miao left a will in her pocket, which began, "Ba, Ma, hello, by the time you read this letter, I will already be in another world living happily ever after."

When I told Miao Miao's parents what I'd learned—that over ten kids preferred to take poison in order to stop Miao Miao from dying, or to die with her—they didn't believe me.

"I can't imagine our daughter influencing someone else to commit suicide," her mother said. "How deeply can kids really feel for each other?"

After the incidents, the provincial government sent down a pair of elderly psychologists. They told me, "Children of this age are especially prone to center their emotions around the judgments of their peers. In tight-knit friendship groups like these, when an important connection breaks, it can be very dangerous."

The center of the friend chain seemed to be Miao Miao. Her photo showed a girl with tender features—like a soft chalk drawing. Her dark hair was tied into a ponytail. Her small curly bangs fell on her snow-white cheeks. She had a pointed chin, and smiling, gentle eyes.

I asked several of the kids the same question: Why do you care so deeply about Miao Miao? They all said, "Because she understands people."

"In your view, what kind of person understands other people?"

"Someone who can listen to others," Little Cai said.

In her will, Miao Miao had told her father and mother to not be too sad. She'd advised her mother to be a little nicer to her grandmother: "Grandpa's gone, Grandma's very lonely. Grandma doesn't say it but I know. She doesn't need money, she just needs your affection and attentiveness." A few days after Miao Miao had passed away, another letter had arrived in the mailbox. The letter read, "When I look at your eyes swollen with tears, my heart shatters . . ." The sender was "Your beloved daughter."

Her parents had thought it must be a forgery, but forensics confirmed it was indeed Miao Miao's handwriting. She had given the letter to her friend, to be mailed after her death. It was the child's innocent way of comforting her parents in their most troubled hours.

When I visited her family, even though Miao Miao was gone, she was still her fifth-grade cousin's "only confidante."

"How do you deal with the things that trouble you now?" I asked.

"Swallow them," said the little boy.

"And when there's something you don't understand?" "Ask myself."

"Have you answered yourself?"

He said nothing. Tears lingered on his cheeks.

"Why don't you talk to grown-ups?"

His voice was so quiet you could've heard a pin drop: "I believe nothing they say."

After Miao Miao died, more than a dozen kids ditched class and climbed over the wall of the hospital to see her at the morgue. The doctor who found them said, "I've never seen kids in so much grief." When they returned to school, they carved the date of her death on the desk: *519*.

After returning from the morgue, a child named Little Sun stopped speaking altogether. His teacher said, "I didn't think there was anything wrong with that." One day, around noon, noticing that he was standing in a daze, his mother said to him, "You haven't eaten after school, after playing all day . . ." His lack of response frustrated her. She grabbed a yellow plastic package from on top of a chest and hit the boy on the head with it. Later, when she spoke with me about the incident, she still couldn't understand what happened next.

"There was something bad in the air those days. Little Miao had drunk poison, so I said, 'Are you going to drink poison too?!' He was so mad he said, 'Yeah, that's right!'"

Turning away from her, he'd found a bottle of pesticide and drank it.

"I didn't even hit him that hard," his mother said. "Why did he do that?"

"Little Sun is my best friend in the universe," his classmate Little Ni, an introverted boy, told me. "I thought he was going to die for sure." He cried all night after Little Sun had taken the poison.

Afraid of more incidents, the school insisted that parents accompany every student coming to and from school. The teachers set up a checkpoint at the school gate. The next day, when they saw Little Ni coming to school alone, they yelled at him, refusing to let him enter the school: "What if something were to happen at school?" they said. So Little Ni squatted outside the gate, then went home, grabbed a bottle of pesticide, and drank it in the wheat field.

After three extreme incidents happening back-to-back, the government put together a task force to investigate the school. These men dressed in police uniforms and interrogated every student who was close to the victims. They conducted the interrogations without parents being present. The police asked Little Yang if he and Miao Miao had had "inappropriate relations." Little Yang said, "I explained that we hadn't, but they wouldn't listen."

That night, he also took poison. After getting his stomach pumped, he survived. He said, "I can't stand humiliation."

The parents didn't understand their children's misery. In 2003, the per capita GDP of Twin City was less than three thousand yuan. The families of the children were either in farming or ran small shops. They worked hard to earn money to raise their children. Miao Miao's parents said, "We fed her well, dressed her well. What else did she need?"

Little Yang's father scolded his son right in front of us: "Why don't you die? You've brought us nothing but trouble." The mother wailed, kneeling on the ground, and said, "We've lost all our dignity because of you."

Lips squeezed tight, Little Yang turned and walked away. I followed him. Pain twisted his face. "Don't tell anyone else," he said. "By the time you finish your investigation, I won't be in this world anymore."

"If it's because of our investigation, I will leave tonight," I said.

"Then you'll never see me again."

The next day, we put our work aside and took Little Yang out to play.

There was a horse park in the area, overgrown with tall weeds. Two bald horses wearing ragged blankets trotted about lethargically with big red flowers on their heads. Two peasants with their arms crossed stood at the entrance selling tickets, five yuan a ride. Little Yang didn't speak and wouldn't ride.

Wearing a pair of cutoff jeans, I jumped onto a horse and encouraged him by saying, "Let me show you how it's done."

The moment I got on the horse and grabbed the reins, the peasant gave the horse a kick, and it went crazy. The bucking horse nearly gave me a heart attack, but when I passed by Little Yang, I somehow showed him a grin with bared teeth. When he saw me like that, he smiled too. Old Fan said, in all those days, that was the first time she saw him smile.

That night, the sides of my calves were full of green and purple bruises. Old Fan, completely lacking common sense, brought me a basin of boiling water. "Soak them," she said. As my legs swelled up in the boiling water, like noodles in a pot, I wrote a letter to Little Yang: "There's no need to be angry or fight back against humiliation—you only need contempt."

Being contemptuous of shame may not be the best way to cope, but that's all I could think of to unleash a young boy's pride so that he could get through the difficulty.

I still more or less remember how the letter ended, because it was also a letter to my fourteen-year-old self: "When it hurts, look at the sky to the northwest, look at the sunlit trees; the comfort they offer is eternal."

After the students had poisoned themselves, the school enacted emergency measures. The blackboard hanging against the brick wall read, *Follow the law; behave yourself.* In a proper and rigid font, the words continued: *Read healthy books, avoid video arcades, avoid forming cliques, never take part in superstitious activity . . .* All the fifth- and sixth-graders gathered for a "Love Life" meeting, a psychological intervention session for suicide prevention.

"What did the teachers say to you guys?" I asked.

"Taking drugs will lead to stomach disease," Miao Miao's brother said.

The sixth-grade teacher ordered the students to scratch out the *519*s carved into their desks to commemorate their classmate. After they refused, he told the school handyperson to repaint the desks. After that, the children could no longer see the numbers clearly. But they could still feel them with their fingers.

"I don't know how to educate them anymore." His hair was a mess and his wrinkles were filled with dust. He said the last time he'd received any psychology training was in 1982. "No one ever taught me how to deal with this."

I thought about my own elementary school. In fourth grade, I had just transferred in. My only friend was my desk mate, Gao Lili. She was nice to me, sharing her raisin water with me. We sat in the front row in class and held our hands under the desk. The teacher screamed, "The two of you, what are you doing!" She broke off a piece of her chalk and threw it at my head. The other students in class chuckled quietly. For the rest of the school day, there was a streak of white chalk in my hair.

I asked the sixth-grade teacher, "If there is something bothering you, who do you talk to?"

He froze for a moment. "I don't talk."

"Then what do you do when something makes you feel sad?"

"Bear it." He answered just like the kids.

The response to the Twin City episode brought me back to my radio days. I received letters from many children. One boy wrote, "My ma and I watched your show together, hugging each other tighter than we ever had before. A girl wrote, "A few days ago, my little brother did poorly on his final exams. After watching your program, I went next door to his room, and we had a long talk like never before."

When I returned home from the office in Beijing, the concierge of my apartment complex handed me a letter. It was from twins living in the community. The letter said, "We saw your program and just wanted to tell you we're happy you live here."

It was the first time I could really see that TV could allow people to connect emotionally.

For the past ten years, Old Fan and I have continued to talk about Twin City. It also became a wound for us. We had revealed the basic outlines of the story in the episode that aired on TV, but it was only a scant outline. The depth and complexity of the emotions the children experienced went far beyond what we had presented.

Mainly, though we'd talked about the party that led to the rumor, we'd left out the details related to this party.

In their grade, there were several students who'd had a crush on Miao Miao. The boy who choked her with a slingshot was always touching her arm and hair during class, which annoyed her. She'd told Little Yang, who'd beaten the boy up. At fourteen, Little Yang was the oldest, and tallest, boy in class. Miao Miao had called him "big brother."

But the two argued shortly before the accident. As it turned out, Miao Miao had also taken to calling a school security guard "big brother." When Little Yang heard this, he was jealous, and refused to speak to her. She asked for his forgiveness. When they ran into each other in a narrow alley, she'd stood in his way and said she was sorry, but he ignored her and continued on. She'd picked up a brick and smashed it on her forehead. Blood and dust flowed. But he didn't stop walking. Miao Miao went straight to the blacktop, where all the students were, and got on her knees. She proclaimed, "I'm sorry Yang . . ." She hoped this self-abasement would earn his forgiveness, but it wasn't enough. Later, at the party where the incident that incited her suicide occurred, another boy who had a crush on Miao Miao wanted to hold her, but she wasn't interested. Little Yang had ordered her to let him. And because this order had come from a boy whose forgiveness she wanted, she obeyed.

That party was a whirlwind of emotions. A girl who later signed the "'til death do us part" pledge, yet denied her friendship with Miao Miao during my interview, made her feelings for Little Yang known at that same party, in front of Miao Miao. Little Yang had known that this girl had always been competitive with Miao Miao, but he did not tell me how he had handled the situation.

Before taking poison, Miao Miao had returned to the classroom and sat at Little Yang's desk and cried. After that, she had asked Little Yang for a photo. When he'd given her one, she'd told him, "Thank you for granting my last wish."

She then carved three numbers on the desk and told him, "Never forget May 19," before walking out of the school.

When Little Yang told me these details, he kept asking me, "Am I really the one responsible for her death?"

I couldn't answer him, but the question would always haunt him.

Rewatching the program ten years later, I saw something in a shot of his notebook that I hadn't noticed before: *She and I parted, but she will always be alive in . . .* And that was where the words ended.

We didn't reveal all these details. Besides wanting to protect the privacy of the children, we also worried their romantic entanglements would make the audience confused and uncomfortable. Maybe they would think, *How can twelve- and thirteen-year-old kids act like this?* As if any of us were different at that age, as if all the struggle, desire, jealousy, and pain that we've been through are worthy of shame.

Subsequently, I read that when Leo Tolstoy was writing *Anna Karenina*, he had begun with a news story about a woman who cheated on her husband, then killed herself by jumping onto a railroad track. In the beginning, he had a moral judgment on her and wanted her story to end with a "good riddance." But as he wrote, without trying to beautify her, but simply by giving her more and more depth through the innate power of human nature, the story branched out with tender new buds; with each new set of branches, new clusters of flowers blossomed more voluptuously than the next. In the end, Anna's death transcended the moral judgment of people, leaving only a tragic echo in their hearts.

The nine days we spent in Twin City were not enough for us to get adequate information to reveal the full truth of what had happened there. And the limitations of my understanding of life and children at the time also prevented me from seeing the full import of the interviews I'd conducted. But, before leaving, we finally found the last child who took the poison: Little Sun. His mom wanted us to talk to him, but he didn't want to talk in front of her. So he ran off, up a mound. I took off my shoes and climbed up barefoot. When I reached the top, the two of us sat on a precipice. The camera pointed at our backs. The boom mic rested in a ditch nearby. Little Sun wouldn't look at me. He gazed into the distance. White poplars circled a village. Wind sent the green leaves twirling, blinding us with their silvery white undersides.

I asked him, "Do you sit here often?"

He nodded.

"Because no one can see you here?"

"Yes." It was the first word he had spoken to a grown-up in days.

He wedged his head between his knees. I squatted in front of him, holding his thin dark arm. His skin was peeling from too much sun exposure. When I wiped the dust off, I saw three pink scars. They read *519*. "What did you carve it with?" I asked.

"A knife."

"Would you have taken the poison if Miao Miao hadn't died?"

"No."

He suddenly stood up and walked down the mound, circled around an ox pen, then around another house. Without ever turning around, he eventually disappeared behind a low wall. The camera followed him until it couldn't any longer.

For more than a minute, I stared at his back. A thought struck me out of nowhere. I wondered if maybe he was the boy who'd held Miao Miao at the party, because he'd reacted so violently to her death, as if not only in pain for her loss, but also out of guilt. I didn't realize the camera lens had turned on me until the cameraman whispered, "Say something." Only then did I snap out of my daze and speak my mind.

"Seeing this child leave during the middle of an interview, we know that there is still a lot more he hasn't said. Perhaps what he didn't say was the real reason behind the suicides. After investigating this incident in Twin City, we learned that the deepest mystery is in fact the inner lives of our children, and the ability to access them is our real challenge."

A nearly two-minute-long shot was used to end the episode. Back when I was working mostly in the studio, I used to think that every segment had to end with a conclusion; then a story would be wrapped up and we could go home. It was like the studio itself rendered the outside world one-dimensional, like I was only an actress playing the role of a journalist. It had never occurred to me that an episode could end without a conclusion at all.

By admitting my limitations in this regard, at some point it reveals that life itself is beyond judgment. And the silence echoes in people's hearts.

Interviewing Yan Qing, who killed her husband with a gun, in Hebei Women's Prison. 2005.

Four
Silent Scream
2005

The winter was extremely cold when I visited An Hua's home. The snow was slow to melt, flowing down from the roof, turning into ice on the eaves. No one cleaned up, the ice wrapped up layer by layer, turning into thick heavy icicles, flashing cold, like a row of sharp blades piercing the ground. Hundreds of empty wine bottles were piled up in the yard, uncapped, half-buried in the dirty snow. It was all that was left of the dead.

The bedroom had been empty for three years. Under the wide roof tiles, inside the narrow windows welded shut with iron bars, not much light penetrated the space. Only after a moment of adjusting could I see the cracks on the concrete walls. The green satin blanket hadn't been touched since the accident happened, still stiffly curled up on the bed. For over a decade, it was the most intimate space for a man and a woman. And then, the killing had taken place here. The police report noted that the floor and walls were covered in blood. An Hua had stabbed her husband twenty-seven times.

The police told me that when the victim died, he was bound with a rope, "covered in blood, barely recognizable. Most cases of homicide occur with one lethal stab. Cases like this are rare indeed." They said the victim died with his eyes wide open and a look of disbelief on his face.

Wind whistled through the empty room like a scream.

. . .

During my time at *Oriental Horizon*, I'd seen a report from the China Law Society that said the majority of serious violent offenders in women's prisons are there for killing their husbands; in some prisons, this category exceeded 70 percent. Behind every statistic are people—men, dead; women, subject to harsh sentences. It was something that had been on my mind for years.

In February 2005, I went to see An Hua at the Hebei Women's Prison.

The moment I saw her, it shocked me that one of her eyes was white. Her husband had stabbed her in the eye with a broken glass bottle until her eyeball almost fell out. In twenty-five years of his beatings, she'd never struck back until the last time. I wondered what had set her over the edge in the end. But she couldn't even recall the moment she'd killed him.

"I've spent five years trying to remember what happened that night, and there's nothing but a blank," she told me with a confused look in her eyes. "I could be crazy."

In Hebei Women's Prison, ten other inmates like An Hua were there for killing their husbands with knives, guns, iron bars, wooden sticks, and concrete blocks. They'd all turned themselves in after committing the crime. They read out their sentences one by one in front of our cameras: death suspended, life in prison, life in prison, life in prison . . .[4] According to official files, all of these women had experienced severe domestic violence before killing. They refused to cover their faces and hide their identities. One of them said, "We want to tell our real life lessons to society."

Another added, "Don't make the same mistakes we did, but please believe we are not bad people, we really aren't." They all cried.

· · ·

---

[4] Death sentence with reprieve is a criminal punishment found in the law of the People's Republic of China. It gives the death row inmate a two-year suspended sentence of the execution. The convicted person will be executed if found to intentionally commit further crimes during the two years following the sentence; otherwise, the sentence is automatically reduced to life imprisonment or, if the person is found to have performed deeds of merit during the two years, fixed-term imprisonment.

Lil' Pea killed her husband with an iron bar; it only took one blow to the head. He didn't even try to block it, never having imagined the possibility of it happening. She was given a suspended death sentence. It had already been eight years, but she still couldn't believe he was dead. She had a pale narrow face and slanted eyes. As she spoke, her head rocked back and forth.

"He can't die," she said.

I was shocked. "What?"

She repeated, "He hasn't killed me yet. He can't die until I die. I'm not dead, so how can he be dead? I don't believe he's dead."

At fourteen, she'd married that man by arrangement with her family, and when they first met, he stared into her eyes. "Are you going to say yes?" She was too scared to say no. The feeling started with the first look and lasted eleven years in her marriage. She said, "The moment I got home, he would interrogate me. He didn't allow me to speak to any other man or even any other woman, not even to my family, because he was worried people might persuade me to leave him. Then, he'd beat me."

"With what?"

"His belt, shoes. If I disobeyed, he'd tie me up and whip me with his belt."

The belt landed on her bare skin with a *pu*. Hanging by the rope that bound her, she turned her body so that the blows would land on her back. She tried not to make any sound so that others wouldn't hear her shame. He beat her calmly, never hitting her face. After all, the night was still young, *pu*, *pu*, *pu*.

In eight years of marriage, she had never once worn short-sleeved clothes because she didn't want anyone to see her scars. What she feared most wasn't the beating itself, but the anticipation, never knowing when the next one would come. One night, she awoke to an icy chill against her neck. Her husband was holding a blade to her throat. He pulled her back by her hair to expose more of her neck. She could only stare at the ceiling, unable to make a sound. She swallowed her saliva, waiting, wondering if the blade would cut.

"He would do things like that, or he'd give me a bottle of pesticide and tell me to drink it."

"Was it because of anything in particular?" I asked.

"He'd say, 'Don't worry about the reason; you're all grown up, you can die now.'" She stared at me in confusion and asked, "Does growing up mean I should die?"

I didn't know how to answer but she kept asking. But there was a question I was mulling over. Though there was a male cameraman behind me, it came out anyway: "During your years of marriage, was the conjugal relation normal?"

"Too painful, I don't want to talk about it."

Nearly a dozen of them answered in almost exactly the same way. "Don't ask me that, it hurts me to think about it."

Accompanying me on the investigation was Chen Min, a medical expert from Canada. She said of all the cases of domestic violence she had ever come across, the women "were sexually abused, without exception." The most unbearable aspect of the abuse wasn't the physical injury, Yan Qing, another female inmate, explained, "but how he humiliated me."

I asked, "In really perverse ways?"

"Yes." Her eyes were red.

They would cry, but no sounds accompanied their tears. Those silent tears were undoubtedly the result of their years of marital torment. After a decade, even if they had wanted to bawl and wail, they didn't feel able to.

The gun Yan Qing picked up was her husband's. He worked in private security at a coal mine and liked to play with guns. Once, he dropped a few bullets on the ground, then picked up one, loaded the gun, and pointed it at her. "When I count to three," he said, "pick them up."

She was eight months pregnant. With one hand on her belly, she bent over as much as she could and picked up the bullets one by one from under the sofa. He kept holding the gun to her back. Later she told me, "I thought he was going to shoot for sure. I could almost hear the gunshot."

He wanted a son, Yan said. "His boss didn't have a son. Because we didn't have money like his boss did, my husband said we needed a son to piss him off. He told me plainly that if I gave birth to a daughter, he would strangle her to death. I said only an animal would do a thing like that."

She gave birth to a daughter. The killing happened the next day. She said, "The room was dark, lit with only one little red light bulb. He said, 'You have five minutes.' His whole vibe was so weird."

"What kind of vibe?"

"I can't explain it. I just felt like the baby and I were done for. He really went after the baby. I grabbed him and grabbed him; he kicked me to the side. I saw him going after the baby's neck so I grabbed the gun; I grabbed the gun, and I shot him."

"What was your sentence?"

"Life imprisonment."

"In prison for the rest of your life?"

"For my baby, I'm willing to die."

Of the eleven inmates, only one wouldn't say her reason for committing murder. So I went to her mother's house. The inmate's older sister pulled me aside and urged me again and again to stop asking: "She won't ever tell you . . ."

Then she seemed seized by an impulse. When the cameramen went elsewhere to shoot footage, as if she wanted to release something that had been suppressing her heart for too long, she clutched my wrist and said, "You want to know why she killed him?" she said. "On the day it happened, he walked naked into their two daughters' bedroom."

"What?"

The older sister tugged on my clothes. "Don't, don't make any sounds."

She turned and pointed to the bedroom door. The dark green latch had been torn from the wall and hung on the door frame by only one screw. "He rammed my door, then he . . ." She didn't continue. Were it not for the broken latch hanging there like a gaping wound and the look of shame and misery on the face of this woman, I wouldn't have been able to believe it. When the inmate fled to her sister's home for refuge, her husband broke in and raped her sister, and on the day of the incident, he intended to do the same to his own daughters, and his wife stabbed him to death. They, out of shame, could not say anything to defend themselves and nobody was able to ask them.

In the courtyard, hundreds of green glass bottles protruded from the dark gray snow, their blackened mouths pointing upward.

While discussing the women's stories with my colleagues, I learned that their plight did not impress at least one of the men: "These women are so stupid," he said. "Pour a pot of boiling water over their husbands' faces while they're asleep, and these men will behave." He believed that these women's cowardice in committing murder had retroactively justified their husbands' violence.

When I was in high school, there was a hooligan who hung around the school. He always looked at people with his eyes drifting up from the ground.

He would wait for me at an intersection in his big army uniform after the evening study session. I didn't tell my family or the school about him; in a small town, it was shameful to be the victim of sexual assault, and I was scared the reaction would be, "Why did he pick you?"

The only person who knew about it was my classmate who would walk me home. He threatened her, telling her with a voice like the edge of a razor blade to go away. But she looked straight at him and said, "I'll escort her."

She didn't turn away until I was almost home, and as I walked, I could hear her whistling in the distance—a way of telling me she was still around.

Eventually I left the town, got an education and a job, and had a voice. But most women I interviewed didn't have those opportunities. They grew up in the countryside and got married in the seventies. They had no education, no skills, no chance to get a job elsewhere, and were trapped in a traditionally patriarchal society as if it cast them in concrete. In my episode, I cited a national survey conducted by the All-China Women's Federation in 2002, which showed that at least 30 percent of Chinese families suffered from domestic violence. Nine out of ten perpetrators were men.

The only refuge for these women were their own families, but their husbands always threatened to burn down their parents' houses or harm other family members if they reached out to anyone. An Hua had sought help from the chief of the village committee, who had tied her husband to a tree and beaten him. But when she returned home her husband made her pay. No one dared to intervene again. After that, the only shelter she had for herself and her children was a public toilet where they hid overnight through the snow and ice.

Abuse is a crime, but in China there is no public prosecution system for domestic violence cases. The victim bears the burden of proof, and even if a conviction is achieved, a perpetrator who abuses a family member to death can only be sentenced to a maximum of seven years.

In countries with successful policies to prevent and punish domestic violence, Chen Men told me that in over 90 percent of cases, abuse is stopped when an intervention is made after the first incident. Police can forcibly arrest a perpetrator, and a restraining order can prevent the perpetrator from approaching the victim again. It sends a message to the offender that society will not condone abusive behavior.

But when I reported on this issue in 2005, a man in China could still beat a woman, stab her in the eye with a glass bottle, point a gun at her back, rape her sister, abuse her child, even in front of others—just because he was her husband.

Growing up, I dreamed about the hooligan I met when I was fourteen. Sometimes, in those dreams, I would hide on the beam above the front door and he would come searching. Just as he was about to rush out the door again, he would stop below me, his head slowly lifting up. Trembling, I would wake up from the nightmare. At fourteen, I could not have fought such violence, and without the help of a girl who whistled for me, I would have been paralyzed in fear, with nowhere to hide and no one to help.

No one was there to blow the whistle for these women.

I studied all the case files. These murders were not premeditated. The weapons were picked up from nearby, indicating a sudden intention to kill. During their interviews, the women all said, "The final night, he was especially strange."

Lil' Pea said, "It was like he wouldn't rest until he killed me that night."

"How could you tell?"

"Because he kept looking at his watch."

"What about that seemed especially dangerous to you?"

"It made me feel like he was waiting for the time to do it. I remember it clearly: it was 4:50 in the morning, the sun would be rising soon. He said, 'Yes. It's almost five o'clock.' He said, 'You tell me: you want to do it yourself, or do you want me to do it?'"

"Did you look into his eyes that night?"

"I looked. His eyes were dull and bloodshot; it had been an entire night of staying up, waiting."

She had one chance to escape. She tried. She opened the door to flee to her mother's house, but he forced her back home at knifepoint. She said, "If I die, will all this be over?"

He said, "Your sister, your parents, your kids, I'll blow them to smithereens."

"I thought, Isn't my one life enough?" Lil' Pea recalled. "Isn't living with him for eight years enough? So I grabbed a metal bar and hit him." Just like that. She wasn't sure how hard she'd struck him. Afterward, Lil' Pea did not even know he was dead. "I said, 'Why are you bleeding?' I wiped off the blood."

Then she looked at his watch and said, "It's time, five o'clock. Get some sleep. I'm going to the courthouse to file for divorce." She picked up her child and walked out. Later, she was arrested in front of the courthouse.

"In all those years, had you ever fought back before?" I asked her.

"Never. It was just that one time at the end."

Human nature will never be only good or evil, but when evil isn't restricted, it will feed on fear and grow, mercilessly devouring what goodness remains within, as if it has been mixed into alcohol and swallowed in one gulp. Violence begets violence.

Lil' Pea's daughter was thirteen years old when I reported on her mother's story. After being separated at the courthouse gate that fateful morning, she'd never seen her mother again. She hadn't had enough money to make a trip to the prison. Aside from a blurred local newspaper picture, she had no photos of her mother. I squatted in front of her and said, "I've seen your mother. You look a lot like her."

Her thin, delicate face revealed a slight smile. Her eyes squinted a bit, a mixture of shyness and satisfaction.

Her grandmother put the child's hand in mine and said, "That's right, two peas in a pod. This child doesn't deserve to lose her mother. Look, her hands are cracked from the cold. They're so cold they're bleeding. I don't ask for anything, only that her mother can come back soon to take care of her child, and send me a little offering at my tomb-stone after I pass. Yeah? I don't ask for anything else."

I didn't know what to say.

"Yeah?" Two hands, one old and one young, rested in mine, sway-ing side to side. The girl's grandmother's voice trembled more and more.

I suddenly felt afraid. "Please don't get overexcited," I said.

Just then, she fell back from her little stool. A group of people cir-cled around her, wanting to help. I intuitively stopped them from picking her up, and rummaged through her pockets. I found a small bottle of pills. I put them in her mouth, but she was incapable of swal-lowing them. The most frightening part of it all was her eyes: there wasn't a hint of life in them. I knelt on the icy floor, holding her body, thinking that she must have died.

Five minutes later, she was awake. Her granddaughter was calm. "My granny always does that," she said.

"What do you do when it happens?" I asked her.

"Look for the neighbor," said the thirteen-year-old girl.

The men lost their lives, and the women lost their freedom, leaving behind only children and the elderly. In the depth of winter, An Hua's home had no heat because her remaining family couldn't afford it. Her mother-in-law, who was sick in bed, said, "Please let her come back, she is a good person, she had no choice, she really had no choice." There was no photo of her son. She had burned all his pictures after the incident. He'd also beaten her when he was drunk.

I asked An Hua's daughter, "Do you ever think about your father?"

"Yes," the fourteen-year-old girl said.

"What do you miss?"

"When he smiles . . . when he smiles at you, it's like he'll give the universe to you."

The scar between her nose and her eye had been left by her father. He'd struck her with a metal corner brace.

It took us two days to find the girl's older brother. He was already nineteen and rarely returned home. He would never say where he ate or slept. Though it was twenty degrees below zero when we found him, he had no coat, only a sweater that was so dirty I couldn't tell what color it was. His hair was messy. He sat on a set of stairs in a stupor.

"Why do you never go home?" I asked.

"At home I miss my ma. Make my ma come back."

I took him and his sister to the visiting room at the prison. When the two kids saw their mother from a distance, they approached with infantile sounds as they cried out, "Ma, Ma!" A policewoman tapped on the glass and said, "Sit down, pick up the phone."

The daughter said, "Ma, Ma, we'll do anything you say, just come home soon."

An Hua's entire face was shaking. "I know, and I know your brother is afraid to say anything, too afraid."

The son buried his head in his arms, crying, unable to look up. The daughter screamed into the phone, "Ma, he says he misses you every day, he can't sleep. He goes everywhere to look for you. He says he misses you."

The mother patted her hand on the glass. "Silly child, where are you going to look for me? I know you need Mama, and Mama needs you."

The son pressed his forehead to the glass. "Ma, don't cry anymore."

The mother said, "No matter how hard it gets, we have to stay strong, we have to survive, do you hear me?"

The son answered, "I hear you."

The policewoman turned away to wipe her tears with the sleeves of her uniform.

After returning from the prison visit, the son left again. His sister shouted at his back, "Big brother!"

He walked away without turning around to look. No one knew where he would go. On the night of the murder, he had helped his mother tie his father up with a rope. When the knife had landed, he was there.

On March 8, International Women's Day, some of the female inmates have a chance to get their sentences reduced for good behavior. It represents the only possibility they might have to see their children grow up. Lil' Pea told me it was her favorite holiday. "But why is there only one International Women's Day a year?"

After our episode aired, with help from various sources, An Hua's sentence was reduced. She was released two years later.

Lil' Pea remained, suffering from mental illness.

From 2006 to 2010, while covering the National Congress and the Chinese People's Political Consultative Conference, I kept seeking representatives interested in domestic violence, because they had the authority to make laws. A male police representative said, "Existing laws can judge injuries, so why do we need a separate law covering domestic violence?" A female representative retorted, "Domestic matters cannot be treated like other personal injury cases."

An argument erupted on the spot. "You only say that because you are a woman."

"It shouldn't be about women caring about women, it should be that human beings care about other human beings."

There was little legislative progress over those years, and I always heard a recurring comment: "These men are the dregs of village society, they don't exist in cities."

In 2011, Kim Lee, an American citizen, posted a picture on the Internet in China. In it, her ninety-kilogram husband rode on her back, pulling on her hair and smashing her head into the ground. After he'd struck her over ten times, she sustained injuries to her head, knees, ears, and more. Her husband was Li Yang, a Chinese celebrity who'd founded a famous English-language education brand. They used to work together.

The day the assault occurred, Kim needed her husband's help with paperwork. She wanted to take their three children to the United States to visit her mother, but her driver's license and teacher's certificate were expired. Li Yang said he didn't have time to provide the assistance she needed because he was only at home two days a month, otherwise occupied with touring the country. After arguing for several hours, he screamed, "Shut your mouth."

Kim said, "Everything in my life is under your control, you can't tell me to shut my mouth."

When he held her hair and pinned her head to the ground, he shouted, "I will end this once and for all."

Had it gotten any more serious, he later admitted, "I might have killed her."

For the first time, it made the violence in elite urban families public and caused a strong social reaction. Kim refused to give any interviews, but when Old Fan sent her the footage we'd shot at the women's prison, she agreed to talk to us. "I did not know that there were so many women living like this in China. If I stay silent, who will be there to protect my daughters?"

In the footage, I asked the female inmates, "When you testified in court, did you talk about the domestic abuse you suffered?"

They all said no.

No one bothered to ask them. The murder of a husband by an abused woman was considered ordinary murder, not "self-defense," because it did not occur while the abuse was "ongoing" and the "abuse" was not considered a long-term process. During questioning, when an inmate wanted to talk about how her years of marriage had been, the prosecutor would interrupt her: "Are we here to listen to your life story? Get to the part where you murdered someone!"

After being assaulted, Kim Lee reported it to the police. A police officer tried to dissuade her: "You know, this isn't America." She said, "Of course, but there must be a law in China that says men can't go around beating up women." He said, "You're right, men can't beat up women, but husbands can beat up wives."

One of her daughters had witnessed the beating. The girl struggled to hold back her father's hands, but he tossed her aside. She has had nightmares ever since, crying in her sleep. "Mama," she said, "I'm sorry, next time I'll use chopsticks, and scissors, okay?"

Kim took her daughter in her arms and said, "You can hate Daddy's actions but don't hate Daddy the person."

Just talking about it, she shook her head and held back her tears, unable to go on at a certain point. The veins in her neck bulged from the effort.

Li Yang once said on a television show that his two daughters had bad tempers, maybe because "when their mother was pregnant, I hit her a few times." He performed a face-slapping motion and the other guests on the show just laughed it off.

When Kim made the abuse public, we interviewed a schoolgirl about it. Addressing Li in front of our camera, she said, "You've touched the lives of so many people. I'm sure Mrs. Kim will forgive you for a few minor mistakes at home."

Kim said, "I have money, I can choose to return to America. But what about these other women? They have no way out."

When I interviewed Li Yang, he did not hide the fact that he was violent to his wife; instead, he justified it: "A woman should learn to forbear." He interrupted my following question, saying, "I didn't invent violence, society taught it to me."

Li Yang and I were born in the same town in Shanxi. When I was young, I'd known his father through family ties. The man was a respectful intellectual who'd helped youth like me. But then he and his wife left their children to their grandparents' care and went to the remote Xinjiang to volunteer, in response to the state's call for "selfless devotion."[5] After being reunited with his parents, Li never called them Mom and Dad again.

He told me, "One night my father said to me, 'Let's share a bed.' It scared me to death. Share a bed with him? I'd rather die."

When he was growing up, the words he heard the most were *idiot* and *pig*. He stuttered as a child and was afraid to express himself. Even when a machine malfunctioned and burned his face, sending him to the hospital for treatment, he didn't dare to scream. The scar remained on his face for life. He said, "I used to hate tough guys, which is why I ended up going this direction. I'm tired of being soft."

After reaching adulthood, he tried to overcome his insecurity by developing Crazy English, a method of language learning that encourages students to shout English phrases in public. Eventually, it became more and more radical, until he demanded that students kneel, girls shave their heads, and tens of thousands of students chant in unison, "Learn English to conquer the world, learn English to overthrow American imperialism."

He said, "Insecurity taken to the extreme becomes arrogance, right? China is like that as well. China is a country of insecurity, a perfect example of this."

Being soft had become a sign of weakness. He openly said there was no love in his marriage; it was only an "educational experiment,"

---

[5] From December 1968 onward, millions of educated urban youth (zhishi qingnian, 知识青年), were mobilized and sent "up to the mountains and down to the villages." One tenth of the urban population shifted to rural villages and to frontier settlements. In these areas, putting down roots there, in order to be reeducated by the poor peasants. The slogan is "go to the countryside, go to the frontier, go to the place where the motherland needs it most."

as were his children, whom he called "Crazy Babies" and groomed into poster children for his company.

"How can a small family compare with service to humanity?" He added with pride, "Success must be the only goal."

"Not love?" I asked.

"Genuine love is to achieve outstanding success," he said.

I asked Kim, "Of all the people in Li Yang's life, who does he feel closest to?"

Kim had to think about the question for a while. "Who does he feel close to? Strangers. When he stands up on stage, his students adore him. And in two hours, he can just leave. It's perfectly safe. No time to make mistakes."

She said that whenever they boarded a flight, Li Yang always waited until the flight attendant called his name on the loudspeaker before boarding. That way, "everyone on the flight would know he existed."

When I visited Lil' Pea's brother-in-law, he grabbed a broom from behind the door. He raised it up to brush the roof beam. An ID photo fell down; he dusted it off and showed it to me. It was the only photo that still existed of his deceased brother. Eyes moist, he said, "Look. It's been eight years. I didn't have the heart to throw it away, but I don't want to see it either."

The man in the picture wasn't a vicious-looking person, but a rather handsome man with a radiant smile.

Lil' Pea said, "We were watching TV, and he suddenly asked, 'Do you love me?' I said, 'What is love? I don't understand it. I don't know.' He, *pia*, slapped me on the face. 'Tell me, do you love me?' What love is, I don't know."

In prison, I asked An Hua, "When your husband was violent, how do you think he was feeling?" I expected her to say satisfied, or cleansed.

Instead, she said, "He always seemed rather hopeless. That's how I knew he was pitiful too." Sometimes, after a beating, he would rub here and there to examine her, asking, "Does it hurt?" That's how she knew he felt remorse, which is what allowed the women to survive for decades with hope. But the next time, the beating would be even worse.

"Did it feel like he wanted to overcome it?"

"Of course he wanted to overcome it. He would say, I don't want this to happen again. He said he couldn't control himself . . . He would ask, 'Why do I have to hurt other people?' That's why I felt so torn. I wanted to leave him, but I couldn't."

It seemed to me that violence didn't come from alcohol, it came from whatever drove people to drink or use violence. They themselves didn't know what it was or how to deal with it. They could only take it out through alcohol and violence.

After the beating that Kim had made public, Li Yang sent her a text: *When I was pulling your hair, I saw a lot of white, just like in my hair.* Deep down, he knew he was wrong. "I do respect her," he said, "which is why every time she criticizes me, I feel terrified; when the fear builds up, it expresses itself in violence."

"Do you feel you are someone in need of help?" I asked.

His eyes squinted to a line, and he avoided my gaze. He stuttered, "Of course I need help. At this moment, I need help with my marriage, and how . . . how . . . how to deal with depression."

Every morning when he woke up, the most terrible and frightening feelings would come. "Work seems meaningless," he said. "Life seems meaningless."

In the end, Li Yang never sought therapy, nor did he spend more time with his family. He gave all his time to media interviews, setting himself up for a role as an "anti-domestic violence activist." Kim filed for divorce.

He tried to convince her that his behavior was part of "Chinese culture."

But Kim said, "This is not Chinese culture. People are all the same. I think Chinese people, American people, all people, are more similar than they are different. We all love our children. We all want a happy family. We all want a good life. If his dream is really to make China a better place, a more international place, I hope he can start with himself."

After reporting on the Li Yang case in 2011, I found that more people were paying attention to the topic of domestic violence than six years prior. Through the Internet, women were raising their voices far louder than in the past.

On February 3, 2013, the People's Court of Chaoyang District of Beijing found Li Yang guilty of acts of domestic violence, and the judge made a personal safety protection ruling based on Kim's application, which prohibited Li Yang from beating and threatening her. Society universally recognized this as the first "personal safety protection order" issued by the Beijing court system. Not long after, in 2014, a draft of China's first-ever law against domestic violence was published. Over forty thousand people had advised in its drafting, including me.

The law was enforced on January 1, 2016. It requires police and medical institutions to produce and maintain evidence of suspected abuse. Procedures for getting and maintaining restraining orders no longer required a lawsuit to be filed. In addition, the law stated penalties for perpetrators of violence: they must be fined or detained for up to fifteen days, or face criminal charges.

Kan Ke, the deputy director of the Law Committee of the National People's Congress, sent a text message to me shortly after: *You said in your 2005 report, "No policy or law can guarantee a happy marriage, but a policy or law should exist to prevent extreme misfortune in marriage." And now, the law is here.*

· · ·

Before my interview with Kim Lee, while preparing my outline, I started thinking about what I would need to pay attention to during our communication—mostly out of old habit. I imagined what I would feel like if I were her.

As I closed my eyes, I thought of something long forgotten. The hooligan who'd had his eye on me when I was fourteen had ambushed me once, while I was walking to school at noon. He jumped me from behind. I fell to the side of the road and couldn't get up. The drunken body pressed against me was as heavy as a corpse. Bystanders laughed as they dragged him off of me. I walked and cried, shaking too much to pat the mud off my denim. The worst part was not the scratches on my head and arms, nor the anger and humiliation I felt, but a sense of self-loathing. People who experience misfortune often blame themselves, as if they did something wrong to bring it on.

I bought Kim a bouquet. She looked surprised when she received the fresh white lilies wrapped in newspaper. She searched for a long time before finding a jar to put them in. Then she brought a few large photo albums out. They were family albums, with notes from English classes taught by Li Yang, and a rose from their wedding anniversary, which her husband had bought at her prompting, though it was delivered by his secretary. The flower was still intact, each leaf still carefully preserved under a plastic sheet, next to a family photo.

She said, "I had to remind myself why I ever wanted this man."

The wilted, bloodless petals spoke to me. People are the same. They have the same desire for happiness, the same need for wholeness. The only difference was that here she was, living like this; and there I was, living like that, all by chance. What is an interview? Interviews are the meeting point of different lives. The more you know about yourself, the more you know about others, and vice versa. Each person has a unique situation, but our destinies are connected, because everyone is embedded in the same world and shaped by its rules.

At the end of the year, the department asked everyone to contribute a quote to the year-end newsletter reflecting what they had learned over the year. One quote came to my mind. In the past, I would have worried that people would think it was too emotional, but this time I just wrote it down: *What others suffer, I too shall suffer.*

Me and my sister, in the first local photo studio opened by the factory. Shanxi, 1980.

Five
Shanxi, Shanxi
2006

The poet Hai Zi wrote a line that touched me deeply: "The sky has nothing / why does it comfort me?"

I was born in Xiangfen, a county in southeastern Shanxi Province, in 1976. When I was in first grade, I was afraid of being late to class. In the morning, at the slightest hint of light against the paper window, I'd wake up in tears. Granny would hold my hand and walk me a part of the way to school long before it would be open, past the jujube trees, the pomegranates, and the old pagoda tree, then around the big dog. Dressed in a milky-yellow pullover, I looked like a plump little peanut standing by the school's still-dark gates, waiting for them to open, alone.

Afraid of the dark, I would fix my eyes on the star-studded sky. I stared at it until the stars faded and disappeared against a cerulean blue. Schoolmates would arrive. I'd open the textbook to read aloud— "Ma . . . Liang's . . . Magic . . . Brush"—before falling asleep with my head on the desk, day in and day out.

A Shanxi girl like me had never seen a babbling brook or a mountain with a verdant jungle. The only way to find anything poetic was to look up at the sky. When the boy I had a crush on in high school passed by, he got off his bike and walked with me, exchanging a few words. After parting, my heart couldn't quiet down. I ran around the school track before sitting down, panting; the sky was endlessly blue, a fat fluffy white cloud above my head turned clumsily on its side.

I looked at the sky when I was happy; I looked at the sky when I was sad. I looked at it most when I was alone, when the sunset morphed in infinite variations, signifying a future of endless possibilities. I wrote in my diary, "The beauty of the earth, clouds and sky is always with me." I loved that the summer storms came unexpectedly. Black clouds rolled in and out in a flash. Only Venus remained unobscured until the final moment. It offered one last glowing wink before being snuffed out. That was when I'd turn and run. The rain chased after me, stirring up the dust and pouncing on me like a creature reeking of mud.

In 2006, I returned to Shanxi to cover pollution issues. Stepping out of the bus in Xiaoyi County, in the middle of Shanxi, my throat itched. Old Hao said, "Oy, reminds me of choking on the smoke from a charcoal stove during class when I was a child."

She was my new partner, the opposite of Old Fan. Short hair, cowgirl dress, shining dark eyes, a sharp tongue but a soft heart, we were like childhood friends, similar in age and we had both grown up in the north where coal was burned for heating. Both the air in our classrooms and the air here contained hydrogen sulfide.

The sky was a burnt wok covering the earth. The air wasn't gray or black, but a burnt brown. We arrived at a small school at the entrance of Tian Jia Gou village. A group of children were cutting out little stars to glue onto the windows. A girl with a round face and bright eyes who was not afraid of strangers came over with a small stool and sat next to me with a sweet smile.

I asked her, "Have you ever seen a star?"

She said, "No."

"Have you ever seen white clouds?"

"No."

"Blue sky?"

She pondered for a moment. "I've seen a bit of blue sky."

"What does the air smell like?"

"Stinky." She made a fanning motion in front of her nose.

This six-year-old, whose name was Wang Huiqin, was talking about the smell of tar. But even more dangerous were the odorless chemicals that she couldn't smell. The level of benzopyrene, a carcinogenic compound, in the air was nine times the safety limit, and on the hill less than fifty meters from her classroom was a coal-coking plant with an annual output of over six hundred thousand tons of coke. Less than a hundred meters away were two petrochemical plants. On her way home from school, she had to pass a coal-washing plant. But even though the factories were very close, they weren't visible. Because visibility was only ten meters.

The roads in the village were covered with coal ash. The crops along the road stiffened under the black crust of the earth. Grass and trees no longer grew. In this dark world, Wang Huiqin's red dress was the only sign of color.

As soon as we entered the city, local officials knew about it and escorted us to a hotel. Looking through the brown-tinted windows in the lobby made the view outside less abrasive. But the smell inside was similar. When we coughed, they made a few coughing sounds too, as if in greeting. They crossed their legs and spread them again, constantly changing sitting positions, unable to break the ice.

An official presented us with a bribe: emerald-green stacks of American dollars. "Thank you for your hard work," he said.

Old Hao and I traded looks. From her cynical wink, I could practically read the girl's mind. "You Shanxi people are making bribes in dollars," she said. "How fancy."

I was surprised that they made bribes in public, meeting someone for the first time. Later, we learned that several journalists had threatened to publish a report about the city's pollution on the front page of their newspaper, which would have ruined the officials' political careers. So, the officials offered them money, and the journalists dropped the story. This bribery system became the norm.

Accompanying us was Wang Jing Long, an inspector from the provincial Department of Environmental Protection. Old Hao called him "Old Man," which was her way of expressing that she thought he was reliable.

In a low voice, she asked Old Man, "Don't they have trouble breathing too?"

Old Man chuckled. "Let me tell you a joke. Two years ago, the mayor of this city went on an official trip to Shenzhen. As soon as he got off the plane, he fainted and no one could wake him up. A sensible old secretary called a car over and pointed the exhaust pipe at the mayor's face. After being blasted with car exhaust for a while, the mayor came to. He sighed and said, 'This Shenzhen air ain't hard enough.'"

The people in the city government listened and forced a dry laugh.

The mayor led us to a conference room. Out of habit, he announced, "Reporting to the honorable ladies and gentlemen present."

He began with history and worked his way to economic development, finally emphasizing the recent progress in pollution control. The local officials smoked one cigarette after another. Old Hao whispered in my ear, "They must have amazing lungs."

I kicked her under the table.

After a long speech, the mayor said, "Through resolute effort, we achieved one hundred days of meeting secondary air-quality standards last year."

There was laughter; it was Old Man. "You're calling that an achievement?" he asked. The statistic meant that the city was polluted for over two-thirds of the year.

The mayor opened his mouth, but no words came out. He continued with his speech.

· · ·

Wang Huiqin's village looked like my old home. The orange clay wall around the village was still standing, inscribed with long-ago dates and the words *in the reign of Emperor Kangxi*. Most of the old houses were made of gray bricks carved into intricate patterns. Some had collapsed, however, and turned back to earth.

All the village's farmlands had been sold to factories. The villagers either worked in the factories or drove the factories' goods for them. Wang Huiqin's mother sat on the bed-stove holding her one-year-old brother. The baby's face was mottled with ash. Embarrassed, the mother wiped the ash from the edge of the bed-stove for us to sit. "Can't ever keep up," she said. "A gust of wind and the ash comes right back like rain." The child was still a tiny thing. As we chatted, he often coughed. There was nothing his mother could do other than hold him firmer and shut the windows a little tighter.

Outside the window, you could see the coking plant's flare stack. When the wind blew, the flame on top of the chimney fluttered. Folks in the village called it a "Sky Lantern." When the factories first came to the village, the children used to believe the burning gas was fireworks.

According to regulation, all factories must be at least a thousand meters away from the nearest village. But factories don't walk on legs. Near the village there were roads and power lines, essential infrastructure. And besides, coking comprised 70 percent of the city's GDP—it was shooting to join the top one hundred strongest economic counties in the nation. The local authority was on the cusp of promotion.

So the only choice was to move the villagers.

"But where can we go?" Wang Huiqin's mother asked me.

The county was one of the first fifty key coal-producing areas in China, with thirty-eight of the forty-seven coking plants built illegally, and zero of them meeting environmental standards. A young person in the village said, "I don't know, I just want to go somewhere far away, somewhere free of this lethal stench."

A person in a black coat passed by. In front of the camera, he said to the young person, "Be careful how you talk, the factory gave you money."

The young person said, "What good is that bit of money? Who's going to pay when you get sick?"

They argued.

The man in the black coat was a factory manager. I asked him, "Are you worried about the consequences?"

He replied, "People just have to get used to it. Humans can evolve."

I thought he was joking, but from the look on his face, he was dead serious.

"What about your children's future?"

"Can't worry about that right now."

Ren Bao Ming, the boss of the coking plant called Red Tower, was originally a peasant from this village. He'd begun processing coke twenty years ago, and now his factory was capable of producing over a hundred thousand tons of coke. It had nothing at all by way of pollution control.

Offended when I pressed him on this issue, he looked into the camera and said, "Why are you only talking about pollution? What about my philanthropy? I give each of the old folks in the village six hundred yuan during the New Year, as well as rice and noodles." He smirked. "Even their own sons aren't as generous as I am."

"Has anyone come to talk to you about the pollution?"

He pointed to a wall of photos showing him shaking hands with officials. "Nope. They decorate me in red and green and parade me through the streets." There was a photo of his oldest son, the operations manager, wearing a big red flower, being given an award for entrepreneurial excellence by the county.

That night, Old Man had dinner with the city government. The officials offered him a toast, but he said no. The party secretary said in

a matter-of-fact tone, "To be frank, despite the chatter around pollution, who really has the guts to slow down the economy?"

"You sent your own kid away," Old Man commented casually. "To
the provincial capital, Taiyuan, was it?"

The secretary pretended he didn't hear the jab. "What country
doesn't develop first and clean up later?"

Old Man said, "At this rate, there won't be anything left to clean
up."

"Anything can be cleaned up with enough money."

"Do you want to bet on that?" Old Man raised his glass of liquor
for the first time.

No one took his offer.

There was a river near Wang Huiqin's house called the Wenyu—a trib-
utary of the Fen River, which flows from the center of Shanxi, and
nurtured the twenty-five-hundred-year-old civilization there.

"Can you still call this a river?" I asked Old Man.

He spoke pointedly: "You could also call it a sewage ditch."

The black river was coated in opalescent oil slicks. The surrounding area had been zoned for heavy industrial use. The effluent from the
coking plant flowed straight into the river. The concentration of benzopyrene in the stretch we were looking at was a hundred and sixty-five
times the regulation level.

I grew up by the Fen River. My hometown, Xiangfen, was named
for it. We called it "Mother River," and when I was a kid, it was yellow. On its banks were lush weeds, cloves, clumps of clover, wild peas,
and yellow and blue stems with crickets, grasshoppers, and frogs jumping among them, and ladybugs inside . . . I can still remember the sight
of a blue-purple butterfly falling to the ground like a leaf, just touching
the earth before flying steeply up again. My cousin would hang a plastic bag on a broken window-screen and go down to catch fish. I didn't
have the courage to join her. But a boy named Chubby would call to

me quietly from outside my kitchen door—"Little Jing, Little Jing"—and hand me a plastic bag filled with black tadpoles, their small tails wiggling. At that time, Chubby was a newcomer in my life. His parents, who worked in a textile mill, rented a room in our house. We never saw him as an intruder.

Everyone loved the factory. My cousin found a job there, and I found outdoor movies, and a barbershop for my first perm. I can still feel that hot yellow plastic bag over my head—the discomfort seemed like a small price to pay for a modern way of life.

When the factory expelled a stream of foamy yellow liquid directly into the river, none of us knew what it was. Once, Chubby brought a cup to the mouth of the pipe, curious enough to taste the liquid. But after one sharp sniff, he ran, and never returned.

When I was in middle school, the river became white, covered with all kinds of industrial waste, but especially a thick layer of paper pulp, which moved slowly. Yet it was still a river. When my crush and I took walks next to it, tracing the winding riverbank, silence was also a form of speech.

The river turned dark brown when I was in high school. In the nineties, light industry's share of Shanxi's GDP dropped from 40 percent to a mere 6. Thanks to coal, coking plants, steel plants, and iron plants flourished instead. Soon there were no more fish. At wedding parties, people started to serve wooden fish to symbolize prosperity. Even then no one complained about the environment. People pulled strings to get their relatives into the factories. In their minds, the industrial use of coal was no different than the way a family burned honeycomb-shaped briquettes in the winter. Sure, there was smoke, but also warmth. And anyway, a small amount of discomfort was easily dismissed once one was asleep.

In 1993, I enrolled in college in Hunan, in Southern China, three thousand kilometers from my hometown. At dawn, when I woke and pulled the window curtain to the side, I was stunned. There were countless little lakes dotted with lotus flowers—did such things still exist in the world? I forgot about my hometown. Subconsciously, I felt that when I went back one day, everything would have returned to the way it was when I was a child.

Years later, when I did go back to face my Mother River, it had become a sewage ditch. Sixty-six percent of the Fen River was so polluted it couldn't even be called a body of water. Yet, every year, three hundred million tons of that water flowed from the Fen into the Yellow River, its COD (chemical oxygen demand) concentration over 7.3 times the national water quality standard, and its ammonia nitrogen content twenty times the standard level.

Old Man said, "First develop, then clean up? Sheer naïveté."

I said, "What if all the pollution stopped right now?"

"The coal mines have left holes in the earth. The vegetation has been destroyed. The soil no longer holds water."

He showed me a report that illustrated the drastic displacement of water by the coal mining industry, which had led to a drop in the water table across the province. This caused wells to run dry, which in turn formed sinkholes. Compounded with severe reductions in the flow of karst springs, this meant that 47 percent of the 7,110 kilometers of waterways were no more.

I asked, "You mean, no matter what, we won't see the original Fen River again?"

He looked at me. "Not in your lifetime."

As if these words weren't enough to break me, he added, "But the most serious problem is the pollution of the underground water—especially where your home was."

Since 1990, my parents had lived in the county seat of Xiangfen; as I went through my teenage years, our tap water had become salty and bitter, like drinking rusty nails. It was the same for all the families living in the area.

The villagers living in the hills drew water from their wells, which were deeper, and transported it into the city in metal coolers welded onto their tricycles. They had signs that said Sweetwater for Sale in bright red letters. It cost twenty cents for a small bucket. My mother bought water that way and stored it in a vat so she could use it to cook porridge. She said we could only use the water in the vat to stew beans.

Later, when I returned to the village, I visited our old family well. It had been there for hundreds of years. In the summer, when I was still a child, my father would put a watermelon in the bucket and lower it into the well to chill it, then turn a winch to pull it back up for eating. When he cut it open and handed out slices, the sweet coldness would make my teeth chatter. I remember Chubby and I poking our heads over the well wall to look into its depths. At the bottom of the dark, mossy tunnel, there would be a circle of light.

But since water had become a business, several pipes had been put into the well, pumping day and night. It was now close to dry.

Yet I didn't hear a single complaint. Everyone just showed me the new plaza, the road, and all the other construction, which of course was thanks to the coal industry. In the ten years since I had left in 1993, the price of coal had jumped from seventeen yuan per ton to over a thousand yuan. Coking became a vast industry, accounting for over 70 percent of Shanxi's GDP. It was the backbone of the economy. And it came at an unprecedented cost.

My father was a doctor of traditional Chinese medicine. After retiring, his patients still came to see him at our home, so he built an herb cabinet. My sister and I would weigh out herbs for him on a small bronze scale. The prescriptions were almost always for Huang Qi, Dang Shen, five-flavor berries . . .

"Aren't these used as supplements?" I asked once, noticing that the patients coming to see my father looked severely ill. They were all farmers, squatting in our kitchen and mashing herbs with stone pestles, silently.

My father said to me, "What they have can't be cured. I can only give them some comfort." He added, "Ten out of ten will die."

I stopped weighing. What was he talking about?

"Lung cancer, liver cancer, stomach cancer . . . they all have serious diseases that large hospitals have no way of dealing with. So people come here looking for hope."

He named the villages where most of the patients were concentrated. All of them were near the river and near factories. They were all farmers who ate their own crops and drank polluted water.

I asked him, "Can they sue the factories?"

"But which one? Water and air flow freely; no one will claim responsibility."

It was only after Old Man told me about the underground water issue that I did some research. I found the answer in my county's public file: "The municipal water supply contains excessive amounts of minerals, chloride, sulfate, and iron." The drinking water of up to two hundred and forty thousand people did not meet safety standards. Cases of fluoride poisoning were concentrated along the banks of the Fen River, where there was "zonal distribution." Crops irrigated with water containing industrial pollutants were then over-sprayed with chemical pesticides, causing fluoride to not only reach the soil, but also seep into the ground and poison the water.

In 2003, the village headman from my hometown and a few farmers came to find me in Beijing. The coal-washing plant on the Fen River had moved, leaving behind dead trees and land that could not be cultivated, and river water that was too polluted for use of any kind.

But they didn't come to me to complain about the pollution; they asked me to help them find investors to build a new plant. My father felt sorry I couldn't help them. But the headman reassured him: "Don't worry, we understand. Look how small her rented apartment is—she has no resources."

·   ·   ·

I interviewed Zhang Xuguang, the mayor of Xiaoyi, in 2006. He had a stern, square face and wore a stiff, Western suit. Eighty percent of the coke projects in his city were illegal, and most of them had been launched during his tenure. But no matter what pollution-related issues I brought up, he always replied that the city was making reforms.

I said, "The city has already paid a heavy price. In retrospect, was this price unavoidable?"

He took a sip of water and looked at me. "The government has always been in control of coke development. So, with our reforms, we will hold the next waves of pressure back."

"Hold them back?" I asked. "Then why are there still thirty more illegal projects coming up?"

He was dismissive. "There was an investment craze, everyone wanted to get in on it. But even under such circumstances, our attitude is resolute."

"If you had a resolute attitude, you would immediately stop the construction of these illegal projects. Right?"

He took another sip of water and sat in silence. We stared at each other for a long time.

In the evaluation of an official, GDP was the most important indicator; it would determine Zhang Xuguang's career. In 2004, Xiaoyi's GDP grew by more than 40 percent, reaching a total worth of sixteen billion yuan in 2006. That same year, as coal became the key industry driving Shanxi's economy, China became the world's largest producer and consumer of coal.

Old Man said to me, "Xiaoyi is the epitome of Shanxi; Shanxi is the epitome of China."

That night at the hotel, Old Hao and I were getting ready for bed when there was a knock at our door.

It was the eldest son of Ren Bao Ming, the factory boss of Red Tower—an illegal project. I recalled that the son was the operations manager there. He carried a sack in his hand that looked heavy and plump. It was tied with a rope wrapped twice around his hand.

He looked at me and said, "Could you give us a moment?"

I said, "As you wish, as you wish," and excused myself to the washroom. I turned the handle to the showerhead and shut the door. By the time I finished washing up, the man had already left. Old Hao smiled at me from her bed.

I said, "The people of Shanxi sure are practical. Skip the reporter and go straight for the director."

We lay in bed wondering just how much money Ren Bao Ming's son had stuffed into that cotton sack.

In the end, the episode we filmed wasn't cleared to air because the pollution issue was "too sensitive."

Hao and I edited the unaired episode anyway, even though nobody would watch it. Then we traveled to Bali for vacation. On the trip, the brightness of the sun, the lushness of flora, and the vivid colors and sounds of the animals all reminded me of childhood. I told Old Hao and Old Fan about it. Pointing to the giant banyan trees growing out of boulders and the lotus ponds covered in leaves, Old Hao teased me: "Are you sure you remember these from Shanxi?"

I began, "Back in the Paleolithic era . . ."

They broke down in laughter.

Not far from the Fen River was the Dingcun Folk Museum. It was about a twenty-minute bike ride from my home. An exhibit panel there explained: "Over a hundred thousand years ago, ancient Homo sapiens lived here. The banks of the Fen River were rolling hills, sedimentary basins, and monocot grasslands. The wetlands comprised bulrushes, river bulrushes, water plantains . . . Along the river were mugwort, lamb's quarters, asters . . . Growing on the east-facing hillsides were broadleaf deciduous trees like oak, birch, toona, sweet olive, and horn-beam . . ." Fossils recorded this lush array of flora. After eons of birth, decay, and geological movement, they had become coal. This is what enabled Shanxi's coal reserves to fuel 28 percent of China.

When I was a child, people dug up sand from the Fen River to build houses. Digging into the river sediment often turned up dragon bones, an ingredient in traditional medicine. My father said they were dino-saur bones, and could be used to stop bleeding. Crushing the fossil with an iron mortar and pestle revealed finely streaked bones and tiny honeycomb-shaped orifices that could soak up a lot of moisture. My sister and I often stuck a piece of white bone to our lips and ran around. Later, I learned these weren't dinosaur bones, but the fossils of mam-moths, rhinos, and hipparions.

The Dingcun Man, whose fossilized upper skull might have belonged to a child, was the first to forge stone tools along the Fen River. He survived by hunting and gathering. The creatures he and his people hunted were mammoths and rhinos.

At the Taoshi archaeological site, which was also close to my house, they unearthed an "alligator drum," which contained bone plates from a Fen River alligator. Four thousand years ago, there were alligators in the Fen River.

It amazed me that this was one of the first places where humanity had practiced agriculture, using stone knives to harvest grain and stone mills to shell and hull it. Nourished by the surplus of these agri-cultural innovations, tribes coalesced into cities, until, around four thousand and five hundred years ago, Chinese civilization was born.

The river's history was equally long. Back in the Zhou and Qin dynasties, it was called the "Great River," and its waters were crystal clear. But as the population grew, forests were cut down so the land could be made arable, a process that was repeated for thousands of years, increasing the potential for erosion. At the same time, fine sand blowing in from Central Asia and the Gobi Desert created the Loess Plateau, which increasingly caused flooding during heavy rains, and washed even more land into the river. By the Han dynasty, the "Great River" had become progressively more muddy, earning the name "Yellow River," of which the Fen was one of two main tributaries.

It was a source of life and a source of worries. And those worries have only grown over the past thousand years, accelerating especially in the last century, as forest coverage in Shanxi virtually disappeared and the province's share of the Loess Plateau became one of the most severely eroded in the world.

When the forests aboveground disappeared, people dug for resources underground; after the middle of the twentieth century, Shanxi became the energy capital of the country, supporting 80 percent of China's energy deployment with coal. Over the past sixty years, twelve billion tons of coal have been mined in Shanxi province, enough to fill a freight train that circles the globe three times over.

The damage goes beyond air pollution. When coal is mined out, caves are left behind. If these caves are not refilled, the rock and water seams will naturally collapse. "Mines occupy one-seventh of the land area of Shanxi," Old Man explained. "By 2020, one-third of the provincial and state-run mines and nearly half of the county and township-run mines will be depleted and abandoned."

After all that history, I don't know what would be left for children like Wang Huiqing.

In 2003, I arrived at Hejin, a mining district in the south of Shanxi.

Under an ash-gray sky, the road was crumbling under the weight of overloaded coal trucks. Wheels sank into muddy potholes, stopping and going. These trucks weighed seventy tons each when fully loaded, and at night, they filled the road almost entirely, crushing what had never been meant to support them.

The village I was visiting was called Old Kiln, where the local mine was leased out to coal companies for tens of millions of yuan. The head of the village paid eighty thousand yuan to his residents every year—with the population numbering about 1,300, each person received less than six hundred yuan in the end.

But whenever it came time for the village election, two candidates would campaign through the night before the ballots were cast, using financial incentives to compete. They hired motorcyclists to pass out fliers. The format of these thin pink sheets were all the same: a list of campaign promises ending with a line for the amount of every resident's cash payout to be penned in when the time came, a kind of bidding war. Fliers would be dropped off at every household—even newborn babies had a share.

The entire village stayed awake with their doors open, eagerly waiting for the sound of motorcycles passing the houses, stuffing papers into the door rings. This candidate offered one thousand yuan, that candidate offered one thousand five hundred, then two thousand . . . two thousand five hundred . . .

When we visited, the candidate offering two thousand five hundred yuan to each resident turned out to be the winner. That very day, he put a gigantic box with over two million yuan in cash on the stage. People's eyes lit up when the box was opened. An old man wearing a fur-lined green army hat pointed at the stage and told me with a wide smile, "Ah, what more is there to say? It's money, real money."

The money was handed out on the spot. A chairman of the town council who was there to supervise the election said to me, "I can't control it. If I try, the folks'll beat me."

The villagers said they saw elections through the lens of economics: "It doesn't matter who gets elected. For us, a ballot is a dividend."

So every person received two thousand five hundred yuan, even newborn babies. The young men were thrilled and chased one another down the village road on their brand-new motorcycles.

Only a hunched old man, practically kneeling, was begging us to follow him. He dragged us up a road to the top of a hill to look at his newly built house. An entire wall had been ripped open. There with a gaping crack. The place was standing, but precariously, buttressed with only a few wooden stakes. His house was on top of the coal mine. The well had dried up. Several red plastic buckets hung on the eave of his roof, collecting rainwater.

When other villagers saw him jumping up and down, crying to us like a madman, they laughed. They'd built their houses halfway up the hill—these dwellings remained stable for the time being. But, meanwhile, the village head and party secretary had both bought houses in the city of Hejin. They no longer lived in the village.

We hiked further up the hill. A tree big enough for a person to hug had withered and died. It collapsed on a crack in the earth. Its branches looked like hands trying to crawl out of the chasm. My homeland is on the Loess Plateau, but this hilltop had eroded into a veritable desert, overgrown with seaberry shrubs. When the wind blew, I could hear grains of sand clicking against my teeth.

Eventually I brought my mother and my younger sister to Beijing; I no longer wanted to go back to Shanxi.

But my father remained. There was a train station near my family's house, with a dedicated platform for coal shipments ten meters from our door. Trains ran all night, shaking the desks and beds. The building was only a few years old, but it was already sinking. I worried that it would topple over. "Move in with us," I begged my father.

He refused. He still had patients to see, not to mention lamb soup and vermicelli porridge he had to drink every day. Walking down the street, he could make small talk with acquaintances without having to speak Mandarin. He was particularly attached to our old house, back in the village. He said, "You guys go ahead, my withered leaf will return to my roots."

One day, he called to tell me that our old house was going to be demolished. Someone had stolen its eight exquisitely carved door panels. Unable to move the pillars, the thief had chiseled off all the flower carvings and taken them away. The blue stone drum that I'd sat on every day as a child was no longer there either. Someone had pried it up from under a pillar and taken it away too, haphazardly filling the hole left behind with a few bricks.

There was nothing I could do. In 2005, some four hundred meters away from the giant Buddha in the Yungang rock caves, a national road—Road 109—was built to transport coal out of southern Shanxi. Each day, sixteen thousand trucks passed through, most of them over capacity, so full that workers couldn't even wrap a tarp over the load. As coal dust blew from the trucks, foreign tourists visiting the cave art would have to put plastic bags over their heads. The stone Buddha smiled with coal dust on its face, soaking in sulfur dioxide and water. As the years go by, the sandstone face will eventually dissolve and disappear.

May the Buddha have mercy.

I closed my eyes and hardened my heart. If this was reality, then so be it.

But then someone cut down the pomegranate tree my grandmother had planted. It happened a few years after she'd passed away. And I don't know what came over me, but I cried and screamed on the phone with my father when he told me—something I hadn't done since I was a child. My father later planted a new pomegranate tree in another location. Two years later, when he visited me in Beijing, he brought me a bag of pomegranates. They were tiny, dry, and hard—one had already cracked, revealing a row of pomegranate seeds like a bitter smile.

In early 2007, an official report from my hometown stated that every day of January and February had met the qualifications for unacceptable levels of pollution, except for one day when the air quality was at a "basically acceptable" level. In two months, people had only seen one day of light blue sky.

When I'd returned home in winter, the visibility was less than five meters. I took a cab with no headlights; only half of the rearview mirror remained from a previous accident. To navigate, the scrawny driver stuck his neck out the window as he drove. After a while, he called out to someone, "Come and take over, I didn't wear my glasses today."

I thought it was a foggy day. He laughed flatly and told me it'd been like that every day.

I had the luxury of coming and going, of revisiting the scenes of my childhood and being able to return to safer conditions afterward. But this place was still my home, and I knew so many people, my father included, who continued to live there. They had to breathe the air, drink the water, and walk on the street every day. Most people didn't wear masks, and those who did had two black dots on the part that protected their nostrils. These dots contained sulfur dioxide, nitrogen dioxide, and floating particulates. The new generation was losing the beauty of the earth, the clouds, and the sky. My cousin wrote to me, *The sparrows no longer make nests under the eaves, never again will there be rainbows after a storm.*

Never again. The words still stun me.

I kept going back to Shanxi and reporting on pollution. In order to increase my odds of getting my findings on the air, I wrote a letter to Yu Youjun, the governor of Shanxi, who had a reputation as a reformer. I told him I was born in Shanxi and just wanted to know what was going on and what to do about it. He seemed sympathetic. We agreed that I would start a new investigation from my hometown, which is part of the city of Linfen. Between 2003 and 2005, Linfen had earned the worst air-quality index ranking in China three years in a row.

When I got there, an official said, "You're from here."

"That's right."

With a sarcastic smile, he asked, "Why don't you do something good for Shanxi?"

"I'm doing exactly that."

• • •

Later, when I came back to Xiaoyi, Wang Huiqin was seven years old. Her hair was shorter, and her skin was darker. She was thinner, too, and no longer so open with me. She stood at a distance—instead of waving, she just smiled. Her village had not moved out of the danger zone, and the factory remained.

At the request of the Department of Environmental Protection, the factory had spent sixty million yuan to install equipment for controlling pollution. The boss wanted us to stand in front of it and take a group photo.

I asked, "Is the equipment running?"

The boss's son chuckled. "Not yet, not yet."

In addition, the county official had demolished a few small coke plants. He said to me, "Reporter Chai, I did this for you."

During the interview, Yu Youjun, the governor of Shanxi, told me he was implementing a "one-vote veto system" to ensure reform. Basically, as long as a region's environmental protection measures were not meeting national standards, the official in charge could not be promoted, even if his region's economic growth rate ranked highly.

I asked, "How do the officials know this isn't just a temporary rule while you are in power? When you leave, couldn't things go back to business as usual?"

He paused for a moment. "It's a matter of government responsibility and accountability. As long as we stay responsible and accountable, I don't think there will be a risk of reversal."

"Why couldn't the public decide on the fate of their own environment before the pollution happened?"

"That's a good question. There needs to be political mobilization. The public needs to know about environmental issues and their own rights, and how to make their voices heard, or else . . ."

He didn't go on.

A month later, after the 2007 Shanxi brickyard slavery scandal, Yu Youjun took responsibility for the event and resigned. Meng Xuenong, the official who'd served as the mayor of Beijing until being dismissed during the SARS epidemic, replaced him as the acting governor. A year later, during the 2008 Shanxi mudslide, which was caused by the collapse of an unlicensed iron mine landfill in my hometown, 277 people died and Meng Xuenong resigned. People back home often used a painful, self-effacing joke to sum up these tragedies: "We finally got to decide on the governor of Shanxi."

After the mudslide incident, thirty-four government officials went to prison. Chubby, my childhood friend, who was then a section chief in the Bureau of Land Management, served one year.

While we were in Linfen, we wanted to shoot some footage at a watershed.

There were only three options in the Yaodu District: Longci, Tumen, and Tunli. According to the Department of Environmental Protection's June 2005 assessment, the mineral and ammonia content in the fifteen wells that supplied the Tumen water network exceeded safety standards; and because of the Tunli watershed's level of pollution, it could no longer be a drinking-water supply. So we went to Longci.

A third of the mountain there was missing due to quarrying. Coal trucks drove back and forth near the watershed. The reservoir was only two acres.

"This is the last," someone nearby commented. "There is none left."

I looked at it from outside of a fence, stunned.

I had never seen Shanxi like that.

A chubby fellow from a nearby village accompanied me. We rested our chins on the iron railing in complete silence, gazing. The water was crystal clear. When the wind blew, wisps of algae swayed as if they were drunk. Siskins and swallows tapped their feet against the water, paused for a moment on a wildflower, then flitted off. The flower bounced back with force, leaving endless circles rippling across the water.

This was my homeland once upon a time.

Up above, an egret flew in a beautiful arc.

Interviewing Zhou Zhenglong, who claimed he had taken photos of a South China tiger in the wild. Shannaxi, 2007.

Six
Paper Tigers
2007

On October 26, 2007, our team of five sat on a train to the southernmost point of Shaanxi Province. The journey took twenty-four hours. We played cards the whole way. The loser in each round had to stick a strip of paper to their forehead. We were in high spirits. No one talked about the episode we were going to shoot—what was there to talk about?

Two weeks earlier, the Shaanxi Province Forestry Department had held a press conference in which it released eight photographs of a South China tiger in the wild, taken by a farmer named Zhou Zhenglong. In all the pictures, a brown-red tiger can clearly be seen sitting among the brush, staring straight at the camera.

The South China tiger originated in China, and the pattern on its head resembles the Chinese character 王, meaning King, and is known as the king of beasts. Per tradition, people used to hang its portrait in homes and embroider the tiger's head on their children's shoes to symbolize the power to drive away evil spirits, but it had been gone for a long time. There'd been three large-scale wildlife surveys conducted since the nineties, but none had produced evidence of the tiger's presence in the wild. Scientists believed it had gone extinct. This was the first time anyone had photographed it. The forestry department claimed the images were proof that, after twenty years of dwindling numbers, the rare animal was once more alive and well in China. The announcement made headlines nationwide.

The next morning, someone with the username "First Impression" posted several of the farmer's images on a photography forum with the heading, "Are these pictures real? The stomach is too white in the tree's shadow." Commenters quickly divided into two camps, and the discussion blew up. On October 16, only a few days after the initial press conference had been held, the Shaanxi Forestry Department responded with a statement defending the authenticity of the photos: "The fact that the South China tigers exist in Shaanxi's Zhenping County is indisputable."

When our team met to discuss the angles of the story, someone dismissed it as small potatoes, to be left to the tabloids: "What's so important about some suspicious photos? You have to find another angle." But Old Hao was convinced that trouble was brewing. Every single person she had passed walking through the CCTV offices had said to her, "Word is, you're covering the South China tiger—so are those pictures real or not?"

The angle was clear.

After the train journey came a five-hour drive up mountain roads. Our arrival in Zhenping was signaled by a four-meter-long billboard that was impossible to miss: "Hear the South China tiger roar, taste the cured meats of Zhenping." In the bottom right corner was a picture of a tiger staring straight ahead. Weirdly, the image hadn't been drawn from Zhou Zhenglong's photos—instead, it was an obviously photoshopped Siberian Tiger. We were hungry and, swayed by the sign, decided to try the local meats, only to find the restaurants had none. Hunting boar wasn't allowed anymore, "to save them for the tigers."

We continued on motorbikes into the Daba Mountains. Around a lush bend in the road, Zhou Zhenglong's home came into view, nestled beneath a persimmon tree, on a flat square of land cut into the slope. There were weeds and wild corn growing in the courtyard, a number of old beehives left by the entrance, and radishes planted on the slope. Zhou's home was the oldest in the village. A mud-brick building with three rooms, it had mud floors and wooden doors, and a stone slab roof with cracks that the daylight seeped through. Inside was a black-and-white television, and on the wall, a bill poster from 1988.

A group of young reporters sat under the persimmon tree on a circle of small, red wooden stools, drinking tea. "You're here too?" they said by way of greeting. Normally, it takes a big disaster of some sort to bring together so many reporters in one place. Since there were no obvious victims for this call, the atmosphere was relaxed. Someone had placed a ladder against the tree to pick the fruit from its branches, and others were helping Zhou Zhenglong's wife feed the pigs.

Zhou himself was in the middle of an interview with a TV station. In his fifties, with narrow upturned eyes, a pointed nose, and thin lips, he was relating with a knife in his hand talking about how he had searched for the tiger deep in the mountains for forty days, before coming across a large paw print next to a puddle. He followed the tracks to a cliffside, where he managed to photograph the tiger—luckily for him, it had just finished eating a wild boar and was resting, unmoving. He lay on his belly fifty or so meters from it and snapped away for a good twenty-five minutes, even accidentally turning the flash on twice at the end, causing the tiger to roar in response. Terrified, he rolled behind a rock to hide, and by the time he came to his senses the tiger had gone.

The reporter asked, "And when you came home that evening you cried for the first time in your life, is that right?"

Zhou replied, "In my fifty-odd years I've never shed a tear, not even when my parents died . . . but the moment I saw the pictures of the tiger . . . I can't bear to think about it."

He was choking up.

Standing to the side chatting, our cameraman Chen Wei and sound man Xiao Hong believed Zhou was telling the truth. Old Hao and I exchanged a look and asked them how they had come to that conclusion. Chen Wei said he had filmed Zhou sitting in the radish patch with a black coat draped over his shoulders, the autumnal mountains in the background, his back to the light.

He laughed. "From that shot, I knew—that's a hero right there."

"I thought the same," said Xiao Hong. "Could a liar stare straight into the camera?"

Everyone has their own experiences and ideas of beauty. We are moved by different things, in different ways. But we can't base our judgment on that alone: without combing through the facts and teasing out causes and effects any comment is a house built on sand.

When we were the only reporters left, we moved two squat benches to the doorway of Zhou's house and started our interview. My first question was: "Are the pictures of the South China tiger real?"

His response was interesting: "I believe they are 100 percent real. Not even a little fake."

"Experts on the species say that the tiger only stops moving when it's near death, yet the tiger you photographed didn't move for twenty-five minutes?"

It was a question he had answered many times already with the same well-rehearsed response: "Ha, well, experts have also said, Mr. Zhou, Count yourself lucky that tiger had just eaten."

I picked up a handful of stones and asked him to show me where he had been in relation to the tree, the rock, and the tiger. He did so.

I was skeptical. "You could see the tiger's ears prick up from over fifty meters away?"

He tilted his head to the side and looked off into the distance. "Eh, that I can't say."

He was unsure how the flash had turned on too. "I just pressed the button like this, and it went *ka-chick*. That's when I dropped the thing."

"You stopped shooting?" I double-checked.

He was becoming impatient. "It roared when it heard the noise. Would *you* keep taking pictures? Of what? The rocks?"

I looked at my materials. "According to the log from your digital camera, you used the flash for the fourth picture, out of over thirty."

"The fourth?" he repeated back to me.

"Right."

It seemed like he'd only just caught on. "So there were twenty more photos after that?"

"Yes, that's what the camera's records say." I handed them to him.

He looked them over while he fiddled with the stones on the ground, his head bowed, rolling them this way then that.

"I can't remember very well," he said, "it's a while ago now."

If challenged, Zhou Zhenglong became very assertive. His nickname in the village was "ol' bludgeon," which is Chongqing dialect for someone who is a bit of a thug, a tyrant even. He had no qualms showing it either, and yelled at his wife in front of a group of journalists: "Dumb bitch!"

One reporter explained how severe the consequences are for fraud. An irate Zhou responded by shouting, "Which son of a bitch said I'm faking?"

I also watched him jab a cigarette toward a young woman reporter for asking a pointed question. "Do you think I won't call your boss right now?" he threatened. When reporters asked if they could take his photos and raw files to be authenticated, he said they were for sale only, a million for the lot, and no refunds no matter the result.

To steer him to admit he was committing fraud, or at least to get the chance to show the photos were fake, was too difficult, and it wasn't our responsibility. Government officials had publicized them. The onus was on them to prove the tiger was real.

. . .

According to Zhou, a tiger had sat in the brush for about twenty-five minutes straight, so there should have been hair, feces, or claw marks around that spot. Regular procedure dictated that the forestry department needed to verify the claim in the shortest possible time. Two or more staff should have surveyed, documented, and categorized any animal traces, produced descriptions of all the surrounding vegetation and geographical features, and interviewed both the witness and anybody else in the vicinity, working to ensure timely confirmation that the information gathered was reliable and comprehensive.

I requested the record of the inspection from the provincial forestry department, only to be told by its deputy commissioner, Sun Chengqian, who had hosted the press conference where the photos were released, that he hadn't seen it. However, the local Zhenping administration had given him their word that an inspection had been performed and documented accordingly. Sun Chengqian told me, "I believe them, they're a first-level division."

So I asked the county government for the record, only for County Mayor Wu to say he hadn't seen it either. But the director of the county forestry bureau had guaranteed to him that there was one. Wu said, "I believe what my official says, I trained him."

So I went to the forestry bureau, where Bureau Chief Tan informed me he hadn't seen any record, but his subordinates assured him it was in safe hands. I asked, "So all of this is based on one man's word?"

"Why shouldn't I trust him?" he replied. "I have complete confidence in my official."

Eventually, we found the person responsible for the site inspection, Li Qian, who up until then had claimed to all media outlets that he'd photographed the site himself. He'd even made Zhou Zhenglong stand for a picture where the tiger had lain.

"The site had basically matched his story," he said.

I asked him to let me see this photo, but he said he couldn't. When I played him the recording of his earlier interview, where he claimed to have taken pictures at the site, he had a sudden case of amnesia. "I can't remember now, I only went there."

"So is there a recording, or any photos?"

"No."

"Written notes?"

"I went, that's it, I've no evidence. I'll admit that much." He looked at the ground, then to the ceiling, but never at me. "I believe Zhou Zhenglong, he's a farmer."

Before the interview, I had joked with Old Hao that the media attention had passed the point where we had to be on our toes in case people doctored the original records or stuck a real tiger in the mountains so they could make a successful report. It never occurred to me that there was no paper trail to begin with. After hearing what I had to say about the situation, Deputy Commissioner Sun told me, "This is the first I'm hearing of it."

County Mayor Wu said, "Perhaps there's been a bit of an oversight."

I imagined that once they knew the truth of the matter they might reconsider the authenticity of the photographs, but County Mayor Wu simply shook his head and scoffed as if I'd told him something absurd. "I'm not sure that's necessary. I believe the pictures are real. Zhou Zhenglong is a regular old farmer, why make him out to be any more complex?"

Since no one else had performed any checks, we thought we would visit the scene of the sighting ourselves. But the way there was sealed off with a metal fence and a sign from the forestry bureau that indicated entry was forbidden. One Beijing reporter, who had snuck in by going around to the other side of the mountain, had been taken into custody by the forest police, who only released him after wiping all the photos he'd taken. Apparently they'd told him, "If you scare our tiger off, what will we do then?"

We asked Bureau Chief Tan what the procedures were for gaining access. He said, "There are no procedures."

"Then how do we check whether the photos are real?"

"We don't care what the media thinks," he said. "The fact that there are South China tigers in Zhenping County is indisputable."

We had come full circle.

I instinctively wanted to return fire, to remind him that reporters have the right to ask questions, but on second thought said, "We all really want to believe there are South China tigers in Zhenping. It's just that we know there are several criteria for confirming a species sighting before it can be internationally recognized. The priority is finding a live specimen. Failing that, a dead one. But there needs to be photographic evidence either way, and a researcher has to have seen the animal."

He stared into space a moment before saying, "This is the first I'm hearing of this." Picking up his glass to take a drink, he unmistakably gulped.

In the past, my line of attack would have been to back him into a corner, to say, "You're the head of the bureau and you don't even know that?" But my job was not to label him a clown. It was to guide him onto the right track. "Before confirming something as major as this, wouldn't a more serious, scientific, and conservative approach be better than assuming everything is conclusive?"

He looked at me, unblinking, as he thought for a second. Then he licked his lips and said, "Leaving some room for maneuvering, a little leeway, might be better, yes."

Bureau Chief Tan never said the word *indisputable* to me again. He swapped it for another phrase: "Still, I have to say that I wholeheartedly believe there are South China tigers in Zhenping."

This reformulation piqued my curiosity. Anyone who refuses to acknowledge an error must have some grounds for their certainty. I wanted to know what his were.

"What are you basing that on?"

"A team of experts produced a report even before the photos were taken, saying that there are South China tigers in the region. Someone was always going to get one on camera someday. If not Zhou Zhenglong, then Li Zhenglong or Wang Zhenglong."

Tigers did use to live in Zhenping. The dense forests of the Daba Mountains were the northernmost boundary of their territory. They lived among the broadleaf forests and thick brush below three thousand meters elevation, far enough from the first mountain denizens who cultivated the valleys below. The earliest conflicts between humans and tigers in the area took place during the last two Chinese dynasties.

Mass migration across the country saw the population of southern Shaanxi increase by over 600 percent in the space of a hundred years. More people meant forests were cleared to make room for growing crops and opening up mines. A single tiger in the wild needs at least seventy square kilometers of forest and a healthy supply of ungulates to live. When territorial clashes eventually broke out, the response to attacks on livestock and residents, and to what official documents referred to as a "tiger disaster," was the first tiger-hunting drive in China's history, which forced the South China tiger first out of the plains into the lower mountain regions, then farther up into the higher reaches. At the beginning of this campaign, in the early forties, the number of South China tigers was over four thousand strong.

In the twenty years that followed, the Chinese population boomed again. As industry and agriculture kept up, vast swathes of woodland were felled for fuel to smelt steel, or burnt to the ground to create wood ash for use as fertilizer. The fight between man and beast intensified.

In 1959, the Ministry of Forestry issued an order identifying South China tigers, along with bears, leopards, and wolves, as dangerous pests and calling for hunters to "dedicate all resources to capturing and killing them." Hunting quickly became a kind of state-sponsored collective action. Every region organized its own tiger-killing team. A record in the Zhenping County gazette shows locals killed two South China tigers in the fifties, and received military-issue rifles as their reward. Meanwhile, across the country, 1,750 tiger hides were traded in 1956 alone. Every "tiger master" was awarded a government commendation at a national conference.

By 1976, the number of South China tigers in China had fallen below two hundred. Three years later, the Ministry of Agriculture listed the South China tiger under first-class state protection. However, poaching remained a serious threat to the species, with tiger hide, bones, and sexual organs sold as consumer goods and medicines. This was when the shortage of tiger prey was already critical. Hunting teams had all but cleared Zhenping's forests of antelope and dwarf musk deer. Zhou Zhenglong had been a member of one hunting team and claimed to have killed a "tractor load" of wild boar in a single afternoon. The delicate ecosystem that the South China tiger relied on to survive in the region had collapsed.

By the time the Wildlife Protection Law was enacted in 1989, the South China tiger was among the most critically endangered species in the world. And after a mountain resident killed the last specimen in the Qinling Mountains in 1964, there have been no further sightings of wild South China tigers in Shaanxi.

In 1998, China implemented a reforestation policy and closed logging areas. Fifty thousand people lived in the region's mountains, with a mere tenth of an acre per capita, and the annual county revenue fell short of fourteen million yuan. Zhenping was classified as a national-level impoverished county. Officials were required during their term in office to lift the local population out of poverty and achieve economic growth. Nature was their sole resource. If they could establish a nature reserve, they would receive investment from the state.

In 2005, Zhengping County Forestry Bureau collected together numerous reports of sightings, which it then passed on to its superior office. The Shaanxi Province Forestry Department then dispatched a team to the area to survey for South China tigers. The team leader, a man named Lu, stated that "for the treasured apex predator to reappear in Shaanxi would be as momentous as finding a Giant Panda in the wild."

Zhenping selected several experienced hunters to act as guides for the survey. Having made his name as a "trap-setter," Zhou Zhenglong was picked to be one of them.

Starting in June 2006, the Shaanxi Forestry Department's team performed three wildlife investigations. The combined time spent was just short of a month. The result was a twenty-page report, which contained accounts of nineteen sightings, including one of a tiger leaping through the mountains, one of a tiger tailing a woman, and another of a tiger devouring a cow. The number who claimed to have heard tigers' calls "were too many to count."

We visited each of the eyewitnesses. Once they were looking down at the camera and questioned closely, their answers suddenly became hazy. "I just saw some large paw prints." "My memory is foggy." "It was a little smaller than a cow." An old hunter was the only one who could convincingly confirm he had seen a South China tiger. Then he laughed and said, "But that was forty years ago."

Those who claimed to have heard a tiger had never seen one, nor did they know what a tiger's call sounded like. Li Qian of the forestry bureau testified in one report that the sound he'd heard had resembled "a saw cutting through a tree," which was later changed to "blowing hard through a bamboo pipe." Bureau Chief Tan Dapeng painted the press an even more dramatic picture, saying, "People throughout the town heard the tiger roar, it was this low, deep, and powerful sound, which started other roars coming in response from the valleys on both sides of the town. This back-and-forth lasted for days."

Of all the witnesses, Zhou Zhenglong spoke with the most certainty. He claimed to have had at least seven encounters with tigers. One was eating a wild boar when he came across it, and another ate his hunting dog whole: "Three drops of blood were all that was left." There was also the time he spotted a tiger beneath a tree. He clambered up the trunk to safety, from where he could easily make out the "王" on its head. He even produced two yellow-black hairs he said were tiger fur.

The survey team didn't collect the hairs for a DNA diagnostic because "one analyst found that there were no follicles on the hairs and, it seemed, no complete cells, so they gave up looking."

Scientific investigations demand material evidence. Eyewitness accounts alone are no good. On December 31, 2006, Zhenping Forestry Bureau released a notice calling for any locals who discovered traces of big cats to report them immediately: "We will generously reward all reliable information and authentic materials."

Eight days later, in a patch of snow in Wanyi, Shenzhou, the wildlife survey team came upon a trail of large paw-prints. An "outstanding contribution" from Zhou Zhenglong aided the discovery.

The prints were the only firsthand evidence included in the report. Yet there were disputes within the team about whether a tiger had left them at all. In early 2007, the heads of Zhenping County traveled to Beijing to submit for appraisal a mold and photographs of the paw prints to Professor Xie Yan of the Institute of Zoology at the Chinese Academy of Sciences. In my interview with Professor Xie, she told me she was "almost certain" they were not tiger prints. "Tiger prints are mostly round."

She told the county heads the same, yet their report featured no details from her verdict.

On July 6, 2007, a group of experts was assigned by the Shaanxi Forestry Department to assess the report. The head of that group was Wang Tingzheng, a retired professor from Shaanxi Normal University. We traveled to Xi'an to interview him, and he explained that neither he nor any of his colleagues had visited Zhenping in making their assessment. They had made their judgment based on the survey team's report alone, in which the sole piece of direct evidence was the paw-print mold. This new batch of experts unanimously agreed that a South China tiger had indeed left the print.

I checked Professor Wang's academic background online. His specialty was not *Felidae*, but *Muroidea*. I looked up everything he had published about rodents. His two main monographs were "Rodent Community Dynamics in Agricultural Lands on the Loess Plateau of Western Henan" and "Research into the Population Age of the Mandarin Vole." I asked him, "Have you published any papers about the South China tiger?"

"I have written none," he said.

"Have you completed any dedicated research within South China tiger territory?"

"No."

"So you're saying that you confirmed there are South China tigers inhabiting the region having neither researched the South China tiger nor inspected the place in question?"

"There's nothing else it could be. And based on my work in zoological taxonomy, I believe the print belongs to a South China tiger."

Seven experts had signed the report. We looked into the specializations of the other six; not one of them researched large animals. And none researched cats either.

I verified with Professor Wang: "Your expertise is voles, Professor Liu's is snub-nosed monkeys, and Professor Xu's is fish?"

"Correct."

"It seems to me like there are some significant differences between those animals and the South China tiger."

He leaned back in his chair and stuck his hands in his pockets. "They wanted experts to meet to make an assessment. Nobody in the province researches this sort of thing, so they found what people they could who work with animals."

"What if the report under assessment was about voles, but they invited an expert on the South China tiger to do it—does that sound suitable to you?"

He paused for a second. "Well it's not ideal, is it?"

He leaned forward and waved a hand in the air, an annoyed look on his face.

"I told them they should take the investigation a step further," he continued. "One must have photos to determine the existence of the South China tiger."

"Yet you all signed the report's conclusion," I said, "confirming the animal still lives in the area. Then you released that report to the public."

His hands went back in his pockets. "We might have been a little hasty, okay?"

Old Hao sat to the side, listening to the whole interview. That evening, she told me, "You go too far."

"What does that mean?"

"Whenever we think it's enough, you always want to push it further, and you take it too far."

"Do you think I'm harsh?"

"No, actually."

"Then what . . . relentless?"

"Exactly."

I considered my conduct—and Wang Tingzheng's. I'd interviewed the former professor at his home. He'd poured us water and generally treated us like we were family. What's more, he was in his seventies. He had a head of gray hair and a kind voice, and was very gentlemanly. In China, it is rude to ask a question that embarrasses an elder when you are a guest in his home, but I asked it anyway. During our conversation, as I pressed him on his assessment, the look of confusion or discomfort in his eyes melted my heart. It even had me second-guessing myself. *I better not ask that question*, I kept thinking. But still I asked.

I stood from the bed and gave her a stern look. "Am I too mean?"

She snorted. "You're alright with women."

"Not always. I have integrity. If it was you in the wrong, I'd be torn up, but I'd buck up the courage and be on my knees begging you to change your ways."

"Get out!"

I paused to think. "Maybe I've not thought it through, but I feel like when it comes to stories, it's a reporter's duty to pull no punches, and when it comes to people, to be tolerant. What do you think?"

She grunted by way of agreement.

The experts selected to assess the report were the provincial forestry department's choice. The person who was responsible for arranging the whole review was the same Sun Chengqian who would organize the press conference where the tiger photos were released.

I asked him, "Do you think the assessment is credible?"

He replied with a question of his own: "Well, Professor Wang Tingzheng was my teacher, and he has worked with animals his whole life. Is the South China tiger not an animal?"

I opened my mouth to answer but he cut me off. "Secondly, I'm confident that the experts I chose understand Shaanxi's geography."

"They might be familiar with Shaanxi's geography, but they're not familiar with South China tigers. How did you expect them to do the evaluation?"

"Who do you think I should've believed then?"

"Suzhou and Fujian both have artificial breeding bases. There are plenty of people there who know the habits of South China tigers. The Chinese Academy of Sciences alone has over a dozen big-cat specialists. Might they have had a little more authority on the matter? Did you think to invite them?"

"I consider Shaanxi's experts able to represent Shaanxi's standards." He hung up.

The conclusion of the review was released on July 6. The next day, great big banners were hung throughout Zhenping: "Experts confirm South China tigers living in Zhenping." County Mayor Wu Ping rallied his departments to seize the opportunity. "Push this project through the province and to Beijing by whatever means," he instructed, "and get us approval for a tiger reserve ASAP."

But things didn't go as he hoped. The Shaanxi media responded that "despite the amount of evidence in hand, without a photograph of a live specimen, the province lacks the confidence to announce the news."

The county still owed Zhou Zhenglong two thousand yuan for his work as a guide. In August 2007, the county mayor walked half a kilometer up a mountain trail to present Zhou with a certificate of honor, along with one thousand yuan in cash, as recognition of his "outstanding contribution" in finding the tiger's paw print. Shaking Zhou's hand, the mayor said, "If only you'd gotten a picture of one in the flesh."

On October 6, Zhou showed some pictures of a tiger to Li Qian and described how he had come to take them. The next day Zhou showed them to Bureau Chief Tan, and the following afternoon, County Mayor Wu Ping had heard the news and decided to report it to Xi'an. By October 10, every division head in the forestry department had seen the photos.

That's no fewer than thirteen officials, across three levels of government, and not one person raised any doubts.

When Zhou Zhenglong presented his photos to Sun Chengqian—a self-proclaimed amateur photographer and deputy commissioner of the forestry department, no less—Zhou said that Sun had "looked at the raw files with a magnifying glass for several minutes, then suddenly leaped up and hugged me, shouting with excitement, 'You've done it, you photographed one, it's real.'"

The forestry department made the decision the very next day to call a press meeting and award Zhou Zhenglong ten thousand yuan.

But he refused to hand over the photographs. He said the experts on the survey team had promised that a picture of a South China tiger would earn him a million. Sun ended up speaking with him late into the night, reassuring him there would be further rewards, and that once the nature reserve was established they would consider giving his son a job there.

At nine o'clock on the morning of the twelfth, the press conference began with the forestry department displaying Zhou Zhenglong's photographs along with the paw-print mold. Sun announced, "The rediscovery of the South China tiger in Shaanxi will go down in the annals of wildlife conservation in China."

On our last evening in Zhenping, we received notice that the media attention was getting out of hand. We had to turn down the heat on the South China tiger story. Such pressure was nothing new for investigative journalists; whenever requests like that came along, we had no choice but to take a step back.

But I felt the need to defend myself. I phoned Director Liang, who was the head of the News center, to ask to continue my investigation. "I don't think we're applying heat. We're just trying to get a clear picture of the matter."

Liang muttered to himself, then told me to wait. He called his supervisor: "*News Probe*'s MO has always been to pursue truth and shoulder the consequences. Let her try."

So, as it turned out, he was prepared to bear the political brunt and risk. He called me back. "Draw up a document for me to look over."

I spent the evening wondering what to write. Before I left the office, someone had said, "It's small-time stuff. One photograph isn't worth forty-five minutes of airtime. It's tabloid news at best."

This brought to mind Hu Shi, the scholar who wrote *An Outline of the History of Chinese Philosophy*. When researching the book, Hu had spent most of his time and energy on the popular novels *Dream of the Red Chamber* and *Water Margin*, much to the disdain of his academic colleagues, who criticized him for neglecting to do serious work. Hu explained, "I wish to make use of these popular literary subjects to propose a kind of methodology . . . Everything needs evidence. Be bold in your hypotheses, and be meticulous in your proving them. This approach topples any -ism and narrow-sightedness and refuses to be bullied or led by the nose."

This time around, our interviews with the survey team ran more than sixty hours, with almost every member subjected to over three hours each of cross-questioning about the timeline, place, persons involved, handling of evidence, and so forth . . . The bureau chief looked uncomfortable in the hot seat.

"That is why we don't want to be interviewed by you," he said. "Your questions are too specific."

But the truth often lies in the smallest details. Bringing a glass of water from the table to your mouth requires no real effort. Moving it exactly a millimeter takes time and energy. Precision is an unwieldy thing.

For Hu Shi nothing the world put in front of him was above questioning. We were empty-handed for the time being, but if we stuck to Hu's advice and pulled at the chain of events, tracing it back link by link, heck, we might have a chance at dragging the monster up from the deep. But first, we needed permission.

The report I submitted to Director Liang began, "The debate around the photographs' authenticity is not only a question of the techniques used up to this point, but also a test of the scientific spirit of everyone involved."

He read it and said, "Go ahead."

On the day we were leaving, County Mayor Wu agreed to be interviewed.

Having previously refused any contact with us, he'd had a sudden change of heart. "Little Chai, you should watch the interview I gave yesterday, you might learn something. The reporters did a great job."

His staff stood in a circle around the dining table and toasted in unison. "You spoke brilliantly yesterday."

Wu sat facing the camera in a black suit and red-and-white tie, not a gelled hair out of place. He rehashed what he had said the day before with a smile on his face. "Ultimately, it's up to the state authority to assess whether the photographs are real or not. But we are certain, beyond a shadow of a doubt, that the discovery of a South China tiger in Zhenping is a glorious moment not only for the region, but also for all of China."

"Why's that?" I asked.

"It's like I said, it's a golden age when China's tiger returns. It's that tiger's roar that will rouse the world." He had said just as much during the other show and repeated it now with a look of pride.

Auspicious signs had played an important role in political tradition in China's dynastic system of governance. Confucianism asserts that Heaven reveals its will to Man through Nature: "A delinquent ruler will feel Heaven's wrath. A sage king shall reap Heaven's auspices." Stars, stones, plants, animals: they could all be symbols of a ruling power's legitimacy. In the Tang Dynasty, there was even a special ministry dedicated to assigning every animal a level of auspiciousness, and regional officials would gather reports of sightings to pass to their superiors in the hope of promotion. China's imperial system had ended over a century ago, but some of its genes remained strong.

"Don't you think—" I said, before he motioned for me not to interrupt.

He hadn't finished.

"Because the South China tiger is China's tiger. A symbol of Chinese power."

Now I could speak.

"Don't you think this is first and foremost an issue of science, rather than politics?"

He blinked. "Of course it's a question of science first."

"Don't you think that while outside controversy and doubts remain regarding the authenticity of the photos—and therefore whether or not there really are South China tigers in Zhenping—the priority should be to get to the bottom of it, before looking for its meaning?"

"I think it all goes hand in hand."

On November 16, when we submitted our program for approval, the station head told us that he, too, believed the photos were fake.

"But," he added, "without proof that has some ministerial clout behind it, it can't be broadcast. Let's shelve it for now."

That day, a set of four photos appeared online of a South China tiger laying in front of a waterfall. The netizen who'd shared them said it was the tiger from the New Year poster on his wall at home. The similarities between it and the tiger photographed by Zhou Zhenglong were immediately apparent. In the twenty-four hours that followed, people posted numerous images of identical posters in cities around the country. They all came from a printing house in Zhejiang. The boss there was soon able to produce the earliest roll of film that had included the picture used in the poster. The date of printing was July 10, 2002.

The Internet blew up. The truth was out, as far as most were concerned—the "tiger believers" had gotten it wrong.

Old Hao wasted no time editing this new information into the program and prepared to resubmit our episode for approval.

A reporter in Zhenping that day said this was the first and only time he saw Zhou Zhenglong flounder. When reporters there advised Zhou to own up, he seemed uneasy and asked them to follow him to the local police station. Then the whole town's electricity was cut off. By the next morning, Zhou had changed his mind. He said he would sue the printing house for copying his photograph. This time, he stuck to his word.

On November 22, the forestry department called an urgent press conference and released a statement that made no mention of the New Year poster. Instead, they reaffirmed their position that "the tiger pictured is a live, wild South China tiger." Zhu Julong, the deputy commissioner in charge of publicity, told the media, "Even if Zhou Zhenglong is pressured to admit they are fake, we will hold firm in our belief that they are real."

Two days later, Zhu Julong traveled to Zhenping himself, where he greeted Zhou Zhenglong with a salute and an audible stamp of the foot. "You are our hero for photographing the tiger," he said as he lit Zhou's cigarette for him and encouraged him to "be strong."

On the spot, Zhou Zhenglong announced that since he had the confidence of his leaders, he was ready to pledge his life for the cause. All he needed were two bullets, a rifle, and a couple months in the mountains, and he would return with the tiger he had shot, sell his home, and hire a van to drive the thing to Tiananmen Square to quiet his detractors.

At this rate, our program would never get the green light. The day turned cold, and teams of reporters retreated from Zhou Zhenglong's home. Someone picked the last persimmon from the tree beside the entrance and took a bite. "Sour."

Usually, when a program can't be broadcast, the director scraps it, sticks the orange *REJECTED* label on the tape, and banishes it to the cabinet before starting on the next program and moving on with their lives. But not Old Hao, not this time. She was determined to find the clear conclusion about the authenticity of the photo which the station head had stipulated, but getting anyone with authority to speak out was easier said than done.

The State Forestry Administration had declined our interview request. As had the Institute of Zoology. And when we went for a first-hand appraisal of the photographs at the Institute of Forensic Science at the Ministry of Public Security, then the Supreme Judicial Identification Center, and then the Institute of Evidence Law and Forensic Science at China University of Political Science and Law, they all said no, on the basis that we weren't a judicial organization.

There was one night when Old Hao tapped out a message to me on MSN: *Chai Jing, I'm at my wit's end.* She said she couldn't stop crying, that she was still crying as she typed. *Nothing hurts, it's the lack of control.* There had been so many other shows of hers that had never reached the air, but not once had I heard her struggle. I had never seen her weak. This wasn't a good sign. If we had passed the pictures off as a farce, an anecdote we could share with friends, maybe we could have laughed about it and gotten on with things. The absurd feeling of powerlessness can break a person.

I had no way to comfort her besides keeping our work going. It was winter already, but the central heating hadn't been turned on. In the deep of night, bundled up in padded jackets and thick hats, Old Hao and I huddled over our laptops, passing drafts back and forth.

We're on a road to disaster, she typed. Then a moment later: *But the alternative only leads to disaster too.*

Well then, we better keep going, I said.

On December 2, the China Photographers Association's digital imaging evaluation center agreed to assess the photographs and the New Year poster.

Photographer Liu Kuanxin concluded that "their postures are identical, and their stripes, eyes, and whiskers are highly similar." He also compared the photographs within the set taken by Zhou Zhenglong. "There's no way a tiger sat for twenty-five minutes with a leaf on its head and remained absolutely still. Even the slightest shift would show it's alive." Another photographer at his side laughed and added, "A little wind or the tiger breathing, and there would be movement."

Their colleague Gao Lei completed a computer simulation and analysis, which judged the tiger to be two-dimensional—flat. They also put the distance between the photographer and the tiger at ten meters. A team from the Beijing Film Academy performed some technical tests of their own and found the white fur on the tiger's chest was saturated blue and unusually bright, while the colors around the tiger remained dark—the opposite to how light usually works. What's more, in the pictures taken with flash, there was no reflection in the tiger's eyes, even though there was a large square of reflected light on its face. Liu Kuanxin said, "There's only one explanation. I would say that it's a flat image, that it was spray-painted. One hundred percent, the South China tiger is fake, from its tail to its whiskers."

Famous wildlife photographer Xi Zhinong was there too. He thought the photo was so fake that it was not worth arguing. All he had to say was, "If those pictures are real, it's a disgrace for wildlife photographers across China."

By three-thirty P.M., we had finished recording.

The conclusions were posted online later that afternoon. The next day, the Shaanxi Forestry Association responded the same way they had been all along: "We firmly believe the fact that there are South China tigers in Zhenping County. Following our assessment, we also believe that Zhou Zhenglong's photographs of the tiger are real."

I interviewed Guan Ke, a spokesperson for the Shaanxi Forestry Department, who had been part of the review team.

"Why is a government department only publishing its conclusion and not its evidence?" I asked.

"We've worked like this for years," he replied.

"So when doubts were raised, why wasn't another survey or review organized?"

"The doubts came from regular folk, not from above."

"Isn't the government above all public-facing?"

"I can't answer that."

"What's your opinion of the public's suspicions?"

"Not even foreign experts have said they're fake, the doubters are unpatriotic."

On December 4, the State Forestry Administration announced that they would conduct a survey in Zhenping to confirm, or disprove, the presence of tigers in the region. But they would not "overrule" the decision about the photos' authenticity. One official compared the South China tiger photos to those of the Loch Ness monster: "People don't know if those pictures are real either, but what they really care about is whether or not the Loch Ness monster exists."

Our last interviewee was Hao Jinsong, who had brought a lawsuit against the State Forestry Administration.

In late November, he had submitted a request that the forestry administration hire a third-party, specialist organization to re-evaluate the photographs. The administration declined to hear his case, so he tried to take it to court. Beijing No. 2 Intermediate People's Court refused too, so he applied to the Higher People's Court asking for somebody at Beijing No. 2 Intermediate People's Court to be assigned to the suit.

"There are a lot of people who think this isn't a worthwhile fight," I said.

"The South China tiger matter is no longer simply a question of whether the photos are fake or not. It has to do with integrity and honesty, with our moral baseline. A society that doesn't pursue the truth is a society doomed to failure. Even if in the future you find South China tigers in the wild, there's no getting around the pictures' authenticity. The people want the truth."

"A Suspect Tiger" aired on December 8, 2007. Old Hao and I felt that the window for it to have any effect had passed, and held little hope anything would come of it. But the intensity of the response reminded me that people never forget a question that needs an answer. When it comes to the truth, there is no nation-specific approach; it is human nature to seek to understand the reason behind everything.

The following day, the State Forestry Administration ordered its provincial body to commission a specialist review of the original photographs and publish the results exactly as provided.

For months, we waited for things to progress. No one was called to account, and no information about the review followed.

In March 2008, a video surfaced online showing a large striped animal with a long tail laying in front of a rock. It shook its head a few times, then stood and pawed at the ground, before slinking off into the woods. The shot lasted nineteen seconds. One news headline ran:

"Suspected South China Tiger Spotted in Pingjiang County, Hunan Province."

The Hunan Forestry Department published the result of its investigation after just five days: the footage was real. The tiger was real. It was a Siberian tiger taken from the circus.

The head of the Pingjiang County Tourism Department and some local tourism developers had colluded to cage the trained Siberian tiger and covertly transport it in a truck to the ravine where the video was taken. Eight people had been needed to lift it off the transport. Once its rope leash had been untied, the tiger lay where they wanted it to, stood when they wanted it to, and even walked on command, all for a reporter to catch on video. An employee at the tourism company said that "when they saw no one had been punished for the Zhou Zhenglong photos, they piggybacked on the South China tiger hype." They figured even if their plot was uncovered, they would simply admit it was fake and use the media frenzy to turn the Siberian tiger and its cubs into stars.

The Two Sessions convened a month later.[6] When representatives from Shaanxi Province were repeatedly questioned on the matter of the South China tiger sightings during the media open day, the vice-governor of Shaanxi said, "This whole affair has turned us into the laughingstock of the nation and severely damaged the image of our government and the province."

They had sent a team to the Madaozi forest zone, where Zhou Zhenglong had purportedly taken the photos, only to discover that the area was two thousand meters above sea level: too low in elevation to

---

[6] The Two Sessions is a key event on China's political calendar, the annual sessions of China's national legislature and top political advisory body, that take place in Beijing. The Two Sessions meet for about ten days each year, usually in March. The Two Sessions make important national-level political decisions.

be a habitat for a tiger. What's more, the area was covered with nothing but weeds and rank grass. There was not a tall tree in sight. A tiger had nowhere to hide there. After measuring the leaf that covered the tiger's head in the photo, they calculated the tiger could be only twenty-seven centimeters tall and thirty-five centimeters long.

Police also found the paper tiger at Zhou Zhenglong's home—he had cut it out of a New Year poster—and a wooden tiger paw, which Zhou had carved himself.

It had taken eight months from the initial release of the tiger photos for the authorities to acknowledge that they were fake.

On November 17, Zhou Zhenglong was given a suspended sentence of two and a half years in prison for fraud and illegal possession of ammunition. The case saw thirteen government staff punished by the administration. But the only one discharged from public employment was Li Qian—the lowest man on the bureaucratic food chain.

In 2010, the State Forestry Administration published the findings of a two-year-long wildlife survey carried out in Zhenping: during the period of investigation, there were no South China tigers present in the surveyed area. The natural environment was unsuitable to support long-term habitation by even the smallest community unit of the species.

That same month, Zhou Zhenglong completed his sentencing. He told the media on his release that he would spend the rest of his years in the mountains searching for tigers.

With "Grandpa" who survived the great earthquake,
which caused about one hundred thousand casualties in 2008, Sichuan.

Seven
Broken Mountains
2008

May 12, 2008: the Great Sichuan earthquake.

I was in a small town in Iowa at the time. There was no Internet, hardly a TV signal, and even buying a newspaper would have required a trip to the state capital thirty kilometers away. I couldn't find out what the situation was in the earthquake's aftermath. I'd heard there were a few hundred dead; the next day that number had jumped to ten thousand.

I called my boss. Zhang Jie said, "Don't worry about coming back. The interviews we shot a few days ago were a waste." CCTV had canceled all their regular programs, including *News Probe*, in favor of live coverage of the earthquake.

But I went to San Francisco anyway, looking for a plane home. Three days after the earthquake, the number of deaths had reached twenty-eight thousand.

I texted Old Hao: *What's happening?*

She didn't know. They aren't letting any journalists go in anymore. Too many people want to go, and there's still too much danger.

I got on a flight back to China. During the trip, I carried two photos I'd torn out from a piece in the *New York Times*.

One showed a Sichuanese couple standing in the rain. The wife was crying with her head buried in her husband's chest. The husband's face was ashen. Wife in his arms, his head tilted toward the sky, his eyes were closed behind his glasses. Next to their feet was a blue plastic tarp covering the body of their child.

The other photo showed a young soldier holding a child, leading a group over a heap of rubble by a river. The roads were destroyed. Next to the brackish green water, people crawled over boulders to make their way forward.

The final count of victims in this magnitude 8.0 earthquake were 69,227 dead, 17,923 missing, 370 thousand injured, and ten million homeless.[7]

I arrived in Beijing on May 19, one of the three national days of mourning for the thirty-four thousand victims who had died in the earthquake. There was a moment of silence when I was in line to exit customs. Everyone in the airport, regardless of nationality or race, bowed their heads. The massive silence hit me harder than any of the news. It was real.

I flew directly to Chengdu, the capital of Sichuan, where the earthquake had happened. There were only a few cars in the lane into Chengdu, but the road out of the city was packed. People were attempting to escape aftershocks. I looked out the window, but didn't see any collapsed buildings. 80 percent of victims were from rural areas, not big cities. During the trip, I carried two photos I'd torn out from the piece in the *New York Times*.

The next morning, I went to the Mianyang municipal gymnasium, where refugees were being temporarily housed. It was overflowing. The major news crews were all there, and a tent had been set up for me on the edge of Min River. While I was brushing my teeth at the waterside that night, I saw the trees on the mountain shining with a terrible white light. They were naked under the moon, like a giant hand had

---

[7] Sichuan Earthquake Relief Records Compilation Committee. "Wenchuan mega-earthquake Sichuan Earthquake Relief Records." *General Chronology*, 1st edition, March 2018. Sichuan People's Publishing House.

peeled off their bark. All the leaves were gone. Only bare branches pointed to the sky, like countless fingers. The river had become extremely vicious, and it roared like endless thunder, pounding in my head all night.

Though I was supposed to be reporting live from the scene, I decided to take an unexpected approach. I used a few objects I'd found in a medical tent to tell three stories: a cracked and dirty helmet spoke of a man who'd come a thousand kilometers on his motorcycle to see his injured wife; a heavy wet boot was from a soldier who'd delayed his own medical treatment because he was too busy rescuing people, which had resulted in his intestines falling out; a watch told of the woman who'd guarded rubble for seven days until her husband was finally rescued.

At the time, Snoopy was also broadcasting from the disaster zone. While I spoke, he stood by the broadcast van, watching. He walked away before I'd finished. After, I asked him what was wrong. He was circumspect, afraid to hurt my feelings.

"You're too polished."

"But I edited nothing. I didn't try to sound a certain way."

"That's not what I mean. When I saw your producer squatting there holding your microphone, my heart skipped a beat. Then, when he was handing you one prop after another, that made me even more uncomfortable. With an event of this scale, there shouldn't be time to set the stage. It would have been fine if those things were just lying on the ground. Or you could've said, Give me a moment and let me grab something. That would've felt more real."

Later, I went online and read some feedback from viewers about my segment. Some people had found it distasteful. So I watched the footage of myself again. As I spoke, it was clear that my focus was on tone, prop placement, and pacing. In short, I was busy telling a story instead of trying to feel what it was like to live it. The sleekness of my presentation felt superficial.

· · ·

On our second day there, Mianyang experienced a magnitude-6.0 aftershock.

We hopped out of our trembling car and ran toward Jiuzhou Stadium, which had been a temporary shelter for around thirty thousand evacuees, though it was nearly empty now in the wake of initial aftershocks. A lone figure sat inside.

I approached him. Sitting with his back against the wall, he wouldn't look at me. I squatted down. "It's not safe here anymore," I said. "Why haven't you left?"

He looked up. The man was in his thirties, with a blackened face and arms resting on his knees. He said, "My wife and child are gone. Why would I run?"

During the live broadcast that night, I mentioned my exchange with this man. But all I received in response was another wave of criticism— this time from my superiors, who'd found the segment too dark.

The dual ire of my audience and my bosses left me feeling beaten. Avoiding tragic details would have been untruthful, but simply telling these stories, with either tears or smiles, was also understandably inappropriate. I thought about how I'd reported on the 2003 Xinjiang earthquake. Though I'd conveyed the realness of the event that time, I was left unsatisfied because the story felt incomplete.

I decided to discuss the matter with my coworkers from *News Probe*. We agreed to stop filming live broadcasts. We would pull back and take time to put together an episode—even if it might not be allowed to air.

On May 24, 2008, thousands of people left the temporary shelter at Jiuzhou Stadium and returned to what was left of their homes. As our investigative team watched the flood of people, a woman walking next to a couple tried to get our attention. She indicated the pair beside her— the man looked about forty years old, with startled, sheepish eyes; the woman was carrying a bucket of vegetable oil with a few packs of instant noodles in it—and said, "This is Brother Ye and Sister Ye. Their son studied at the elementary school in Beichuan. He was the monitor . . . the entire class, including the teachers . . ." She couldn't go on.

Sister Ye finished for her: "No one's made it out."

Beichuan, with a population of 170 thousand, had lost 19,956 citizens. It was the worst-hit county in the earthquake, located right in the fault zone, and most of its casualties were concentrated in schools. The disaster had struck at 2:28 P.M., when students were still in class. Brother Ye and Sister Ye's son, along with 466 other students, had died in the collapsed primary school. The middle school next to it was completely buried in smashed mountain rocks. Over a thousand students had died there; only a flag and a basketball hoop were left.

We rode home with the Ye family. They lived in Willow Field Village, which was on the mountain near the county seat, in a narrow canyon sealed off by fallen rocks.

The road up the mountain had collapsed. Boulders and slabs of earth the size of houses had crashed into the pavement. We had to climb over the debris, then ride two to a motorcycle. At a bend halfway up the mountain, a part of the road had crumbled and fallen down the cliff. A motorcycle lay precariously at the edge. We continued to ascend to an altitude of around fourteen hundred meters. Thick fog flowed like a river, pierced only by our headlights.

The Ye home was nestled under a pear tree. Deep in the cold mountain, the pear flowers were still in bloom. Approaching from the back, we saw that the gray brick wall of the house was still intact. But once we got around to the front, everything was gone. The foundation wall and footing had all shattered. It was the first time the Ye family had seen their house after the quake. Dumbstruck, they dropped whatever they were holding in their hands. Sister Ye whispered, "That's it?"

The camera froze as well. No one spoke for a good four minutes. It was quiet in the mountain, only the shy chirping of birds and raindrops tapping against the toon tree leaves.

Brother Ye walked into the rubble and found something. After brushing off the dirt, he stood still. I walked closer and saw that it was a chess set. He and his son had played the day before the quake. A string of origami cranes hung from a beam, gently swinging. They were clumsily folded out of green graph paper, the kind used for doing homework. Two months prior, for International Women's Day, Sister Ye's son had made them for her.

On the day of the earthquake, the mountains all around their home shook and shook. After massive sounds, like explosions, there was an expulsion of earth. No one could see anything because the sky had turned dark with all the dust. The women working in the fields thought the mountain gods were angry, so they'd lain prostrate, praying in all directions. The ground wasn't shaking; it was turning. At first, Brother Ye leaped out of his house to hold the pear tree. But with a loud yell, letting go of the tree, he dashed down the hill. At the bottom was the old part of town, where Qushan Elementary School was. His son was in class.

The road in had crumbled. A boulder the size of a building blocked all passage. The crushed hood of a taxi poked out from under it. Undaunted, Brother Ye grabbed tree branches and shrubs, half running, half jumping down the hill, "like a madman." He reached the town in just over twenty minutes.

The town was wedged between Wang jia Peak and Jing jia Peak. The narrowest part of the canyon was only a kilometer wide. There'd been massive landslides on both slopes, and the only road into the canyon had been destroyed. Rescuers were moving the wounded out along the edge of the cliffs, passing them down the line one by one. One of the wounded was passed to Brother Ye.

He could have backtracked to look for another route to the school. But after a moment of hesitation, he reached out.

Ye had put his son's life into the rescuers' hands, but there were too few rescuers, and the majority of buildings across the town had completely collapsed. Almost half of the thirty thousand people in the county seat had died, and many were injured. The smashed road made it impossible for outside rescue vehicles to enter with any speed. So most of the work was left to the town's two thousand survivors, who tried to save whoever they could with their bare hands.

One of them was a reporter at the local television station. He'd rushed to the school first, drawn by the smell of blood. When I interviewed him later, his voice was pained. I could barely make out what he was saying.

"Right under that big concrete slab . . ." he said.

He sat on the ground, so I sat with him. In the hoarse whisper of a mute, he said, "I heard a little girl's voice: 'Uncle, please save me.' I said, 'I will rescue you, but I can't move the slab.' I tried anyway. I screamed, but I couldn't move it, Chai Jing."

Children were crushed under multiple layers of heavy concrete slabs. But most of the professional rescuers in town had been buried along with their equipment. Only a third of the police officers and local officials had survived. There were no doctors. The seven-story hospital had completely collapsed. Only three staff members survived.

"All I could do was give her two white rabbit candies . . ." said the reporter.

He turned toward me, face purple, his mouth opening wide. He was breathing heavily, as if he couldn't get enough air into his lungs. Then he stuffed his fist into his mouth to block the sounds coming out. Veins bulged on his forehead. I worried he was going to choke himself. I placed my hand on his back. It was as if a cork had popped out of his throat. He bawled to the sky: "Only . . . two . . . candies . . ."

Brother Ye and Sister Ye leveled the area in front of the house and lined the edges with broken chunks of concrete to keep water from seeping in. Their emergency tent hadn't arrived, so they hung a raggedy yet colorful sheet from the pear tree before retrieving a mattress from the house to place under the sheet. The drizzle picked up, wetting our heads.

I asked Brother Ye why he hadn't stayed at the temporary shelter for a little longer. He said, "Unlike all the wounded and maimed, we still have our hands and feet. We can rebuild our house. I don't want to wait."

With two rocks and an iron wok, he boiled some of the water that had collected in the drinking pond and made some instant noodles.

He and his wife sat on an old log and ate while they told their story. Sister Ye was almost forty years old. She said, "In the future, when I have another son like that, we will raise him as well as our first child."

Brother Ye added, "Just like the first one."

I heard someone swallow a breath behind me. It was my editor, Luo Chen. He was about the same age as the couple and also had a son.

We stayed on the mountain for a few days. Chen Wei, my cameraman, assembled a temple. There was no running water, electricity, or cell phone signal. Each day, we took a short hike and, with a small bowl, collected water from a mountain spring that had nearly run dry. I learned how to use one cup of water to wash my hair and face. When we sent in the material we'd shot on the first day, we brought the tape down the mountain and transmitted it back from Mianyang, and I called the director there. Director Cao said the higher-ups thought it was too dark. It couldn't be aired just yet.

"So what will your theme be?" Cao asked.

I said, "I don't know."

I used to be afraid of the words *I don't know*. Before working on an episode, if I didn't have an outline or a thematic direction, I would feel uneasy. But this time, I really meant what I said.

"So what are you going to do?" Cao was responsible for getting something aired. "Do you want to find a village party secretary and do a bird's-eye view of the situation?"

I said, "I want to wait."

.   .   .

Sleeping at night, it was quiet in the mountain—so quiet that it was hard to sleep.

Knowing about death and experiencing it are two different things.

In the winter of 2003, my grandmother passed away. No one back home told me over the phone; they only said she was ill. But from my little sister's voice, I basically knew what had happened. When I returned home, the house was full of people. There were many things to take care of and many people to comfort. I waited for a moment to look at Grandma when it wasn't so crowded.

Now there was a dark, heavy coat over her and a checkered green handkerchief on her pillow. I leaned in and smelled the soapy scent of the freshly washed handkerchief, which had just been dried by the stove. I remembered the way she had breathed with her lips slightly parted. Listening to her breath, I would sometimes feel afraid because it would seem to stop. I'd have to reach out to touch her face, to feel the warmth of her skin, to reassure myself. Whenever I'd thought about what it might be like if she died, it'd bring me to tears.

I reached into the coffin and softly caressed her cheek with the back of my hand.

Death is inescapable. There is no other way to deal with the pain but to endure.

I knew that for the Ye family, an interview was out of the question. What would I even ask? It was enough that they allowed us to keep them company. Sometimes there were hours where no one spoke. Still we kept the camera on. There was only the sound of fire crackling and the image of embers flying past people's faces, a spell of warmth followed by a spell of cold. Sometimes the couple discussed their future, how they would rebuild the house and go on with their lives, full of determination. Sometimes they were silent, too distracted to do anything. This was real life. It was beyond what words could express.

A few days later, the Ye family helped their neighbors harvest garlic scapes. The neighbor's wife had passed away in the earthquake, leaving only father and son. The son was twelve years old. His name was Wen Chao. Of the eighty-eight families in Willow Field Village, twenty-two were lost to the quake. Of the houses that had collapsed or been seriously damaged, only around 5 percent had met the design requirements for withstanding seismic events. Most people, including the Ye family, had had no idea about these requirements. The construction in rural areas was not under the national supervision system. Four million rural families lost their houses in the quake, and accounted for 80 percent of the victims.

Unlike the communal villages of the North, Sichuan mountain villages were more dispersed. Far-apart houses were connected only by the bonds of kinship. All who could come to the harvest had shown up, but that was only about ten people.

Wen Chao wore a red shirt with a round collar. His knees were covered with bandages featuring little bears. He wasn't talkative. He'd escaped from the collapsed school. Since then, he always kept silent, never asking about his mother, not once.

After harvesting the garlic scapes, Brother Ye showed up wearing a yellow hard hat with a broken brim he'd found somewhere. He'd pulled a hunk of cured ham from under a pile of concrete rubble. Pleased with himself, he said, "Boy am I glad nobody stole this."

We all pitched in to build a stove out of stones and gather firewood. Using a stone shard, someone scraped the dirt off the cured ham before putting it into a wok to boil. Then the ham was scooped out and brushed forcefully, until its charred exterior had turned a waxy yellow. I cut the meat. When the knife sliced through, hot steam rose from between the large chunks while a clear rim of fat sizzled.

Sister Ye turned to shout, "Go look for some potatoes in the field."

The men came back with over a dozen potatoes, which were quickly cut into chunks to be boiled, then stir-fried. One family managed to find, from under their collapsed ceiling, a plastic bottle of rice wine. That lifted everyone's spirits.

After clearing out some more rubble, everyone set three short tables up outside. The sky was getting dark. The villagers didn't want to waste wood on starting a fire. By glimmering starlight against the ink-blue sky, they crowded together around the tables. A dog crouched behind me. If I didn't feed him something, he would poke at my waist with his nose before sitting back with pitiful puppy eyes. Brother Ye threw a piece of skin at him and smiled. "It hasn't seen humans in days."

Chen Wei had to keep filming. He stared through the camera from several meters away. But the villagers didn't seem to think about the fact that we were there working. They were used to the camera being there, as if it were just a shovel. They called to Chen Wei: "Come and eat."

He sat on a rock, still behind his machine, and waved his hand. He was holding a cigarette. "Let me finish this smoke."

Wen Chao's younger uncle, Zhi Quan, raised the bowl of wine and announced, "This is the first time we have had so many familiar faces together since the earthquake. Let's call it a reunion. Cheers."

The wine burned in my belly like a fire.

Once, when we went to collect water with Zhi Quan, we ran into a villager we didn't know. This villager waved hello at Zhi Quan and let out a long sigh. Then he turned to me and explained, "He was the one who dug my son out from the ruins."

Zhi Quan's face was blank. Afterward, as he walked in silence, he grabbed a branch and whipped a nearby rock, as if the man's words drew out the pain inside him.

It wasn't until that night that we talked about what had happened. Zhi Quan's daughter had also gone to the elementary school in town; he'd been nearby when the earthquake happened. When he rushed to his girl's school, he found that the three million cubic meters of earth that was once Wang Jia Peak had pushed all the buildings at the school intersection forward and piled them into a four-story-tall ruin blocking the way. The heap was full of wood, rocks, and thorn-like steel bars, cars, and corpses. At the very top, there was a plane tree that used to be by the sidewalk. Over sixteen hundred people were buried below.

Zhi Quan had climbed up on all fours, desperate to search for his daughter on the other side, but stopped when he heard other people screaming beneath him. He went back down, and helped to rescue as many survivors as he could.

He said, "My wife still blames me for turning around. I was a soldier by training. She thinks that if I hadn't gotten distracted, I would have been able to save our daughter."

I wanted to comfort him, but words seemed pointless. The Sichuanese have a saying: "You don't know the pain of being burned by fire until it lands on your feet." Pain plagued him, tormented him. He said the worst part of it all was that he felt his child wouldn't have even blamed him for what he'd done. "If she were alive, she would write an essay for homework: 'My Dad.'"

We were sitting by a fire. It didn't give off enough light to film, so Luo Chen sat to my left, holding a candle that we had brought. Hot wax melted onto his hand, but he didn't move. Drip, drip. The flame wavered in the breeze.

Zhi Quan said, "That morning, she'd said, 'Daddy, buy me an ice cream.' I didn't buy it for her. I regret it now. It was only a two-buck ice cream. Why didn't I buy it for her?"

Wen Chao lay his head against his uncle's knees and sobbed. Zhi Quan caressed his nephew's hair. "Your grandpa came here as a twelve-year-old beggar. That's how our family started. You have his blood in you. Don't cry."

· · ·

A kitten showed up in the ruins—an earthquake survivor, recently born, who couldn't find its mother.

The little thing was so weak it couldn't stand straight. It buried itself deep into my camouflage shirt, desperately trying to suckle as if the dark warmth was its mother's. Its tiny claws dug into my skin, and I yelped. Chen Wei took it away from me and held it up in front of his face. With a cigarette in his other hand, he pointed at the kitten's white belly and gave it a scolding. The kitten didn't make a sound, staring at him with its sad little face. He sighed and put it down.

Wen Chao poured the milk we gave him into a plastic water bottle and dipped his finger in it to feed the kitten. The kitten's face wasn't much bigger than the blue bottle cap. Its tiny red tongue lapped and lapped. It was the first time I saw the little boy smile. When we ate, Wen Chao handed bits of bamboo shoots to the kitten to work on its teeth.

"The villagers think it doesn't stand a chance of survival. What do you think?" I asked him.

"I'll try my best."

"Why?"

"Because it's alive." He held it in his arms.

Wherever Wen Chao went, the kitten wobbled behind. By the time we left, it was big enough to stand in front of the dog's big nose fearlessly, unwilling to budge.

Victims of disasters do not need to be patronized or told to sing "My Grateful Heart," as they were sometimes asked to do. We shot the episode with an attitude of utmost respect.

The village was running out of grain. There wasn't any food left for the pig to eat. So the villagers bound its feet and took it down the mountain to find food. It was wedged between two people on a motorcycle. The person riding in the back grabbed the pig's legs with one hand and an ear with the other. Despite the manhandling, the pig did not make any sound. It looked docile after the disaster, staring back at me with frightened eyes, a red wound between them where it had been hit in the earthquake. It seemed to fear what would happen next. It watched me until the motorcycle turned the corner and disappeared.

The government building had collapsed, so officials had to work by the roadside. There were only three of them in charge of distributing grain to the town. One was a plump woman with a perm who was covered in dirt. Another was so thin that his face had become concave and his eyes were sunken in. He had a wound but didn't wrap it, and he walked with a limp. His foot was so swollen that shoes no longer fit him. Hundreds of people surrounded him as he distributed oil and grain. A truck drove by, filling the air with dust. He had to shout at the top of his lungs to be heard, his mask pulled down over his chin.

After he finished and the crowd dispersed, he spoke to me. He hadn't gone home in days. I asked him who was taking care of his family members. After a long pause, he said, "They take care of themselves."

I asked, "What about the other officials?"

He said, "They were having a meeting when the quake hit. They didn't have time to escape."

"How many?"

"Over thirty . . . too many died." He blinked nervously, heaving for breath. "I don't want to talk about it."

Approximately one-third of the officials in Beichuan had passed away. Eighty percent of the survivors were injured. After five months of constantly working without a break, the director of the disaster relief office in town hanged himself. He left a note that said, "I can't take it anymore, just want to take a rest." His twelve-year-old son had died in Qushan elementary school. One of his colleagues did the same thing months later; he had also lost a child, a nine-year-old, who'd attended the school. He wrote, "Death is the happiest thing for me, son. I ask your mother to scatter my ashes under the tree in front of your school. Daddy will always be with you. We will never be apart."

It was raining on the morning of June 1, Children's Day. The Ye family couldn't concentrate on anything. Their son used to come back home on that day with gifts from school. Brother Ye said, "I've been thinking about him all morning. Just look at how clumsy I am, doing this for a bit and that for a bit . . ."

Sister Ye said, "Every time I hear a motorcycle, I think it's him, being brought home to us."

Wen Chao came to them. He'd been their son's best friend and called them godfather and godmother. He spent much of his time at the Ye home now, sitting, holding the kitten. I asked him why he hadn't gone down the hill to attend the elementary school reunion. He said he hadn't wanted to.

His aunt said, "Everyone else went. He's the only one not going. We told him to go, but he wouldn't listen."

Sister Ye said, "He didn't want to leave his father."

I asked him, "Is that true?"

He cried, covering his eyes with his sleeve.

After lunch, the sun came out. The fir trees glistened with droplets that dripped onto the roof, gathering into tiny meandering streams that flowed along the broken tiles before cascading down. Brother Ye wanted to cheer the boy up, so he brought out his son's chess set and laid it out on the ground. They played a game. Brother Ye was so distracted that, after only a few moves, he began mumbling to himself: "Did I lose? Have I lost yet?"

Chen Wei shot the clip with the camera far off in the distance. Beneath the noon sun, cicadas filled the air with noise. Tree leaves scattered shadows on the ground; a chess set lay among them. Two silhouettes, one small, one large, sat against distant foggy peaks, empty sky beyond.

One day, while sitting at Brother Ye's house, we heard people shouting somewhere uphill.

"Boy, are they having a fight?" Brother Ye asked.

We hiked up.

An old man with tousled hair and a sun-bleached blue apron was climbing up a ladder to lay tiles on a damaged roof. Below him, his son was yelling at him. As it turned out, the old man didn't want to live in his son's house and insisted on fixing up his own home, refusing any help.

I wondered why he hadn't at least summoned the carpenter. Brother Ye speculated that the carpenter wouldn't have been in the mood, having lost a son of his own.

This son, who was in his fifties, shouted in desperation: "Just wait until I tear this house down!"

When the old man saw our group appear, he grew annoyed and climbed down.

I asked, "May I ask how old you are?"

He was riled up. Eyes bulging, he waved me off. "Not old at all."

The village head was there mediating. With a chuckle, he said, "He's eighty-three." He turned to the old man. "These are reporters from Beijing."

The old man couldn't care less about what reporters did, but the mention of Beijing caught his attention and quelled some of his anger. "Oh, all the way from Beijing—was there an earthquake in Beijing too?" His face showed deep concern. I felt moved.

After chatting for a bit, the village head said, "He sings a mountain song like nobody else."

I egged him on. "Sing us a song."

The old man was stubborn. "No song." It didn't matter who asked him.

In the following days, he continued to live in the half-collapsed wooden house. Light pierced through the cracked tiles, dotting the floor. He kept a fire going during the day and sat with a couple of fat cats around the flame. Hair tousled, face rosy from the light of the red flame, he wiped his hand on his blue apron. He was hard of hearing and couldn't understand Mandarin, so every time I visited him, I simply shouted, "Grandpa." That word he could understand. He offered a joyful toothless smile.

One day before leaving, after finishing dinner, the villagers all came to talk to us. The sky was getting dark. A throng of dark gray silhouettes squatted by the road and sat on rocks. The men talked about what was happening in town. The women listened, drawing lines in the dirt with tree branches, sometimes whispering among themselves, sometimes grabbing a cat to play with. Faces were no longer visible in the dim dusk light. The scene quieted down to no more than the sound of warm breaths. That's the way they said goodbye.

Grandpa suddenly came down the hill. He stood by himself and broke into a song. When the song was finished, he turned around and walked away. We nearly tripped over ourselves trying to capture it on camera. Luckily, we caught the last few lines.

Later, Chen Luo edited the old man's song into the beginning of every segment of the episode. We couldn't understand the lyrics, so we asked the villagers for a translation, but they said they didn't understand it either. During that period, every time I daydreamed, I would hear those lines. He was singing, *Something, something, Willow Field, oh . . . village, oh.* My heart rose and fell with his tune.

Chen Luo stayed up three nights straight in post-production. I told him to take a nap and wrote the ending voice-over. Then I showed it to my producer, Zhang Jie. "Let me read the voice-over this time,"

I asked. He gave me a skeptical look. I had a cold at the time, so my voice was rather nasally.

I said, "If you don't let me do this I'll kick your butt."

Returning home after recording the voice-over, I placed my muddy boots on a shoe rack and wiped off the stains left on my desk by a storm. I found a notice telling me to pick up a package, crumpled it up, and threw it in the dustbin. Cleaning the bathroom, some toilet detergent splashed onto my wrist and left a gnawing sting. I unpacked my luggage—a set of binoculars, a flashlight, a headlamp, an emergency vest—and put everything away. Washing up, I noticed that my face and hairline had changed shade. My arms and neck had tanned to a dark brown.

I ordered take-out because the fridge was empty. Outside my window, people were returning from their ball games. Boys with white jerseys patted one another on the back and laughed heartily in the golden sunset.

I didn't return any phone calls because I didn't know how to speak.

I'd worked so hard to separate the world I reported on from my daily life, but it was impossible to look and not see, to hear and not feel. The pain was inside me and I didn't want to be free from it. It felt like I could only have peace in that small tent on the cold mountain.

After the episode aired, a director on CCTV who I had never met called me and said, "I've arranged for you to recite a poem."

I interrupted her. "No, I don't recite poetry."

She was surprised. "But it's dedicated to the great earthquake."

"I'm a reporter. I'm not suited to reading poems."

She continued her pitch.

"I know it's a good poem and a good project," I said. "It's just that I'm not the right person."

I have nothing against poems or reciting them. I just don't like the feeling of being "arranged."

The following week, I packed again and went back to Sichuan. People had already started building houses—the same unsafe structures in the same unsafe places. The Ye family, at least, planned to rebuild their apartment in the county seat, though it would cost all of their savings. But the county seat was hardly safer than the village; it was still located in the earthquake fault zone. The broken mountains left behind were so vulnerable that I could crush one of the small rocks there with my bare hands. When the rainy season came, the slopes would undoubtedly crumble into deadly mudslides.

My new episode would be about the selection of a reconstruction site for the residents of areas severely affected by the earthquake. I knew it would be a highly controversial issue. The political and economic costs for any entire county to rebuild, let alone relocate, are inherently high. I just wanted to present different points of view before any decisions were made.

The intensity of the arguments went beyond what I'd expected. Yang Bao Jun, the expert who was leading the reconstruction planning, told me he was under huge pressure. Some insisted that the city should be completely relocated, even though it would require a lot of land, money, and the redistribution of administrative powers. Meanwhile, other experts believed there was no risk of further earthquakes soon, since a major earthquake had already occurred.

On September 24, a massive mudslide ended the debate. Fory-two people died, and two-thirds of downtown Beichuan was buried, including the Ye family's future apartment. Luckily, the buildings were empty at the time.

Beichuan became the only city to relocate after the earthquake.

· · ·

A year later, we discussed returning to Willow Field Village for a follow-up interview. Some were opposed. After Luo Chen did some planning work, he was worried. "Nothing has happened in the village."

"Perfect," I said. "Let's shoot nothing then."

"Sister Ye tried to get pregnant and failed . . ."

Years of working in the media made us want to give the story a bright ending—but everything that happens in life is real, and reality weighs a million tons.

We ended up going back to the village during Tomb-Sweeping Day, at the end of March. Cutting through the cobalt-blue mountain ranges was a sliver of rapeseed flowers that were shedding their petals. They were growing from the barren cracks I remembered from the previous year. The chilly mountain air was still stunning; charcoal burners continued to smolder.

The road had been repaired. We drove right up to the entrance of the village, and the dog came to greet me. The women showed up first. I couldn't hear them out because everyone was talking and joking. It was the first time I sensed that they were actually typical Sichuan women, bold and vigorous.

Zhi Quan's wife, Gui Fang, put a newborn puppy in my arms.

"Look how funny he is, it is the first time he's opened his eyes," Zhi Quan said. "He knew that Little Jing was coming." People all laughed.

Little Jing. Nobody had ever called me that except my family. The little black puppy licked my hair. It did feel like a family reunion. The mother dog watched it caringly, wagging its tail at me. I gave the puppy back, and she licked her baby again and again.

I went to the old man's new house, knocking at the door. No response. I shouted, "Grandpa! It's me!" The door opened suddenly, and an old man with messy hair shouted back, "The girl from Beijing!"

His hearing had further deteriorated, so he couldn't communicate. But, cheek to cheek, we took a photo together just for fun. He looked at the reflection on the camera lens, saying, "You are not bad. I am old, not pretty anymore."

I made fun of him. "Last year you said to me you were not old at all."

Suddenly, he sang a minor tune: *"Seventeen and eighteen years old, I was pretty and sweet."* People burst into laughter. The loud sound was not something I'd heard the previous year.

The only person still in silence was Wen Chao. The boy was in the fifth grade and had grown taller, reaching all the way to my shoulder. He was more introverted, too. The kitten was gone; he'd parted with it after he'd started going back to school. His father wanted to remarry, but the child wouldn't entertain the idea. The thing that worried his father most was the silence; the boy still hadn't mentioned his mother, not once.

The ground was a slippery mess of mud, sand, wood, and water. Families were busy rebuilding their houses. My crew sometimes helped the villagers chop wood. They'd gotten loans for reconstruction from the state, along with the state's design layout. Seismic fortification could not be lower than seven degrees. Everything was new. The only old thing left in Brother Ye's house was the pear tree. He said, "I will keep it for my future children as a reminder of the earthquake."

One day, Brother Ye asked if we knew what his son looked like. I shook my head. I didn't know. I hadn't asked. He glanced over at Sister Ye, testing her reaction, then walked to the bedroom to get something, but stopped in front of the door, watching his wife. She was motionless, and he had to say, "Give the key to me."

"You locked it up?" I asked Sister Ye.

She smiled awkwardly and pulled out a ring of keys, explaining to me, "I don't want him to see the photos."

Brother Ye opened the locked door. Inside was a locked chest that could only be opened with a smaller key. He pulled out a bundle tied in a red handkerchief with a burnt corner. In the bundle were the child's prizes and photos. He opened the bundle to show us. It was the only thing he'd dug out from the collapsed apartment after the earthquake. Most of the objects were damaged. With a smile, he pointed to a photo of his son, who had just started elementary school with a new backpack, proud and shy. Sister Ye laughed. "I joked with him that he looked ugly in that photo."

When Brother Ye got to the child's last photo, from 2008, she jumped to her feet and left, standing at the door, with her back to us. Brother Ye tried to lighten the mood by making a joke. "She can't let it go." Then his voice trembled, and he said it again: "She can't let it go."

Suddenly, he stood up and approached her, patted her on the back clumsily, as if he was patting away dirt. "It's okay, it's okay, go back to warm up."

A while later, Brother Ye returned. He was yoking buckets of well water on a pole. I walked up to greet him. Chen Wei manned the camera from inside the house.

I said, "In the few days that I've been here, you've been drinking a lot, much more than last year."

Brother Ye tapped his foot lightly on the stone path. "I never used to drink before, but now there's no one supervising me. Before, when he was around, he'd say, 'Daddy, don't drink so much, just a cup when there are guests . . .' I hope that one day, when we have our next son, he'll speak just like our first. Yeah, I had it good, I sure had it good."

I said, "But Brother Ye, you are trying to have a child now. You shouldn't drink, right?"

Sister Ye kicked up the same rock. "He doesn't listen. He just won't listen."

"I will listen. I have to listen. I want to listen," Brother Ye said.

I said, "You should accept the supervision."

"Alright," he said.

I said, "You have to promise us."

"I promise," he said.

Wen Chao was watching everything with a smile.

Such everyday small-talk was included in the episode in full. I used to despise this type of interview. I thought that reporters shouldn't express their opinions, shouldn't enter into discussions, shouldn't get involved in the lives of the interview subjects. I had so many rules that I set for myself. Now words just came out of my mouth.

April 1 was Tomb-Sweeping Day, when Chinese people commemorate their loved ones, so Beichuan city was open to locals for the first time since the earthquake. Brother Ye was shopping for paper offerings near the entrance. Chinese people burn items made of paper for the dead on this day in the hope that they will use them in the other world. He picked a paper backpack, a red one with Ultraman on it. Then he put it down, opting for a blue one instead. His son's favorite color.

The ten-kilometer road was lit with flares, two parallel lines of fire meandering beneath a blue-gray sky. Most families were mourning a loved one in the absence of a body. There was no grave, no tomb. So they mourned them under the ruin. On a boulder by the river, facing the unrecognizable school on the opposite bank, a middle-aged woman sat gazing, motionless.

The Ye family knelt behind the police tape, burning incense wedged between a few rocks, and the paper offerings in the direction of the school. As Brother Ye stared at the billowing ash, he mumbled, "You always loved to wear new backpacks. Do you like this one?"

Wen Chao turned around and walked off on his own. After a long search, Zhi Quan and I found him standing silently in front of the East district of Qushan elementary school. I didn't want to convince him to leave; I just put two hands on his shoulder. Zhi Quan said to me, "He jumped out from the second floor. Then he watched as his classmates tried to free themselves; only their heads made it out of the rubble."

The school had been a three-story building. The first floor was now gone, replaced by the second floor. The poor design was obvious: classrooms were extremely wide, with few columns in the corridors. All the brick walls on the first floor were broken and disconnected from the main structure. It had been a quick collapse, leaving students little time to run out of the classrooms. I looked for stairs. But they'd collapsed, designed without consideration for seismic dangers. There weren't even escape ladders—no way out or in. People had pulled down the basketball hoop to use as a ladder for sliding down injured children. Wen Chao had witnessed all of this, until his tearful father had come, alone, to take him away.

I held Wen Chao and said, "Let's go home."

We returned to find his father burning offerings to his mother, a desolate smile on his square face. He was muttering, "In the past it was always you who led the ritual. Now I'm giving it a try. Tell me if I'm doing it right."

I looked to Wen Chao. But the boy was gone again.

I found him in the woods. The camera was far away; nobody could see us. The boy told me that he often dreamed about his mother yelling, "Baby Chao, come eat." Tears streamed down his cheeks. He said, "I was too afraid to ask about her, because I didn't know how to face the answer."

After dinner, I took a walk by myself. It was dark and silent in the mountains, not a light in sight. As time passed, I could slowly see the outlines of clouds tumbling above.

I looked to the north.

Usually on this day, I returned home to sweep Grandma's tomb. After weeding around the grounds, I would sit in front of her tomb for a while. The carved words on it said that she had enjoyed ninety-four years of life. I'd think back to when I'd first learned arithmetic in elementary school, and calculated her lifespan in a notebook. She was born in 1910; I'd wanted her to live to 110. In the squiggly handwriting of a child, I'd practiced addition: *That means she'll live to . . . um, the year 2020.* It had been six years since she'd passed away. I still didn't want to talk to anyone about her. I didn't want to look at her photos. I didn't even want people to mention her in front of me. Whenever I finally saw her again in a dream, I felt at peace. *See, she's not dead, I knew it.*

People tried to persuade Wen Chao to accept his father taking a new wife by saying, "You need to forget about the pain and move on." But I knew forcing a child to forget his pain would be like forcing him to forget the person he loved; it would just make him angry. The fire was on his feet. What I could do was to stay with him, helping him with homework. When he got questions right, we both ate a piece of candy, holding it in our jaws and sucking all afternoon.

Eventually I asked him about the kitten he had cared for the year before. Wen Chao said one day some wild cats had showed up, and the little one just followed them. I asked him if he'd wanted the cat to stay. He shook his head.

"Didn't you want its company?"

"It needs its own company more."

"You wanted it to be happy?"

He said gently, "Yes."

I know I didn't have to worry about this boy. He would grow up, and one day he and his father would be fine.

Zhi Quan's wife was four months pregnant, and she needed her first ultrasound. Zhi Quan asked me to stay with her, because he was too nervous to face the result. I had never seen an ultrasound before. When the doctor showed me where the baby was, I was amazed. I went out and dragged Zhi Quan in. "You must see this!"

Zhi Quan opened his mouth wide as he watched the screen, confused. The doctor realized he didn't see anything, so he pointed everything out. "Here, little hands! Legs! The baby is moving."

Zhi Quan stood there, his mouth still open, motionless. Then he said, "Move—keep moving, little fellow."

When we got back, the women were busy in the kitchen. They were preparing a meal for the workers hired to build their new homes. On the stove above the crackling firewood sat a small black wok gurgling as it boiled. The smell of meat, Sichuan peppers, and star anise filled the room. Zhi Quan's wife joined the cooking and didn't talk much. She busied herself with scooping hot peppers and lumps of salt into the wok. Fire from the woodstove lit up part of her face. After a while, I asked her what it'd felt like when she'd seen the baby on the sonogram. She didn't answer my question, just told me that she'd dreamed of her daughter the night before. In the dream, the girl had bought her candies, eighty pieces of them. When asked where she had gotten the money, the little girl had said Daddy had given it to her.

Zhi Quan's wife smiled at me then and said, "As long as the child is safe."

She crouched down to stoke the fire. At that moment her smile turned into tears.

Over six thousand families in Sichuan who'd lost children in the earthquake wished to have new babies. The day we left, the Brother Ye and Sister Ye went to the hospital to check their fertility. They both were in their forties. Pregnancy would be a long and hard journey for them.

The rain was light and sparse, quietly soaking the dark green mountain ranges. Spring grass wobbled in the fissures left from the year before. The inky green canopy of the firs stood in layers along the dark, wet hillside, accented by bright white pear blossoms. Birds chirped, water trickled.

We watched Brother Ye and Sister Ye climb onto a tractor with their best clothes on. They waved to us as the dog came around to see them off. The tractor drove further and further, turned into a small dot, and disappeared. The dog was still waiting, motionless.

The hillside that'd crumbled and shifted last year had regrown a layer of grass and shrubs in its huge cracks. Inside this mountain canyon, new houses were being built. After experiencing pain and difficulties, everything was regrowing, one leaf at a time. The spring rains were coming.

Behind the endless woods and the winding mountain road, the tractor showed up again. The dog wagged her tail, gently.

In this photo taken on Wednesday, Oct. 14, 2009, suspects involved in mafia-style gangs are escorted by police to stand trial at the Chongqing No.5 Intermediate People's Court in Chongqing, China. The trials of the gangs are exposing sordid, deep-seated connections between organized crime and corrupt officials and police in the central mega-city of Chongqing.

Eight
Truth Is Often
Lost in between Tears
2009

"Get a hold of yourself," my editor-in-chief, Yuan Zhengming, would say after reviewing my episodes. "Don't let the audience see your sympathy and anger."

I'd tell him that the audience wasn't complaining. They rather liked it, calling it "appropriately moving."

He was unimpressed. "How you express yourself in your life is your own business, but in your work, you can't do that."

"So you're saying I should be more mature?" But I was not old yet.

"It's not about maturity," he said, "it's about what your profession demands of you."

He even gave me a copy of the Vajra Sutra, a Buddhist classic. There's a line in the book that says, "When a feeling arises, know it, and then don't follow it."

I secretly gave him a nickname inspired by one of the characters in *The Shaolin Temple*, a movie I'd watched as a child: Abbot. At one point, the abbot says to Jet Li: "Renounce all lust . . . do you abide by this?"

When Jet Li looked at the token of love in his hand, his brow furrowed. His beloved watched from behind a door, her eyes swollen with tears.

The old monk was not finished. "Do you abide?"

". . . I abide."

The girl turned away.

I didn't like that abbot, a fervent heart, telling me why I needed to abide.

In March 2009, my boss, Zhang Jie, handed me a letter signed by nearly three hundred factory workers, their names accompanied by bloody fingerprints. It was a traditional Chinese form of grassroots protest. It meant that the disadvantaged had nothing to fight with but their own lives.

The facts were clear: In a recent auction, the land on which the workers' factory was located had been sold off for about one hundred million yuan below market value. Police had investigated a gangster named Chen Kunzhi in connection with kidnappings that were alleged to have violently manipulated the auction, and found him to be guilty. But, although he was arrested, he was released soon after, and the case was closed. The result of the auction remained legitimate.

Now, armed with sticks, the workers were confronting those who wanted to take over their land.

My team and I arrived on the scene. One worker said, "They are thugs with knives." Their fearless expressions touched me. The workers were filled with righteous indignation, and more and more of them gathered in front of our camera. There were fists waved in the air, and tears. "We will defend our factory with our lives!"

My cameraman, Li Ji, gave me a look. He'd thought it would have been better to sit down with a few workers and have them describe the situation, together with their evidence. He'd said, "The only message you convey when talking to a big group is an emotion."

But I found the victims' voices to be very powerful. What was wrong with hopeless workers who'd suffered injustice for so long expressing themselves to the media? Maybe it was the only language that people with power could understand.

· · ·

"He had a gun," said Mr. Wu, a key witness in the investigation of Chen Kunzhi. "He put it to my head and made me sign a contract."

After Wu had borrowed ten million yuan from Chen and couldn't repay it, Chen had locked Wu up in a hotel for twenty days, then seized the company's official seal and used it to sign a collusive auction contract with COFCO, a large state-owned enterprise in China. Mr. Wu said he had been in hiding for the two years since the incident. He warned me that interviewing Chen would put everyone in danger. "He would have killed me. I don't know if CCTV can handle this."

The judge who'd overseen the land auction also refused to show his face on camera, fearing for his safety. When more companies had tried to bid, some men had stopped them from entering the auction site and dragged them away. The judge brought in six police officers, but Chen Kunzhi countered with six times as many, and each one had a knife. These gangsters called the judge's superiors in front of him to put on the pressure. "You're just a minor figure," they told him. "Who do you think you are?"

In a last-ditch attempt to save his integrity, the judge called off the auction. But his superiors demanded that he start it again ten days later. When he acquiesced, it was the same situation as before: the other companies set to participate in the bidding didn't show up, because they were afraid of the "complications." The only two companies that took part in the auction were Chen's company and COFCO. After four bids, the land was finally sold to COFCO for 37.1 million yuan. A year later COFCO announced it would offer the land up for 140 million.

I wanted to interview Chen myself. But my boss knew it would be dangerous. He asked me and each member of my team to use disposable phone cards to avoid being followed in retaliation. He said, "If you don't interview Chen, will the story still stand?"

"The basic evidence is already there," our producer, Jian Feng, said.

"Then the interview might not be necessary. We have to think about security first," the boss said.

I worried that security would be the least of our problems. If the interview went poorly, the whole show might be endangered. Chen Kunzhi was not a traditional street thug. He'd been a police officer for fifteen years, and after being removed from the force for assault, he'd started running a casino. After escaping a homicide charge, he went into the loan shark business. As China's urbanization continued to speed up, Chongqing's real estate industry was desperate for capital, financing some 90 percent of its expansion with funds borrowed from loan sharks. Chen Kunzhi had already made over a million yuan in profits, according to Mr. Wu.

Unlike any gangsters I had interviewed before, Chen was one of those men who controlled the economic lifeline of the city through the underground economy, armed with ties to the entire judicial system, which allowed him to escape justice despite obvious evidence of lawbreaking.

My fear was that once I interviewed Chen, the huge forces behind him would stop the episode from airing. It would be like a cigarette dropped into a toilet—a soft hiss and the flame would go out, only to be flushed away, worthless. So we decided to leave without the interview.

My team and I had packed our bags. Our flight back would leave in a few hours. We sat in the hotel lobby looking at one another; I sensed some misgivings about what we were about to do. I started to question myself. Our show was meant to give voice to every side of these conflicts.

I felt guilty for leaving without giving the other side a chance to talk, then I tried to convince myself that reporters were on the side of justice.

But what is justice? Is there a standard that is agreed upon by all people of all places? If so, I hadn't experienced it. No matter what stories I produced, there were always some people leaving comments under my blog in defense of justice. "Anything CCTV reports, I'm against," they would say. As if an organization of over ten thousand people was entirely absent of credibility.

Jian Feng understood why I was hesitant. He said, "How about just a quick phone interview, then we leave?"

Good. Then we could go back to Beijing and work around the clock to edit and broadcast the episode before any intervention came and cut us off.

At four P.M., I called Chen's cell phone number. No one answered. Jian Feng and I looked at each other, relieved and disappointed at the same time.

We decided to try once more.

The phone rang. This time, the connection was crystal clear. "Hello."

I said, "I'm a reporter from CCTV, here to do interviews on the land auction. I'd like to hear what you have to say. Can we meet?"

I was sure he'd hang up or say he was busy, in which case we could get to the airport in time for a bowl of chili oil vermicelli. As it turned out, he said, "I'm doing sports and exercise right now."

"Where?"

"South Mountain Golf Club."

"We'll be there in half an hour."

Chen stood in front of the doors of the Nanshan Golf Club, Chongqing's first "international community for the rich."

He was tall and stout, with a square face and thick hair. He wore a purple polo shirt with the collar turned up. He'd tucked the hem into his pants to show off a designer belt. He wanted to be seen as a wealthy businessman, not a gangster with a shaved head and a gold chain around his neck. His face was expressionless as we sized each other up. I was still thinking of what he'd said on the phone: *I'm doing sports and exercise*. It seemed like an indication of vanity—a way to speak with sophisticated language usually reserved for written communication, so as to appear educated. Mostly I thought it sounded overdone. A person like this needed recognition to relax. So I shook his hand and introduced myself first.

He used a tone of voice like he was from the upper class. "I've been waiting for you to arrive for a long time—no one listens to me in this process."

People may find it strange that a man like him would give a television interview. Mike Wallace of *60 Minutes* once said, "You may think someone is a bad person, but deep down, they don't think they've done anything wrong."

Chen's brow furrowed, his eyes widened, and he made a childlike expression of resignation.

"They make all kinds of distractions and threats against me, always like flies and mosquitoes buzzing around."

"Who?"

He looked at the ground to avoid eye contact—a kind of weakness and nervousness beneath the bluster. "Gangsters, hooligans, those who only know how to fight and kill, very low people."

I wanted to laugh. It was hard not to show some sarcasm when I heard something so ridiculous. Once, the manager of a factory where pollution had killed three workers told me that his factory was not polluting, and I said, "Then how come there's a strong smell here?"

He'd sniffed and said, "My sense of smell is not as acute as yours."

I'd said nothing, broken into a smile, and leaned back in my chair. That was the end of the interview. But later, when the reviewer watched the clip, he made a comment about my expression. "Ask, don't challenge."

I said, "I can't even show a little irony? But what about the dead workers?"

He said, "Your job is to provide facts, not feelings."

Now I realized the danger of emotion; if I couldn't control my expressions and body language, it would stimulate Chen's self-defense and make the interview risky. The audience expected journalists to reveal the world, not swing fists at anyone. So I calmly said, "Tell me why."

As if I'd skirted around his worst fears, he relaxed, leaned back in his chair, spread his legs wide, and admitted almost proudly what he had done. When I asked him if he had stopped other companies from bidding on the factory land, he said, "If the bidding hadn't worked, we would have received nothing. I wanted to not only prevent other units from bidding, but also stop COFCO from withdrawing."

Chen wanted to show that he was not a low-level gangster who took orders from his superiors, but the real boss who controlled the entire auction. In his view, "rigging the auction" was a successful business activity. He even felt justified because he had done his "fiduciary duty"—that was why COFCO paid his company seventeen million yuan after the auction.

"What was the seventeen million for?" I asked.

"Whatever is written on the check." He narrowed his eyes, testing to see how much I knew.

"It said *demolition*. Did you ever demolish something for them?" I asked.

"No. Not a single tile." He let out a giggle, as if he'd been waiting for this moment to hit the nail on the head. He enjoyed the thrill of toying with everyone and making fun of them, as if crime was a skill he couldn't help but show off.

Clearly, he was declaring victory. "I've consulted with lawyers. Everything I've done is above board. If it wasn't, I would've been arrested, wouldn't I?" Tilting his head with a sarcastic grin, he asked me, "Do you think all those law enforcement officers are trash?"

We were sitting on a large bow-shaped golf course with green grass and wet fog covering the hills. He treated me like I'd come to listen to a hero's story. I later learned from the local media that when our show aired on April 18, Mr. Chen invited his friends to watch in a large private room at a nightclub.

After asking if we needed his black Maserati to take us to the airport, Chen Kunzhi walked us out after the interview. He had no qualms about any of it. He lowered his head close to mine and said in a voice only I could hear, "I graduated from the police academy. That's how I play the law."

I used to believe in a black-and-white world of the exploited and the exploiters. But after verifying the information Chen Kunzhi gave us, I realized that the people I had interviewed earlier were not simple victims.

Mr. Wu, who'd been kidnapped by him, was the first to sign an agreement with an ex-factory manager and COFCO, ensuring that COFCO would get the land at an appraised price of forty million yuan and extract a commission of over fifty million. It was this collusive agreement that was destroyed by Chen Kunzhi.

Tao Yilu, the manager who'd said he would spill his own blood to the last drop to fight the initial agreement—and who'd suspended the auction after he was elected—was later bribed by Chen Kunzhi into restarting the auction. The appraisal came in at thirty-six million— even lower than the price he had previously opposed.

The workers who'd written to us were also more than the simple victims I thought they were. A significant portion of the plant's workforce had inherited jobs from their fathers and rarely worked. When the former manager had struggled with layoffs while trying to take the business public, the workers demanded compensation high enough to bring the factory down. As I stood in the abandoned factory and watched over one hundred million dollars' worth of imported equipment being discarded, they told me that this was their way of protecting the factory. But the truth was, they sealed up the machines themselves, stopped producing goods, closed the factory doors, and kept vehicles out to disturb the reform. They rounded up the former manager for thirty-nine hours and he had to piss on the spot in the conference room. When the factory broke down, they divided the land into many small pieces and rented it out.

This was not what I imagined the exploited working class to be like. They were not nameless, faceless workers who looked exactly the same as on the propaganda posters, but individuals pursuing their own self-interest.

In one of my interviews, Chen Kunzhi said, "No one is on the side of justice, don't make it that way. Everyone is in it for their own benefit." It was the law of the jungle. "The big fish swallows the small fish."

After reviewing the land auction program, Yuan, the editor-in-chief, said, "This one was sharp and calm." It was the first time he'd ever praised me.

The complex and contradictory reality taught me a lesson. The slogan of our program was "Hunting the truth." But sometimes "the truth" is like the bottom of a bottomless pit. The only way to ensure an independent perspective is to be alert to all points of view. And "hunting" can be continuous. One must keep questioning, keep dispelling illusions, keep breaking down and reconstructing events in order to avoid being an accomplice to bias.

The abbot was right, as it turned out. Monks, just like journalists, needed self-control.

Those who cannot or do not want to abide must find another business.

I expected little in the way of justice when our episode was broadcast on April 18. Usually reports involving high-ranking officials were met with backlash and accusations from local authorities.

Yet two months later, on June 20, 2009, Chen Kunzhi was detained. A few days later, Wu Xiaoqing, director of the executive bureau, and Zhang Tao, vice president of the Chongqing High People's Court, were investigated in connection with the land auction case.

Rarely did we get such a swift and thorough response to our reports. I received a message from the Chongqing Municipal Party Committee's Propaganda Department inviting me to follow up on the "fight against blackness and evil" campaign, which had apparently begun on the day Chen Kunzhi was detained.

Then I read a report in the Chongqing media. "The episode of *News Probe* aired and key Chongqing leaders watched. Then, on June 4, 2009, Zhang Tao was taken down." The leaders in question were Bo Xilai, the party chief of Chongqing, who'd started the campaign, and his right-hand man, Wang Lijun, the new police chief. Wang was known as the "hero of the fight against underground society," and he was sending over two hundred thousand letters to citizens, asking for tips on organized crime syndicates (known in China as "triads"). It was a campaign of unprecedented scale in China's most populous city.

The crackdown in Chongqing quickly became national news. The factory workers I'd interviewed asked me to follow up on their story. They were excited to see "the bad guys" finally going down. They told me that some people in Chongqing were beating drums and setting off firecrackers to celebrate. "This is the will of the people calling for justice," they claimed.

It was my responsibility to follow up on the story, because there were still some facts that were not clear. However, before long, Chen Kunzhi was officially arrested, along with sixty-seven chief members of triad-related gangs and nearly sixteen hundred other suspects. Nearly five hundred fugitives were hunted down as well, dovetailing a massive anticorruption campaign that saw sixteen top police and judicial officials investigated. I took responsibility for the facts of the land auction case, but the other cases were beyond my reporting.

I understand people's long-suppressed passions and desire to cleanse society. Perhaps these campaigns can punish many who deserve it. But historically, when judicial campaigns try to fight crime and corruption in a short time, concentrated arrests requiring police to work jointly with prosecutors and courts end up sacrificing suspects' right to defense for the sake of efficiency.

I had interviewed several innocent people who were wrongly convicted in such campaigns. One of them, Xie Hongwu, had been imprisoned for twenty-eight years, starting in 1974, on a mere detention warrant with no files. When I interviewed Mr. Xie in 2004, he had lost the ability to speak because he had been held in solitary confinement for nearly three decades without being allowed out for a single day. I handed him a pencil and my notebook to see if he could write something. He had lost his mind and could only write two words: *Chairman Mao.* I could do nothing but look at him. He pulled my hand over to touch his knee. There was emptiness underneath the fabric; someone had gutted his two kneecaps a long time ago.

I declined the invitation from the Propaganda Department, and along with it the leads that would be given without digging, the numbers that would be given without verification, the interviewees that would be put in front of me without convincing, who might not be free to tell me the truth. I decided to follow up on the story later, when the trials were over.

Bothered by concerns that still felt somewhat vague, I did not put the episode on my blog to discuss with readers as I usually did.

On February 6, 2010, I saw Chen Kunzhi on TV. He was standing in a courtroom wearing a yellow prison uniform, the hair on the back of his head almost falling out. He was charged with leading a triad organization, committing intentional homicide, gambling, conducting illegal business, loan-sharking, bribery, and illegal detention.

Chen was sentenced to death with a two-year stay of execution. It looked like the sentence was lighter than he had expected. He said in court, "Thank you for the kindness of not killing me."

During the Chongqing gang trials, fifty-seven people were sentenced to death. Thirteen of them were executed, including former deputy police commissioner Wen Qiang. A fourteenth death was added to the tally when the prison claimed that Wu Xiaoqing, the director of the executive bureau involved in the land auction, ended his life with a cotton thread from the waistband of his woolen pants. Official reports said he avoided the detention center's cameras and that his cellmates were asleep when he committed suicide.

The TV news said the court found that there were seventeen other people in Chen Kunzhi's "triad organization." There were men who I'd thought were involved in the illegal detentions that had plagued the land auction. But most of the defendants were from a company called Guo Heng, which I had never heard mentioned during my interviews.

All the defendants argued they were not involved in the triad. Some claimed their only job had been to deliver checks and collect interest. One of them said, "I'm sure I'll go to jail, but I'm not pleading guilty."

Their lawyers argued that Chen's illegal detention schemes and collusion in the auction occurred before he became a shareholder in Guo Heng—and criminal law does not prosecute private lending. Further, there was no evidence of violence or threats when other company shareholders had lent money.

But the lawyers' voices were rarely heard. Several were called *Dog Head Consultant,* a highly derogatory Chinese term meaning "one who advises the bad guys."

Gong Gangmo, who had worked with Chen Kunzhi, told his lawyer, Li Zhuang, that his confession had been made under the torture of being hung for days until he became incontinent. When Li Zhuang tried to defend Gong by citing the illegal circumstances under which the confession had been obtained, the lawyer himself was arrested in Beijing and detained the next day. He was arrested the day after that. By the fifth day, he was transferred to the prosecution, and on the sixth day he was charged with falsifying evidence, for which he was sentenced to two and a half years. The case aroused collective solidarity from the legal community and the media, which tried to rally to Li Zhuang's defense, but to no avail.

Chen Kunzhi's trial marked the end of the campaign, and on March 16, 2010, during a meeting of the National People's Congress, Bo Xilai spoke to the media about the crackdown. He said that Chongqing's law enforcement team "was brave, combative, and intelligent in this fight," dismissing the controversy surrounding their methods as merely "a murmur."

When Chen Kunzhi escaped judicial punishment, I had a duty as a journalist to report on it—and if he or people related to him got more punishment than they deserved, I also had a duty as a journalist to report on it. But by the end of the trial, I had lost my job as an investigative journalist, for covering another case and could not report on it.

Direct criticism was also impossible by any means. One producer at CCTV lost his position after airing an episode that questioned the judicial process in Chongqing. But I could at least talk about a mindset, starting with my own. I wrote a blog post.

"When I watched movies as a child, the moment a new character showed up, the group of kids sitting with me among the pile of empty shells of sunflower seeds loved to ask the question: 'Good guy or bad guy?' When the climactic confrontation came, our tears welled up for the good guys and our fangs flashed to the bad ones."

Television programs have a habit of casting one person as the protagonist and one person as the antagonist. But dividing the world into the powerful and the exploited—attributing the successes and failures of history to any single individual—placed moral judgment above the truth.

A reader asked, "So you don't have an ethical responsibility?"

I said that balance is the ethical responsibility of journalists. Give each party a chance to speak—especially the party being testified against. "We may not have had the opportunity to interview the accused, but were we ever even skeptical of the one side of the story that we heard? Could we have put ourselves in the shoes of the accused to question the accuser? Did we exhaust our technical resources to discover evidence supporting the accused to the best of our ability? 'Can't be done' indicates a technical problem. But 'not necessary' indicates the blind logic of an eye for an eye."

I had a friend, Lin Bai, who used to be a radio host. One day, the program was discussing Hu Wanlin, who had caused many deaths because of his illegal practice of medicine. Hu Wanlin called in after hearing the program to express his views, and a listener was furious. "He is a liar, how can you let him preach his views?"

Lin Bai said, "Thirty years ago, there was a man who was imprisoned without trial and denied medical treatment when he fell ill. A nurse hit him in the face with a stethoscope. That man was Liu Shaoqi.[8] If we don't give a liar a chance to speak today, we may not defend ourselves one day when we are wronged."

In April 2010, I went to Chongqing to see what would happen after the campaign.

As I sat in the cab at the airport, I saw many big trucks passing by, one after the other, carrying trees. The driver said that three hundred thousand ginkgo trees had been planted in Chongqing to replace the

---

[8] Chairman of the People's Republic of China (1959–68) and chief theoretician for the Chinese Communist Party (CCP), who was considered the heir apparent to Mao Zedong until he was purged in the late 1960s. In 1968, Liu disappeared from public life and was labeled the "commander of China's bourgeoisie headquarters," China's foremost "capitalist-roader," and a traitor to the revolution. He died under harsh treatment during the Cultural Revolution, but was posthumously rehabilitated by Deng Xiaoping's government in 1980 and granted a national memorial service.

ancient banyan trees that had taken root there for so long. When he mentioned the cost—fifty billion—I practically jumped out of my seat. The thin man laughed, having enjoyed the reactions of different passengers to this figure many times. He told me that after getting rid of the "rich gangsters," working-class people were about to become wealthy themselves, and the city would look new. The government was going to build a lot of public housing and he was going to apply for it, even though he didn't meet the "low income" criteria. He smiled and said, "There's always a way."

I asked, "Where does the government get the money?"

He didn't know. "It's not my money," he added.

"Maybe it is yours." I laughed.

He laughed too. "But it's not going into my pocket anyway, is it?" Then he asked if I had any connections to get ginkgo saplings from the north. "We can get rich together."

At noon, I saw a dark green parasol on a black pole. It was on the street, and a police officer was standing next to it. There was a new reform in Chongqing that allowed police to work twenty-four hours a day in the open air through the use of five hundred of these street platforms. The purpose was to "deter crime." The platform had been created by police chief Wang Lijun, and carried twenty-seven of his patents, including the umbrella sitting in the corner. I took out my phone to take a picture. The police officer pointed his finger at me. "What are you doing?"

My local friend stepped forward to explain. The police officer was full of displeasure and didn't say a word. His overreaction surprised me. To create a "peaceful" atmosphere in Chongqing, Wang Lijun had abolished over one hundred police stations and sent all the police to the streets for twenty-four-hour law enforcement in the open air—yet there was a huge tension behind this policeman's distrust of a citizen who wanted to take a picture. I learned later that someone had gone to jail for a year because he'd taken a picture of a drunk man handcuffed to one of these poles. The man had been completely naked.

While eating hot pot with friends in the evening, a female police officer caught up in the ecstasy of the revolution—she had just graduated from the Chongqing Police Academy—told me that Secretary Wang had removed all the old officials from the deputy to the full division level on the spot. Over three thousand positions were open for registration. His plan was to add ten thousand new police officers that year, with new bases, intelligence monitoring equipment, and funding for study abroad. "There's even going to be an exclusive hospital for police officers," she added.

I was curious about where the money was coming from and soon learned the answer. By the end of 2010, the Chongqing Police Department had opened 375 triad cases, and the core figures being targeted all ran well-known businesses: transportation, meat, motorcycle manufacturing. All of them were fined over a hundred million yuan, and Chen Kunzhi was fined three hundred million, the highest figure.

State-owned companies controlled their assets in trust until the courts pronounced their sentences. So their money was already at the direct disposal of the police, including their family money, equity, properties, and cars. Chen Kunzhi's black Maserati was placed in the police compound along with over fifty other luxury cars from the "triads" as part of an exhibition on the fight the department was waging. Shortly after the trial, the police station said that the newly built women's traffic patrol unit would be "equipped with world-class police patrol cars such as Lamborghinis, Bentleys, Porsches, Mercedes, and BMWs—all beautifully painted."

The private entrepreneur association in Chongqing pledged over a hundred million yuan to the "Chongqing People's Police Martyrs Relief Fund," advocated by Wang Lijun.

In September 2010, when meeting with some bloggers, Wang Lijun said, "Robbing the rich to help the poor is the way of the world." He took Putin as an example. "If there were ten people, Putin would shoot the two richest ones, inspiring the two average rich people to contribute what they had to save themselves. The remaining six poor people would say 'well done.'"

His statement was the same as Chen Kunzhi's: "The big fish swallows the small fish." The only difference was that he had appointed himself a shark.

On February 6, 2012, I read a message on Weibo that Wang Lijun, the police chief of Chongqing, had driven about three hundred kilometers to the U.S. consulate in Chengdu to apply for political asylum. He'd turned himself in to Chinese authorities thirty-six hours later.

Two days after, the news released by the Chongqing Municipal Government Information Office made the story even more dramatic: "Wang Lijun is undergoing vacation-style treatment for serious physical discomfort because of a high level of mental stress caused by long-term overload."

On the same day, Li Zhuang, the lawyer who had been detained by Wang Lijun and held for eighteen months, posted that he was willing to defend Wang Lijun for free. He reminded Wang's future interrogators not to extort confessions from "patients" under torture. If they did, he would apply for the exclusion of illegal evidence in court to protect his client's legal rights. He said, "I want those in prominent positions of power, those who despise the judicial system, the lawyer system, and the defense system, to feel the value of the role of lawyers themselves."

Six months later, Wang Lijun went on trial for treason, abuse of power, and embezzlement. The details of his downfall were sordid. The trouble had started when Gu Kailai, Bo Xilai's wife, poisoned a British businessman with close financial ties to the Bo family. Wang Lijun covered up the case, keeping the evidence for himself as leverage. But when

Gu tried to involve herself further in the coverup, Wang became concerned. He tried to take the matter up with Bo Xilai in January 2012. But Bo did not react well. He punched Wang in the face and fired him from the police chief position, then arrested and tortured his subordinates. When Wang felt his life was in danger, instead of seeking protection through his own country's judicial and administrative systems, he dressed up as an old woman and fled Chongqing to the U.S. consulate.

Wang's eventual confession led to Bo Xilai's arrest. On the last day of the proceedings, before the former Chongqing party secretary was sentenced to life in prison for embezzlement and abuse of power, he pinned his hopes on the rule of law in a speech: "The current law has designed a system of checks and balances between the public prosecutor and the law, including defense lawyers, to prevent wrongful convictions, and if we only listen to the prosecutor's side of the story, it will lead to many wrongful convictions."

There are many different lessons to be learned from everything that happened in Chongqing. I learned mine. In reporting on what seemed like an isolated case of land auction manipulation, I'd failed to discover its deeper roots, which only became clear to me later.

I should have reached back all the way to the 1950s, when the planned economic system was established in China, purging capitalism and centering economic control with the state. Private property rights were soon abolished, all resources were nationalized, and the Chongqing Cosmetics Factory was founded under collective property rules rather than private ownership for the sake of idealistic utopian ideals.

The experiment failed; the factory encountered operational difficulties. After the reform of the market economy had begun, factory leadership established a new brand, Olive, in a joint venture with a Hong Kong company in 1991. Olive grew rapidly to become the only enterprise in China that could compete with Procter & Gamble, but collective property rights hobbled the company. External market competition was fierce, and everyone's decision being counted at Olive equaled no one's decision being enacted. It was yet another failure of the government-monopoly style of managing supply, as well as the marketing model on which it relied. Despite strong performance in the nineties, the company eventually ended up on the verge of bankruptcy due to internal leadership struggles. The government had no reform program for companies with this type of ownership.

The owners in Hong Kong finally left the enterprise. They wanted to sell the land they had bought for the factory, so as to recoup what was owed to them by the leadership in Chongqing, but because the land had been registered collectively in the factory's name, there was a long dispute over whether they had the right to do this. The former manager from the Hong Kong company told Mr. Wu, one of their debtors, to find a buyer who would purchase the land cheaply, then resell it at market value, so as to generate proceeds that would be passed along to the Hong Kong leadership in the form of agency fees that would repay the outstanding debts.

Wu had to take this route, because he had already been borrowing money just to maintain Olive, and he couldn't get another loan from the bank. Private companies, which contribute over 50 percent of Chongqing's tax revenue and support over 80 percent of its employment, can use only one-third of the credit resources available to them. So Wu ended up borrowing money from Chen Kunzhi, whose loan shark resources exceeded four hundred million yuan. With an enormous amount of money coming to him from state-owned institutions as well as black market enterprises involving court presidents, police officers, and government officials, he could get loans at very low interest rates.

In short, unclear property rights and unfair financial policies gave Chen Kunzhi room to manipulate the eventual land auction through underground operations. With his connections to those in power, the big fish ate the small fish in a continuous cycle.

In countries that have transitioned from a traditional planned economy to a market economy, there is often serious organized criminal activity. The absence of the rule of law stems from a government that is failing to fulfill its role as the guardian of a functional market economy.

But without sufficient analysis of these root causes, pathos and righteous indignation encourage people to pursue simple solutions with a black-or-white moralistic mentality: removing all the "bad guys" at the expense of the justice system and demonizing the privatization process in favor of a state-owned economy is a nostalgia for utopia, to narrow the gap between rich and poor.

In Chongqing, during the ten years between 1997 and 2007, the private economy rose from 22.64 percent of GDP to 45.5 percent, an average annual increase of over two percentage points; but in the four years between 2008 and 2011, when the "crackdown" was at its worst, the private economy grew by less than 1 percent per year. Many private enterprises began to flee Chongqing, taking capital along with them.

Bo and Wang were punished as "bad guys." But it did not solve the problem. Among their successors, another Chongqing municipal party secretary and two police chiefs were jailed, all involved in corruption. If the world is divided into only two camps, black and white, moral and immoral, it becomes like a cube. Once you roll it over, it's still the same, just with a different side facing up.

For years, I favored highly confrontational journalism, with strong emotions, hard-hitting like a storm of copper beans; everything had to be big, forceful, earth-shattering.

But although rain fell on the ground, the water could not seep into the earth to nourish the roots of plants. Now I see the results of this approach. On the dry dirt, cracked like a tortoiseshell, moisture vanishes as soon as the storm ends.

At the end of my blog post, I quoted something a reader had written to me:

"I'm guessing that when Chai Jing writes her programs and her blog, she does so with hot tears welling in her eyes. To be frank, tragic emotion and righteous indignation are psychological ways of feeling good about oneself. Feeling good about oneself is expedient, it is addictive. But to have self-control over such feelings is a worthy achievement. Behind every headline is a hidden, long, winding chain of logic. From out here in the audience, these chains of logic all feel uncannily similar. It is because of this unspoken yet widely acknowledged secret that we need to remind ourselves: don't travel halfway across the chain of logic and start bawling."

He said, "Getting it right is the most important aspect of your craft. And feeling good about yourself is the biggest enemy of being right. The truth is often lost between tears."

Talking with Lu Anke.

Nine
The Power of the Powerless
2009

Eckart Löwe lay on the grass. Children played and rolled around on his chest, stomach, and legs, hitting and pushing each other. I instinctively caught one by the hand. "Don't do that."

"Why not?" said the boy.

I almost replied, *Because I don't like it*. But I caught myself and tried to persuade him instead. "You'll hurt him, he'll feel bad."

"No he won't," giggled the child. Even the kid being hit was beaming.

Buried beneath the pile of children, saying nothing, Löwe smiled at my helpless expression.

"I wouldn't be able to stop myself from telling them to quit it or scolding them," I said. "It's my natural reaction. But not yours?"

"I know what they've been through, and what they're each like. I understand them."

"But is understanding enough?"

"If you understand them, you'll speak to them completely differently than if you're just annoyed."

What could I say to that?

Löwe was from Germany. In China he was known as Lu Anke. At the time of our first meeting, he was teaching at Banlie Elementary School. He'd spent ten years in the country as a voluntary educator in rural areas.

Banlie is in a mountainous region of Donglan County in Guangxi Province. There was no highway that led to the village, and 80 percent of the students at the local elementary school were known as left-behind children.

In the mid-nineties, when travel between cities and the countryside became much easier, farm laborers migrated in the millions to economically developed cities to find work. This phenomenon lies at the core of China's economic miracle. Yet because of the limits set on hukou registration for city residence and the high cost of urban living, many parents left their children in their rural hometowns and villages. They returned to see them once a year for a brief stay during the Chinese New Year. There were over sixty million such children left behind in China's countryside—one in five nationally.

Löwe taught at the school. He didn't have any relevant qualifications, and rather than follow an official curriculum, he painted, drew pictures, and sang with the children, keeping them company. During his decade in the country, he refused to be interviewed by the press. Beside his email address on the homepage of his blog, there was a note: *I spend little time online. Please keep your correspondence to five sentences.*

I read his blog, all several hundred thousand words of it. It served as his manifesto on education. There were no stories or details, just abstract terms like *belonging* and *feeling* . . . Reading it, I felt helpless, like I had been plunged into an ocean far from land, with wave after wave washing over me. Old Fan wanted to convince Löwe to accept an interview. But the task made her apprehensive. She didn't know how to approach the request. She hesitated a long while before finally typing, *You remind me of a song by the rock singer Cui Jian—"The Power of the Powerless." How the powerless are sometimes a hundred times stronger than the powerful.*

Old Fan had a knack for intuiting what it took me an eternity to realize.

. . .

Traveling from Nanning, the capital of Guangxi Province, to Banlie took four hours by car. Karst landforms predominate in the province's northwest region, where the roads hug mountainsides and zigzag so sharply that every corner pitched us passengers this way then that. We had no hope of sleeping en route. The whole way there were mountains as far as the eye could see, tall mountains and dried-up streams. The earth was a brown lime. It was a long time before we saw even a meager patch of sweetcorn growing.

From the county-town, we bounced along a bumpy dirt road for an hour before we arrived in Banlie, just in time for the market. At a few open-air stalls spread around an area of only twenty square meters, butchers hawked their goods with knives in hand to mostly elderly customers. A gaggle of toddlers and five-year-olds played off to the side. Seventy percent of the village's young adults worked in manual labor in Guangdong or Hainan. A baby strapped to the back of an elderly woman, who was picking out some tiny pink trainers, could only call out the first word he knew: Grandma, not Mom.

Löwe appeared from behind a small store and met us on a thin stretch of dirt track. Standing nearly one-meter-ninety, even with a slight stoop, he looked malnourished in the dirty, knockoff Lakers jersey that hung off his body. His curly hair, a pallid blond, was uncombed, and his eyelashes were nearly white. Deep wrinkles lined his face.

He didn't greet us. He just smiled and turned to lead the way. That's when our cameraman lifted the camera—the signal for any reporter that the interview has started, and any small talk or chatter from now on must "have a purpose." I always feel sorry for the shoulder schlepping around several dozen kilograms of hardware.

I searched for topics for us to talk about, but Löwe's replies were terse, and he didn't speak unprompted. I had the sense that going in full of pep and verve had missed the mark, but I couldn't tell the cameraman to "put it down"; that would have been trying too hard as well. I had never felt awkward in front of a camera before that moment.

Banlie Elementary School looked almost brand-new. It had been renovated in preparation for an official inspection. The standardized building had large rooms joined by wide corridors lined with white ceramic tile. As soon as the children saw Löwe, they screeched and squealed and whizzed up to him, climbing on and hanging off his body like monkeys, four or five of them zipping under his arms and butting him with their heads.

The cameraman lowered the camera. "What do we film now?"

This was a typical question—everything followed a plan, every segment we shot had to fit the story. It's how we had always operated, only this time the question bothered me. But we had to make a decision, we couldn't have everybody standing around carrying gear for nothing.

"Let's film your room first," I said to Löwe. "Is that okay?"

He was very easygoing. He showed us to a small room with a bed, a desk, and an old computer, and a red candle for when the power cut out, which it frequently did. Old Fan and the cameraman went about rearranging the space, moving stools and checking where the best light was. Normally this was my chance to converse with the interviewee, to build a rapport and a better understanding of them, so I chatted with Löwe to see what details I could find out. But he was reticent, and he didn't answer some of my questions at all.

As the noise of moving furniture grew louder and louder, my skull felt like it had split right open. Every sound scraped across my exposed nerves. I couldn't work out why I felt so uncomfortable.

Our first interviews that afternoon were a sister and a brother, of fourteen and ten. Their parents worked in Guangdong while the children lived up the mountain with no neighbors in sight and looked after themselves. The boy planted and maintained the vegetables, and the sister cooked. This was all made much harder by the lack of tap water. They had to siphon spring water with a hose, which passing cows often trampled and split. But the children didn't complain. The girl said their parents were making money to pay for their schooling.

The inside of the old brick building was gloomy. Dull light came from a single bulb, which I turned on by pulling the cord to the right-hand side of the doorway. There was no furniture except for a broken mirror hung on the wall. The first thing the young boy did once he'd come through the door was squat to turn on the television, an old thing smack back in the center of the room. Their lives revolved around it.

He was tan and had a brightness to him, a mettle. His forehead already put me in mind of other mountain folks I'd met. Securing with his foot a tree trunk as thick as his calf, he hacked at it with a hatchet and all his might. Everyone agreed it was a touching shot to behold. But it wasn't long before the fire died down, and it became too dark for clear footage. We stopped filming and asked the boy to feed the fire, and when we had finished, I asked him to show me his vegetable patch. He said no. "Why?" I was a little taken aback.

"Go yourself." He didn't look at me. He went over to Löwe by the fire and whispered in his ear, then shot a sharp look my way.

I wanted to try to smooth things over with a joke. I said, "You're plotting how to test us, I know it."

The boy kept whispering.

Löwe laughed. "No way, city folk like them won't enjoy it."

I had just about caught what the boy said. "You want us to play in the mud?" I said.

"Will you?" asked Löwe.

"Of course." I thought I might like it. My image of myself was someone who still loved to roll around in the mud and jump in puddles in a downpour.

But by the time the interview ended, it was already evening. The sky was about to turn dark, and we shivered in the cold air as we got ready to head down the mountain. On the way up, the boy had squeezed in next to me on the front passenger seat, but he refused to do the same now, taking off down the steep road instead, his feet hardly seeming to touch the ground. Löwe started after him, but not before he stopped and asked me warmly, "Are you coming? We're going to play in the mud."

"Now?" I hesitated.

I never expected my brain's first reaction to be, *I only have one pair of jeans with me.*

I'd have been lying if I'd said again that I would go. If I had forced myself to join them and ended up caked head to toe in mud . . . it could only have been an ugly sight.

I agonized over my decision for the rest of the night. "Did I do something wrong?" I asked Old Fan.

"What?"

"With that boy."

"No," she said, "I thought he was very welcoming."

"Not true, there was definitely something up."

"You're overthinking it," she said. "Anyway, can you do Löwe's interview tomorrow?"

I frowned and blurted out, "No, leave that 'til last." I could tell she was eager to have the big interview done so she could relax. That was our routine. I couldn't tell her I was holding on to hope that we might never do it. That something would come up, or he would refuse in the morning.

Usually, before any interview, the two of us discussed our line of inquiry, but this time we didn't say a word to each other. Looking frosty, I wrote the outline while, from the next bed, she occasionally glanced at me, waiting for me to say something. I was pricked by these looks, again and again. They almost drove me to hate her. Anger is the pain we feel when we're powerless.

The next day, we continued to film the children.

Banlie Elementary School had 240 pupils, 180 of them boarders. After their parents left, lots of children, four or older, lived in the school dormitory. Each dorm contained four bunk beds, half of which were empty because the youngest slept two on a bunk, so they could play together and keep warm. The quilts the kids had brought from home hadn't been washed in a very long time, and their upper halves were a shiny black from wear. On a metal shoe rack there were a dozen or so pairs of shoes, mostly sent by parents, whom some children hadn't seen for four years. I asked them how their parents knew how tall they were, and one of them said, "I'm one-twenty. I measure myself with a folding ruler." Another child had bought himself sneakers, which were clearly too big but dearly cherished. He had whited them out with chalk.

Each of the children had their individual character, but they all stuck to Löwe like glue, without exception. Four managed to lie across one of his legs, giggling and chirping and calling him Daddy. I wondered whether this was them competing for attention in front of outsiders, but it soon became clear they were just like that, whether they could see us or not. In the center of the school stood a tall, broad cotton tree. Staring up at its branches, one kid said, "Teacher Lu, will the hornet's nest fall down?"

"I don't know," he said slowly.

Another child tugged at Löwe's arm and stretched his sleeve so long he had to lean to one side. "Will the hornets sting?" another asked. Then another, with something green stuck to his front tooth, prodded the first child and giggled, "They'll sting you." The two started wrestling on the ground in a tangle, rolling this way and that. Löwe paid them no attention and continued to talk about hornets with the other children.

Deep down, I envied these children. Not their relationship with Löwe, but how rational and natural they were. They never had to stop to think about what they were doing, they said what they wanted; they wore their emotions on their sleeves. They were uninhibited.

Wherever people gathered, Old Fan would never be far away. And wherever Löwe went, she was never far behind. "When will the cotton tree flowers bloom? They're bright red, aren't they? Do you have any pictures of them I can shoot? Anke . . ." She didn't mind how he replied, she was just happy to be there.

I watched them from afar. My task was to interview this person, and to do so I wanted to get close to him. But the moment we were face-to-face I became self-conscious. This thing, my "self," which I had known for so many years and always relied on for protection, now left me embarrassed, filled me with an anxiety I couldn't pinpoint.

Yet the show must go on.

We usually shot main segments indoors, with lights and a screen in place, and a bounce board turned toward the interviewee's face. For Löwe, I chose the hilltop where he spent a lot of time. While we carried the chairs up, the school official warned us it was too cold to sit outside in winter. *No*, I thought, *I won't feel strong unless I can sit on the ground and touch the grass.*

With the school below us, Löwe and I sat on small stools, burning charcoal in a broken enamel washbowl at our feet for warmth. He wore old sneakers with holes and no socks, so his ankles were exposed. Before I could ask why, he said in a kind tone, "Let's not talk about that."

The red light came on the camera, and the operator gave me the signal. I began with Löwe's story, thinking that was solid ground.

"Tell me about what happened in Nanning."

"I don't remember."

"Why did you come here?"

"I can't explain it."

He looked at me calmly and repeated the two answers.

A voice in my head screamed, *This interview is a disaster, it's over.*

I tried a few more questions. Finally, when I asked why he came to the countryside he replied, "City people think too quickly, I can't keep up."

"Is quick a problem?"

"They ask too many questions for me to process. While I'm thinking over one, they're already onto the next topic."

Even though he wasn't referring to me, I knew in my heart of hearts
that I fit his description. I scrambled for a follow-up. "Right, they've
moved on before you've thought through the previous question."

"Mhm, or they've told me the answer already."

When the program was broadcast, I couldn't muster the courage to
look at my expression on screen. Shame drains your face of color. It
reminded me of when another presenter, from a different station, managed to coerce Löwe into an interview using her own life as a bargaining
chip: "If you don't accept, I'll jump off a building." Löwe agreed to the
interview, but it never aired. It made sense to me now what had happened. They couldn't edit the footage into anything coherent. The
usual media conventions were as good as useless with Löwe. He wasn't
doing it to make anyone feel awkward or embarrassed, he simply
wouldn't reply to crafted questions—at the start of any interview a
good reporter has a plan and narrative in mind, and has predicted
what the interviewee's answers will be, at what points their boss will
nod, when the audience will shed a tear.

The coal at our feet crackled. Every time there was a pop, the black
rock ruptured into red. I scrunched my notes into a ball. All these
years interviewing every person under the sun, honing my professional
craft until it was second nature—it all fell away.

"Yesterday . . ." said Löwe suddenly.

I looked up at him.

". . . at the children's home, with the fire, you complained you were
cold. He was trying so hard. He would've chopped wood until you said
you were warm. Then he realized you had an ulterior motive. You
wanted a good atmosphere for the interview, an action shot, and the
light from the fire. He knew you hadn't given 100 percent of yourself

to him, so he would not accept you either. That's why when you asked to see the vegetables, he wouldn't take you."

It hit me like a punch to the gut. "I know. I thought about it all night yesterday, I knew I'd made a mistake."

"He blamed me for bringing you up here, and said he wanted to kill me. I ran back down with him to show I was sorry."

Oh god.

"It's my fault, I made a mistake, I don't know what to say."

"Goals are good, but they're empty."

"Empty?"

"If a goal is your reason for doing something, you'll get nowhere. You won't achieve anything. It's fake." He spoke deliberately. I had never heard anyone speak into a camera so slowly.

"Do you mean others will ignore it?" I mumbled.

"When your goal is to influence someone, you can't, because they can tell that's what you're trying to do."

"Often our biggest challenge lies in saying that we . . ." *No, there's no "we," no "us," no "our," only "me."* I corrected myself: ". . . saying that *I* don't know how."

"It's what the students do that's important, not your own goals. Remember that and you'll be okay."

Sitting on the stool, he had to hunch over to be at my eye level. His hands were clasped on his knees, his eye sockets so deep I could barely make out the expression in them. A journalist's job is to observe. The profession forces me to take the lead, which serves as a kind of protective shell for me. Löwe never said my name or indulged in empty courtesies. Of everyone I had interviewed, he felt the most distant. But under his gaze was the first time the shell broke open to expose my fragile head, snail-like, to the world.

When we moved on to his life, I asked him about what the villagers had told me. I wanted to know how—when he didn't drink, didn't smoke, earned no money, and had no romantic partners—he found pleasure in his life. He smiled. "There're greater joys than those."

"For example?"

His smile grew bigger. "Yesterday when the boy accepted your interview, there was joy then. I watched his reaction to you, and I understood. I also saw that you were powerless, because you don't understand his situation. There's joy in that too."

I smiled back at him. Having someone see straight to my weak points normally leaves me embarrassed, let alone when there's a camera pointed at me. And I was getting it wrong in front of tens of millions of people. But I didn't feel ashamed. *This person bears me no ill will, but he has no sympathy for me either. He just wants to understand.* "Is it really that scary to make a mistake?" he said. "Is that not how we learn?"

Before I knew it, I was telling him the story of when I was in elementary school and I had memorized the eye chart so I would pass the next test, because I was afraid of being diagnosed as nearsighted. How I had made a rule for myself never to bring my personal feelings into an interview. At this point in the program, I looked down at the floor, awkwardly, like I was eight again. My colleagues were all around me, but it didn't matter. "My biggest fear is being different. How do you overcome a fear like that?"

"I didn't want to talk to any journalists before," he replied, "I didn't want to let anyone else see what I am doing. Then I read something Mandela said. He said, if you shrink from doing something you think you should, for fear that others will see, if you hide away, play small, you are saying that nobody else can do that thing. That's why I accepted your interview."

The day before, we had picked sixth-graders from Löwe's class to interview. "The little guy with the gentle eyes looks quite sincere," I had said. *Unlike most of the other boys* was what I meant. He was the only one who stood in their way when they chopped at saplings with the machetes they carried. They made fun of him in return, but there wasn't a trace of hate on his face. One rainy day, when they passed a virgin forest that had been felled, Löwe told the boy that the trees on the mountainside were important because their roots held the soil in place and protected the houses from landslides.

Old Fan had suggested "the kid with the little round cheeks." He was one of the cuter kids of the bunch. A piece of his writing titled "Pig Riding" was displayed on the classroom wall. We had him read it aloud to us.

"It was spring, and my family were raising a big, fat, and strong pig. One day I had a strange idea. I couldn't go horse riding, so why not try riding a pig? I went straight to the pen and coaxed the pig out . . . When the time was right, I leaped onto its back and the pig set off running. My dad and granddad chased after us, and my mom and grandma stood in our way waving sticks. When the pig finally stopped, I slid off its back, took a breath, and patted the pig's rump. 'You did good buddy,' I said. Dad screwed up his face and said, 'You did good too buddy.' I knew I was in trouble, so I ran off." He babbled through the story in a voice as crisp as a ball bearing dropped in an agate bowl. I couldn't help but smile.

Then there was the tanned-face boy who followed Löwe around, who was extra cheeky, and poked his little face into every conversation. "What are you talking about what are you talking about what are you talking about?"

He ran off before I ever had the chance to answer and often was already on top of someone, scrapping, when I turned to look. During our conversation, he rocked back and forth on the bench until, at the end, I sighed and said, "Go on, go play." He barged his way to the center of a group of schoolgirls and threw his lunchbox at the feet of one of them with a clatter. "Give me food," he said as he zoomed away. The girl was his big sister. She and her friends rolled their eyes at him.

Over on the grass, he started tumbling around and climbing on Löwe with a handful of other children, hitting and pushing each other. "Sir will get tired," I said.

"Oh," said one child and let go, then looked up at Löwe while pulling on his arm and asked, "Are you going to die?"

"Yes."

The little boy with the tanned face said. "So die if you're gonna die, it's nothing to me. If I'm okay, that's all that matters."

He had a fiendish look on his face. I was at a loss for words. Löwe scooped him into an arm and smiled. "That's right, worrying too much is tiring."

Already Old Fan and I had favorites. Even though it was unprofessional of us, there was only so much we could do not to show it. Did Löwe not have any? That made no sense to me. When he hugged the tanned-faced boy and the round-cheeked one in either arm, did he really feel the same about both of them?

"What do you think a child should be like?" I asked.

"For a teacher to spend time imagining what they want their students to be like is the biggest barrier to education. That dream student would be a wall between the students and me, so I don't think that way at all."

I couldn't follow. "But there are lots of teachers who say they want their students to be creative and imaginative. Not you?"

"What if a student isn't either, should the teacher just give up? Won't they blame the student?"

I was stunned.

Some children smoked, some stole his money and screamed and shouted in class, some even swore at and made fun of him to the point he had to stop the lesson. But when he felt like blowing up, he restrained himself. "I can't risk losing it." And restraint always calmed the class quicker than if he snapped. When one boy said, "I can't control myself, let me out." Löwe opened the door and let him out.

I relayed to Löwe what the children had told me. "They say you're too soft, it would be better if you were stricter."

"Some people have thin skin. When others shout at them or mistreat them, they can't bear it, so they lash out. They don't want to hit anyone, but they have to. They lack self-control because they aren't mentally free."

He believed that any child who doesn't learn autonomy and control from an authority figure they can turn to—which most left-behind children don't have—will grow up lacking the strength of will to do what they should. "Absolute freedom in childhood means an adulthood without any." He wanted to be an authority figure who wasn't there to put pressure on the child, just to lead by example.

"Some people think you're not really teaching the children, you're just spending time with them," I said.

His answer still rings around in my head: "Education is something that happens between two people, whether intentionally or not."

I had to ask: "When that boy said he doesn't care if you die, you must have felt bad?"

He smiled, and the lines on his face bunched together. "I've given my life to them. It doesn't matter how they treat me, I can take it."

After two days at the school, it became clear the children only ever played one game: fighting. Without their parents around, there was no one to keep the left-behind children in check. So from the beginning they were up trees, jumping on one another, wrestling, sword-fighting with sticks and sometimes even sickles, rolling around on the ground, hitting one another in the head with stones. They flew into a collective frenzy when they returned to the dorms. At times, they were like critters at play, and other times it was downright dangerous. I watched one kid yell at another, "Why are you trying to hit me in the eye? Bastard."

I asked them why they fought and the tan one replied, "Itchy fingers."

One boy said, "Don't do that, it hurts." The boy replied, "Then you do it to me." When I asked him why, he said, "Life's boring without pain."

Violence was a fact of life in the poor mountain region. Children worshipped the heroes they watched in TV dramas who fought for glory. They looked up to the kids who swam in the floodwaters when the river burst its banks. They didn't fear death, only boredom. Boredom is the main cause for so much bad adolescent behavior. They wanted to feel something, to have an intense experience, and Löwe refused to deny them that. He wanted to give that feeling meaning.

For him, all the slashing at trees and bullying birds and hitting one another stemmed from a feeling that they were superior to everyone and everything else. They didn't think about others having feelings, birds having feelings, didn't know that nature has its rhythms and laws. Someone without a sense of how a thing takes shape will only consume it and break it. He wanted to show the children there was another way. So when his class was in the third grade, he took them up the mountain, put blindfolds on them, and instructed them to touch the bark of different trees. They pipetted ink into a stream to observe the water's flow. They drew each of the stages of a flower in bloom.

There was a colorful gouache painting on the back wall of the classroom, which the whole class had created together as fourth graders. It depicted a story Löwe had come up with for the children, titled *Sword of Peace*, in which a tree person tries to fight off invaders with a precious sword the invaders have come to steal. But the blood of the tree person's enemies poisons the forest where the tree person lives. So, to save its home, the tree person destroys the sword, and since its enemies can no longer achieve their goal, they never return. The children spent a whole year drawing the outline of each scene in the story, adding color and inserting the details. Collaboration can seriously test your willpower and, to begin with, the students were so excited they kept on ruining the picture a matter of minutes after starting. But through repetition, one session after another, they slowly formed a routine and built patience. They learned to work together. When the picture was hung up, they could see the result, the consequences of their actions.

A picture had grown into a story, so the next year Löwe had the now fifth-grade class film the TV adaptation. Everyone wanted to play the leading role, but being a hero wasn't as breezy as they had imagined. Doing take after take of an action scene where the hero climbs a slope left them exhausted. Heroism wasn't about flaunting their brute force either. The hero had to say no when his drunk friend threatened, "If you don't join me, you're not my friend anymore." And when the enemy pushed him into the cold mud, he had to stay cool under their mockery. Löwe said, "The strong don't conquer, they endure."

The 105-minute show took the children a semester to shoot. They wrote the dialogue, choreographed the performance, drew the animations, and designed the stunts, all by themselves. Those who rose to the task earned respect, and those who bullied their classmates lost it. Everyone had had an equal opportunity to show the best of themselves.

Production-wise, *Sword of Peace* was basic. My first viewing tested my patience. Then at every home I went to in Banlie, the child there proudly produced the DVD for me to watch, as if it were the pièce de résistance of the visit. Their mouths would grow wide as they reminisced about being up to their chins in slush. The story was their creation, and people treasure their own creations like nothing else.

On the day they wrapped filming, everyone was sapped. When the boys sang, instead of the usual clamor and yelling at the top of their lungs, they managed something quite beautiful and gentle.

Löwe said: Civilization is stopping to think about what you're doing.

There was only one time when the tanned, mischievous child would quiet down and stop hitting the others, even if they hit him. That was when he hugged Löwe, when he would nuzzle in like a little bear for a dozen minutes or more. Löwe, who had been at these children's side from first grade through sixth, who had watched them grow up and would soon watch them graduate. The children wrote a song together, to commemorate their time at the school, contributing a line each. "I stand alone in the cold outside the window . . ." "A brave man doesn't need pride . . ." They each pieced together a melody on the electric keyboards, and Löwe tied all the pieces together. "Creation is always messy," he said, before the tanned-face boy cut in, "Do you want to hear mine?"

His lyrics surprised me so much I took his arm and asked him to repeat them.

"*For you / I will grow / More than I think's possible.*"

"Who did you write that for?" I asked.

"Him," the boy said, pointing at Löwe.

During a break in one interview, the village head invited us to eat with his family. He had his wife cook a large hot pot with fatty pieces of lamb inside and stir-fried lamb kidney and offal on the side. He was a loud fellow whose thick neck blushed red after a few glasses of drink. He hollered at each of us to join him for a glass. In fact he insisted vehemently, but he never bothered Löwe.

In the dry, infertile soil of the rugged slopes, where severe deforestation had resulted in low water retention, the locals had to string wires between high cliff faces and vats far below for drops of water to travel down, so they could collect enough to grow their crops. But the maize that they planted in the cracks in rocks barely grew to a meter tall and produced cobs no larger than a fist. It was also only really fit for fermenting corn wine, so we saw more than our fair share of people, drunk, swaying along the mountain roads. Löwe told us the locals' drinking habits had put him off at first until it occurred to him that the adults were no different from the scrappy children. "They've no outlet for their emotions. Their lives don't allow them one. It's too hard to face everything sober."

Löwe fished some greens out of the soup, and the village head turned to his wife. "Go fry Lu an egg." Löwe didn't eat meat. His diet was much the same as his students'—the school was poor, and a week of food for a student cost only two yuan. For lunch every day, I saw they had nothing but sweet potato leaves on their rice. The local ten-year-olds were no taller than six-year-olds.

Old Fan and I offered to buy some cheap, thick cotton socks as a present for Löwe, because there were none big enough for his feet for sale in the village, but he told us not to. He said that any gifts from the outside would create inequality between him and his students. He lived on what little he made translating books and what his parents sent him. A hundred yuan a month altogether—around fifteen dollars. When I asked him why he had turned down the wage a county official had offered to pay him, he gave no explanation beyond what he had said in his blog: "I don't dare ask the school for pay because I'm worried they'll ask for the students' grades."

"Don't you like material things?" I asked him.

"It's not that I don't like material things, I just like freedom."

He had lived in Banlie for a decade. As a new arrival, he had been put through the ringer: he received accusations from some residents of being a foreign spy, became the face of someone's business application without his knowledge, and was a victim of theft when someone else stole his money and flashlight. But he never reacted to any of it. "That's how I became a useless person," he said, "and now I'm free." Now when he walked through the village, smiling grandmothers turned to show him the babies on their backs, and while he and the men talked little, I didn't sense there was any animosity there, and they let him get on with his life.

One evening, I walked with him up the hill to gaze out at the Nanling Mountains, where they descend toward the southwest into a deep valley that winds between the high peaks. The Hongshui River makes its way down from those great heights not by flowing, but by leaping off sheer cliffs with a roar, as if freed from the bonds of the earth. As night fell, quiet followed, and the air filled with the fecund, mulchy smell of red earth and thick foliage. The sparse dots of light I spotted against the pitch-black canvas brought a feeling of loneliness.

Löwe was some forty years old, his youth having passed into middle age in a mountain village in Guangxi. He told me he had no family, no home, no children. He walked alone in the mountains and, sometimes when tiredness struck, slept there beneath the stars. I asked him, "Are you looking for love?"

"I don't know what love is, I've never felt it."

My chest tightened.

"I saw it on TV, and it was strange," he continued.

"Strange?"

"I don't know what love on TV is based on. What is it they say, 'I'm yours'? I can't imagine that kind of feeling."

"But there's a sort of love, a closeness or a fondness, in the children around you that seems instinctual. Don't you think that's natural?

"The sense of belonging they feel with me differs from the you're-mine-I'm-yours one of love. One can be let go, the other can't."

"But what's being let go?"

"When the students leave, they're able to let go, they're not dependent on anything here. But the love I've seen on TV is a trap. It hurts if the other person wants to leave."

"And that dependency isn't for you?"

"No."

I could understand this at an intellectual level, but my instinct was to recoil from it. "Can you really bear so much freedom?" I asked.

The hint of a smile formed on his face. "I'm willing to."

. . .

I wondered how someone could so easily resist their human urges and thought I might find some clues in his story.

Born in Hamburg, Germany, in 1968, he was an introverted child like his twin brother. The reason he never resisted when he was bullied? "The pain had a use," he wrote in his blog, "it was through it I gained the strength to face future problems."

His father left engineering behind at forty-five to become a teacher, so he could educate his children himself. People often told Löwe's mother that her sons were weak and had their heads in the clouds and that they needed straightening out. But the parents were in no hurry to make his brother or him become any kind of person and preferred to let them grow in their own time. Every birthday their parents gifted them wood gadgets and models they had made themselves.

They put the brothers through a type of schooling that had no exams and had the children write the textbook themselves. Löwe said, "My parents and teachers didn't treat me like I was stupid, you know, by making me 'match the words.' Those exercises bring creative thinking into line, they blunt it. But neither did they act like I was smart and push me to act intelligent too early."

Since he failed the foreign language section of the middle school entrance exam, his parents sent him to be an apprentice at a sailboat yard where he designed sailboats and took part in international sailing competitions. "Sailing doesn't require you to think. All your reactions on the water are intuitive, as you search to balance the wind, your weight, and the waves. It's so much easier with your eyes closed." Later, he applied to the Hamburg University of Fine Arts, where the professors' response to his product designs was, "Once he learns the know-how to go with his creativity, he'll be able to bring to life all the ideas in his head." He attended college without having passed his high school exams, and with his classmates there built a glider that broke the world record for flying the farthest. He had figured out the dimensions for the aircraft by touch alone while making a model. "If you have a feel for something's mechanics, it's easy to sense where there are weak points."

After graduation, he had no interest in earning money, which made his parents worry he didn't have what it took to survive. He worked a job loading and unloading goods for two months until his parents told him it was beneath him, to which his reply was, "The job isn't cheap, it's just not worth working for money." To which his father said, "In that case, it would suit you to serve others."

A big part of the reason he was able to stay in China, so far from his parents, was their belief that "your children never belong to you." His father was a retired teacher, and his mother a housewife, while his twin brother worked for Greenpeace around the world and his little sister volunteered in Namibia. He himself volunteered as an educator in his home country first, then in Brazil, while he researched psychology in his spare time. He traveled to China in 1990 and stayed. "There's little to do in Germany. Whereas in China things are just getting started."

The next ten years were a series of "failures" for Löwe. Teaching English in a middle school in Nanning in 1999, he tried, rather than simply follow the textbook, to give his students a feel for the beauty of the language. "If they could've written a sentence like, 'Run like the kite; I can fly like a bike,' just how much more imaginative would that have been." But a sentence like that would earn them zero points in the end-of-term exams. When his class's English grades came back as the worst in the year, with only six students passing, the parents were less than thrilled, so he left.

He then gathered a group of uneducated teenagers in a village near Aidong Town and taught them about how to change their lives by changing their environment. He showed them how to draw maps and repair roads, but he soon found that they were already too old to do anything but complete the tasks assigned. They had grown beyond learning independent creativity.

"I failed at every turn," he wrote. "Failed miserably. But if I had succeeded, all the lessons I missed out on would eventually have loomed too large, and I would have become somebody I don't like. Destiny uses failure to put us on the right path."

He moved to Banlie in 2001, a place only accessible by foot or tractor, with no electricity and no running water. There wasn't half the competition there was in the city, and the school didn't demand immediate returns from him. It wasn't success-oriented. The students were young, he had the time to make things happen when they were ready to. Early on, he tried to apply the German education model to the students' lives, but soon abandoned that approach. "I don't think Western education works here. Students lead different lives depending on where they live. Their environment influences them differently, and the education they need is different. How and what I teach I came up with by observing the students."

"Does that mean you have no experience to draw from?" I asked.

"Knowing a model is not the same as having experience," he said.

That's when it clicked for me. When he said he didn't remember the past, he was telling the truth.

"Little by little, you withdrew to the countryside . . ." I said.

"I don't think I withdrew," he cut in, "I moved to where I wanted to be."

Old Fan told me that most people's first response when they heard about Löwe was to ask, "What's this German really doing in the Chinese countryside, anyway? Has it worked? Who are his success stories?"

"I struggle with questions like these," she said. "Löwe's teaching method can't be explained according to the usual notions of 'success' or 'standards.' If we have to think in those terms, then he falls under the category of 'failure.'"

The middle school dropout rate for children in China's countryside is 63 percent, and it's even higher for left-behind kids. Eight years earlier, of the forty-six pupils in Banlie's fifth-grade class, only eight graduated from junior high school. Most of them moved to the city to find work. One had married before even finishing seventh grade.

A father of one child had told Löwe to his face, "Because of you, my son's turned honest, and now he gets taken advantage of all the time."

During the program, Löwe said the biggest problem for the people of China, whether in the countryside or the city, was that they're too hurried.

"They want results before they've had the time to lay any groundwork."

"Some people might think that the alternative takes too long," I said. I was one of those people—I was talking about myself.

"Elementary school teachers work with new classes almost every year and rarely see the results. If I want to see China's current situation change, then doing what I do with my eye on the results alone, well, there would seem to be no use doing it at all."

"If we're not trying to make change, then what are we doing?" I was sounding worryingly nihilistic.

"Change will happen by itself, but it shouldn't be our goal. And nor is it our responsibility. It doesn't rest on our shoulders to make it happen."

"You used to be in a hurry once, too. What changed?" I asked.

"I came to understand why things are the way they are, which made me think things can only be this way." Listening to him, I felt that the wall I had long been stacking higher and higher in my mind collapsed— it wasn't some Zen-like awakening that knocked it down, but a strict logic that had removed each brick individually until the whole thing toppled.

"There's a danger, though, that once people fully understand the reason behind the way things are, lots of them will give up resisting." This was my worry.

"When we think we have to change things, as soon as we hit a barrier, we give up. I can't change anything, but I don't need to, because change happens of its own accord."

"So what *do* we do?"

"We do what we do as best we can."

•   •   •

A common feeling characterized the comments left beneath the program online. It seemed what Löwe did for people wasn't move them or bring them to tears. He left them sitting there the whole night, puzzling to themselves, "What am I doing with my life?"

One lunchtime, when the dinner table conversation moved onto Löwe, the official sitting beside me seemed to perk up. "We can't have many more people like that around," he said.

"Why?"

He looked flustered. "He causes too much controversy . . . he's subverting our order."

He was referring to what happened when people learned about Löwe, how their inner conflicts came to a head and they couldn't help but question ideas and values that were previously set in stone. But Löwe wasn't tearing anything down. He only lifted the slabs of your life to let you peer underneath.

I asked Löwe, "Isn't it dangerous to be the cause for so many questions?"

"It's dangerous if you're afraid of freedom," he said. "Freedom is unsteady ground."

"Where can people find the strength not to be afraid?"

"If you only have material things, you're setting yourself up to live in fear. If you have something more important, there is no need to be afraid."

Then he brought up when the boy asked me to play in the mud and, as if he knew what I was scared of at that very moment, said, "When you've no barriers in your mind, that's freedom."

The summer after the program broadcast, students from three colleges and dozens of volunteers traveled to Banlie to give extra classes at the elementary school. After the party they organized, Löwe wrote on his blog, "First be clear: did you only come because of me? If so, there's no way you can be honest with the students. So they'll reject you. If you came for the students, you could have chosen a school without a volunteer there already."

It wasn't long before people flocked to the town looking for Löwe. Some begged for him to leave the students a while and take a well-deserved rest, others asked him to write this or that, others made him the face of some initiative or other. He had no choice but to sequester himself away at his students' homes for fear that he might wake from his midday nap again to find some stranger sitting on his bed, waiting for him, or another woman come to request his hand in marriage. His response to all of them was, "I wish you'd realize I'm not what's important, it's my teaching methods you need to pay attention to."

The reply: "I don't really understand your teaching methods, but I understand you, inside and out."

"My biggest fear," he wrote, "is being admired. Admiration is so often based on illusion and only ever leads to disappointment."

People marveled at his "divine nature," but that's not at all how he saw himself or anyone. For him, there is nothing mystical about humans. I had mistaken him for a believer of some sort at first as well, but when I asked about his faith, he only smiled and said, "For the sake of my soul and for a god who can unburden me? That's too self-important." Most of the time, faith derives from superstitious, constrained thinking, he explained. "I reap what I sow, I will accept the consequences of my actions"—as far as he was concerned, this is an essential misunderstanding within education; trying to influence the spirit of humankind by following any fixed strategy is pointless. He had translated dozens of German psychology books into Chinese during his time in the mountain village so that others might understand this, as well as how the mind is formed. "People must trust science if they want to think independently, if they want spiritual freedom."

If that's what it takes, everybody can achieve both.

Löwe received more than a thousand letters daily throughout that period and clicks on his blog numbered in the hundreds of thousands. "There are lots of people who need me to tell them how to live properly, but I can't do that. Students can see right through a teacher who ignores their own feelings and works from knowledge alone. Is there even such a thing as right and wrong? Follow your feelings, that's the right thing to do."

By feelings, he didn't mean desire or emotions or motives. He was referring to "observing things from an honest and equanimous standpoint."

Löwe didn't want people to live according to how he lived. He simply wanted to free them from the "inhuman" experience society forces on us, so they could embody themselves. It was no good looking to him for their superego. The answer lay in not blocking out their inherent humanity.

The Chinese government requires all volunteer teachers from abroad to have a teaching certificate. Löwe didn't have one, and so as the public and media attention around his work grew, his semi-legal status came under fire. He closed down his blog with a statement that he had no qualifications to be a volunteer or a teacher, which only stirred up the frenzy further. One reporter texted me, *Give me Lu Anke's phone number, please. He can have a full-page spread. I want to help.* I replied, *He has a public email address, write him there first.*

Full of confidence, he answered, *No, I'll call him directly. Sincerity can move mountains.*

I told him Lu doesn't have a phone, and we should respect his wishes.

I'll go to him then. Sincerity can move mountains.

I didn't write back. Half an hour later, the reporter messaged again, saying he had boarded the train. Then, like a broken record, *Sincerity can move mountains.*

I received Löwe's permission, which I'd requested by letter, to release a public statement—his life and work in Banlie were normal; he hoped the media and the public "will put no further pressure on the Guangxi Public Security Bureau and education department."

In the letter I had asked whether we should contact the local government to request they resolve his status.

In his reply, he wrote that lots of people were trying to help him, "But if any problem arises, people will rush to find who's responsible, which makes the higher-ups nervous there'll be a scandal and so want to have everything in check. Why ask for so much in the first place? These demands only bring us less freedom."

Then the matter took on a different shape entirely. One day during a break from work, someone with a strange look in his eyes pulled me aside. "You did the show about Löwe, right?" When I replied yes, he hunched nearer to me, his face close to mine, and whispered in an overly familiar tone, "I think he's a pedophile." Right then, a feral cat came skulking over, searching for something to eat. The man snapped upright and shouted at it, "Get lost. Scram!" His eyes wide, he lunged at it and kicked it in the head with the point of his leather shoe.

In 2010, Löwe left Banlie Elementary School to return to Germany, a move that was met with shock and regret by many people. But slowly he and the hubbub were forgotten about.

After the Spring Festival that year, I received a letter. Löwe had returned to Banlie on a tourist visa. I wasn't surprised. Six years prior he had been in a serious accident in the village while riding on a farm vehicle with a friend. A wheel had come off, sending the vehicle rolling dozens of meters down a hillside. It narrowly avoided falling into the Hongshui River because a large tree stopped it in its tracks. Löwe's friend was killed, and Löwe's spine was compressed three centimeters. He didn't recover for a long time. During our interview I asked him about it. "Don't events like that usually prove too much for people to bear?"

"What else is there but to bear them?" he said.

"You could choose to leave."

"And would leaving mean no more accidents?"

I responded instinctively, "But at least you wouldn't be in a strange place, where there's no money and you can't get medical treatment."

"I think of that car accident as having tied my life to this place. If I leave, then my life's over."

Since a lot of parents didn't return home during the Spring Festival, he wanted to be there with the children. I felt some relief at that, tempered by the guilt I felt for the trouble I'd caused him. In his letter he wrote, "I am confident in my ability to endure, only this test requires that I learn even greater endurance than before. But don't worry, I'll learn."

I didn't write back. He didn't need my comfort. And more than that, I was afraid the moment my pen touched paper I would pour out thanks he had no use for. He had already told me, "Believing your name can give others strength is the worst kind of delusion or heresy." But there were many moments when seized by my weaknesses I had struggled free by thinking, "What would Löwe do?" Change for the better is often impossible, but his way of being had ingrained in me an idea that had not occurred to me before—by giving of myself, I can follow my destiny, embrace the inevitable, and be free.

In late 2012, three years after the program aired, I received another letter from Löwe, along with a copy of the children's new show, *Mindset*. The note said, *This is maybe the last thing I get to make with my students.*

Old Fan and I made the journey back to Banlie. In a blue vest, Löwe sauntered out of the rice paddies to meet us. He still wore no socks inside his sneakers, but he was thinner than before, and his wrinkles deeper when he smiled. His golden eyebrows had turned white, such that the only color left in his face were his bright blue eyes. "How are you?" I asked.

"Up and down," he said, "you know."

Engraved into one of the school's walls were two large world maps and the caption, *Cherish the motherland, look to the world.* Children squatted in front of them, eating. In three years, the proportion of left-behind children at the school had skyrocketed to 90 percent. The volunteers who had turned up in Banlie after seeing the program had all left. The children said that one art teacher "went without even saying goodbye, so we tore up all our pictures. Since she left, I don't want to draw anymore."

Löwe said that it would have been fine had the volunteers only stayed a short while to play with the kids, but giving classes is another matter entirely. It takes time and stability. What they did was give the students a taste of attention, then abandon them and take the youngsters' hearts with them.

We sat on a pile of hay together with the boys leaning beside Löwe. Whenever the girls came near, the boys would still excitedly shout, "Boys and girls must not touch." But the girls seemed to have relaxed a lot. They sat to the side stripping stalks of straw to whistle through and handed one to me to see who could make the loudest sound. Löwe had watched these kids grow over the last three years. He'd watched them shoot *Mindset* too, and this time it was the enemy who wielded the powerful, eponymous weapon, which they used to deflect others' intentions back at them, so any attacker would have their own goals strike them down. Save for Rong Cheng that is, the only child with a heart so pure that "mindset" had no effect on him. I asked why he was the hero, and all at once the children shouted over one another, "Defeating the mindset wasn't his goal!" Then one of them added, "His mind is clear!"

But when I asked again, they said, "I've forgotten!"

We all laughed. They hadn't quite gotten it yet, I said to Löwe. With his arms around the boys, he replied, "There's no hurry. Life isn't about rushing." One of them at Löwe's side turned to me. "Take it one step at a time and don't rush," he said in a reassuring tone. "Rushing gets you nowhere."

We first interviewed the students when they were in sixth grade. By our return, the half that remained were in grade nine, but the other half had left the school, and the village, to work. The little boy who chopped wood for us was now thirteen and had the first signs of facial hair. His parents had used their savings to build a three-story house where the one had been. It was an impressive concrete structure with a shiny metal door, but it was empty inside. There was no glass, no furniture, and the child had no way of organizing his day-to-day life. There were things thrown all over the place, and potatoes heaped in a pile on the dirt ground.

His older sister had gone to work in the city, and he wanted to leave too. To leave his home far behind, like his parents had. To leave behind an empty shell. This worried Löwe. "Lots of the children join gangs in Guangdong. They've no one to guide them, so they become wild. Without boundaries, they can't control their behavior, so the gang becomes a kind of necessity for them. They can't integrate into the wider community, so they join whatever small one they can."

The migrant labor wave in China started around 1995. That first generation of left-behind children had already become adults and were trying to make their own way in the world by the time of our second visit. Since 2000, the number of juvenile offenders sentenced throughout the judicial system had increased by an average of 13 percent annually, consistently accounting for 70 percent of all crimes. Gangs of left-behind children were some of the worst offenders. Löwe said, "China's left-behind kids will become an out-of-control element unless we can give them some sense of belonging. That's the source of our strength."

"What about order?" I asked.

"Order isn't strength. Belonging is essential for our mental health. Order is something only society demands. We need to feel we belong before we have any desire to care. When a person who has that arrives in the city, it won't matter that others have money when they don't, they won't think they've missed out or been let down. They'll have the get-up-and-go to build a life for themselves."

The boy had his heart set on somewhere far away. I asked him what he would remember most about his life at the school, and he replied, "The sense of achievement I got from working together with my class-mates." Old Fan and I looked at each other. We were two outsiders from Beijing, but we weren't immune to this sentiment from a taciturn young man from the countryside.

He was on the cusp of adolescence, and it was more than just his appearance that had changed. The plucky boy of before was long gone, replaced by a shyer teen who looked away when he spoke. Löwe had held his hand through a lot, gently rocking it back and forth, and now Löwe was leading him through the final stretch before saying their goodbyes. "My students have to find their own way in life. What that should be, I don't know, I can't know. I just want to give them all the strength and tools they need to make it."

That evening we had dinner at Xiao Luo's home. He had been the quiet-est one in the class. The boy took out a spanner and turned the knob on the broken electric rice cooker a few times before placing the rice inside. The only dish available was some Hyacinth beans, which had clearly been left strewn across the table for a long time. Löwe absent-mindedly broke apart a pod, not saying a word.

I said, "I wondered on the road here if you were going to be in a different place than before, mentally."

He nodded.

I dropped a handful of the beans into an aluminum pot. "Could this really be your last time here?"

He didn't look at me. "I'm worried there's a chance it is."

I gazed up at him. "I remember during our last conversation you said that this place is your life, and if you leave here, you'll have no life anymore."

He jolted his head up and stared at me. It was as if I had pricked him, and it was the first time I'd seen him taken aback. Then he told me that in 2010, he had married a Chinese volunteer he had known for eight years, who now wanted him to leave Banlie to work at a factory in Hangzhou. It was an unexpected twist in the story, but one that, on second thought, made sense. "Do you understand your wife?" I asked.

"I understand her, she's a woman."

I heard Old Fan sigh by my side.

He stood to chop wood and light a fire while Xiao Luo stir-fried the tomatoes and beans like an old hand. I asked the boy who had taught him to cook. "I taught myself, with practice," he said. The flame from beneath the pot illuminated a foot-long burn on his arm, which had scarred. I turned back to Löwe. "How will you explain it to them? The children."

He bent down to light the fire, sending smoke funneling upward. "I'll just tell them it was my wife's decision."

"Will they accept that?"

"No." Then a beat of quiet. "What should I do?"

I didn't respond. I couldn't. I had never imagined him having to ask others about his own inner turmoil, and it rocked me to my core. He went to chop more wood. Squatting down, he held the block still with his left hand and swung the hatchet with his right. Each time he raised the hatchet, the chunk of wood came with it, before slamming down on the ground again and again and again. I crouched nearby, collecting the shards and adding them to the fire.

For a long time, the only sound was a pop as the wood split and spat sparks.

Löwe and I were the only ones eating. My colleagues had to film, and Xiao Luo refused to eat while others weren't, which made Old Fan uneasy. She insisted he eat something, until Löwe said, "Don't push him. He's the host. If there are guests who aren't eating, he won't eat either. Let's finish up quickly and he can relax."

When we left, Old Fan regretted how we had handled the situation. "The boy rushed around for us all evening, shouldn't I have at least taken a bite as a token of appreciation and given Xiao Luo some praise? When I cooked as a kid, everyone had to tell me it was good." Löwe said, "He probably won't care."

"Don't all children need praise?"

"No. They need people to be real with them."

Ya Hanyun was another sixth-grader, the naughtiest in his class, according to the other teachers; he was a bad influence on the other boys and often led them into trouble. As a result, he had earned himself the nickname "Kingpin." Löwe said, "But he doesn't want to be anyone's kingpin or boss. It's just everyone expects it from him now, so he plays up to the role so as not to let them down." He smiled. "He's in a bad place, and it's his reality that has put him there. He never wanted this for himself."

Hanyun had played the role of Rong Cheng in the show they shot. It was the hardest part to take on. During filming, he had to lie in the mud for over an hour, shivering with the cold, but he never complained. Löwe said that the naughtiest children always have a self-sacrificing streak, so handing responsibility over to them gives them a chance to show what they can do.

Hanyun had seemed nervous when he agreed to the interview. He sat stiffly at the table with a ladle in his hand and insisted that Löwe should stay with him.

I asked him a string of questions: "Why did you play Rong Cheng?" "What's his personality?" And to each he replied, "I don't know," or, "I'll think about it." He had his eyes shut and rubbed his face hard with his hands. "Don't know."

I realized then that he really didn't know. I turned to Löwe. "I think we're all done." Then the boy screwed up his mouth and said, "My tummy's unwell." Holding his stomach, he slumped onto the table and said it hurt, and with his head on his forearm he cried, pushing against his stomach with a balled-up fist. I poured him a glass of warm water. He didn't drink it. I asked him if he wanted medicine. He shook his head.

Löwe squatted beside him and rubbed his back. "When I have to interpret from German," he said, looking at me, "my tummy hurts too." I thought I knew what he was getting at, so I bent down and asked the boy, "Is it because my questions are putting you under pressure? If it is, then I'm really sorry, Hanyun."

He wiped away his tears with his sleeve, shook his head and, as if bracing himself for great pain, said, "It's okay, keep going."

Löwe remained at his side and said gently, without looking at me, "This is the countryside, nature is powerful here. If you ask him to climb any mountain, he'll climb it. But asking him these questions about himself is hard-going."

Löwe walked with him back to the dorms. Old Fan saw my expression but knew it was best to ignore me for a while, so she led everyone outside to film. I sat by myself, in the empty sixth-grade classroom, seething. *Three years, three whole years, and I'm still making mistakes, how can I be so stupid to ask the wrong questions again?*

I sat there for thirty minutes wringing my hands before I went downstairs to eat. Mr. Pan, another teacher, had killed a duck and cooked it in a hot pot that was now bubbling on the table. Löwe had saved a bamboo stool for me next to him. After eating a few mouthfuls to find the food still steaming hot, I slowed down and asked Löwe quietly, so no one else would hear, "Why can't I seem to get better at things?"

"If it were that easy, what would we need such a long life for?"

That afternoon, Löwe led our group and Hanyun up the mountain road on a three-hour walk. Then to catch crabs in the caves after the rainfall, then to lie in the grass where we stayed until sunset. "Talking with him is no use," Löwe told me, "doing things together is what works. Creating things is similar: you work together on something and naturally something always comes of it."

For our dinner, Hanyun killed a duck and washed its innards under the tap while Löwe squatted and held an umbrella over the boy's head. Later, as we readied to leave, Hanyun took out the leftover rice and bowls and chopsticks to give us seconds, so Löwe would stay a little longer. But the time had come to say goodbye.

Löwe walked by and rubbed his back. "Bye," he said softly.

Hanyun didn't look up until Löwe had stepped outside. He waved at Löwe's back and said "bye." Then he started to cry.

Around the corner, Löwe stood still and gazed out over the endless mountains and at the setting sun. He cried too.

I knew then why he had written to me. He wanted to leave something for the children, to remain in his place, and now they would have the program we were shooting. "I hope creativity can be the source of authority they need, that the children will find belonging within themselves."

Once the interviews were over, Löwe wrote back to his wife saying he was preparing to head to Hangzhou. "This is a new responsibility for me, a family, a home. I'm accepting it whatever the outcome." I told him he made it sound like a heavy sentiment.

"I don't know why I'm here, what my purpose is, but maybe in a few years I'll find out," he replied.

"Do you see this as a test for yourself?"

Something in him responded to that idea. He said he did.

"Are you afraid at all that the people who expect things of you will be disappointed?" I asked.

"Any hope you find in other people is illusory. It's pointless. If you don't do something yourself, then you've no hope."

Before he left the village, he disowned his Chinese name, Lu Anke. In the last post on his blog, he wrote, "Nothing in this life is necessary, there are only unnecessary expectations. A life without expectation, without the need for respect or admiration, is the most beautiful and free life you can lead, because without that noise you can listen to your heart."

There was a storm on that penultimate day. In the calm afterward, the bright light illuminating the world, I thanked Löwe. "Life is full of changes. Maybe in another three years we'll see each other again, talk some more. Thank you."

He smiled. "Thank you too."

The thunder was loud. Rain fell heavily around the concrete platform we sat on, in the middle of a paddy high up in the mountains. Luckily, there was an old umbrella for us to take cover under. It had been left by the farmers a few days before, when they harvested the wheat. Löwe opened it as wide as it went, which was enough room for us and five children, plus a curious farmer, to stand beneath. Xiao Luo helped by holding my book of interview notes against his chest. Soon water streamed off the sides of the umbrella. The mountains brightened, then darkened, brightened, then darkened. Everyone huddled close together and scanned the storm-whipped greenery around us. It was a long while before a beam of light broke through from behind the eastern mountains and the blue-black clouds billowing overhead jostled for the horizon.

It was then that I knew how to end the show: "One tree shakes another tree, one cloud pushes another cloud, and one soul awakens another soul. Education is something that happens between two people, and between one and oneself. And it happens constantly. As long as this cycle of transmission and awakening never ends, we will never have to say goodbye to Lu Anke."

Yao Jiaxin, a college student who majored in piano. With these hands, he stabbed a woman to death whom he had hit in a traffic accident. Shanxi, 2010.

Ten
Interviews between Patients
2010

In late 2010, a car hit a twenty-six-year-old woman named Zhang Miao while she was riding her electric bike at night in Xi'an, the capital of Shaanxi Province. Instead of running to her aid, the driver stabbed her eight times until she died. One stab was directly to her palm, supposedly because she was trying to block the knife.

The murderer was Yao Jiaxin, a twenty-one-year-old college student who studied piano at the Xi'an Conservatory of Music. In a brief interview with a local TV station after his arrest, he said he had committed the murder because he was afraid a rural woman "would be hard to deal with" and pursue him for compensation.

His words angered a society that is deeply divided between the rich and the poor. Some people believed that a college student who could afford to learn piano and drive a car must come from a wealthy family that had spoiled its only child too much. It didn't help that his parents remained silent for the eight months leading up to his trial. Many believed they were trying to get their son off the hook, as had happened in some previous cases. Some said they would attack the court if it did not sentence Yao Jiaxin to death. The incident threatened to spiral out of control and affect social stability. Even journalists were banned from reporting the case.

Yet it was the focus of everyone's conversations. The debate, even among friends, was very heated. There were several people who took it as an occasion to advocate the death penalty. Others thought the death penalty should be abolished. Soon after the incident had taken place, I was at a gathering where the issue was being discussed, and I said, "Since we have not abolished the death penalty, we should respect the existing law, otherwise we cannot talk about justice."

My friend He Fan, who worked at the Supreme People's Court, said, "Yao's parents sent their son to turn himself in—and he's their only son. Shouldn't you consider the parents' feelings?"

Most people disagreed. "That justice is too flexible. Otherwise, how can you establish authority?"

I thought one shouldn't consider the family background or the pressure of public opinion, but should simply evaluate the matter.

"I remember that criminal law states that if the crime is 'particularly cruel' and the consequences 'particularly serious,'" I said, "a defendant can't get a lighter sentence even if he turned himself in. Right?"

He pondered for a moment. "This situation . . . is it considered 'particularly cruel'?"

There was a surprised laugh from among our group. Someone interrupted him: "This is not 'particularly cruel'? These are not 'particularly serious consequences?'"

He said, "How does this compare to a well-planned and calculated killing?"

I answered as I understood it. "Intentional killing targets a specific person, and I, as a bystander, have nothing to fear. But when you hit someone with a car and then kill them, anyone could be a victim and the social danger is great."

He said, "That's how you feel."

I said, "Aren't laws made based on people's experiences?"

He Fan said, "I just think that sometimes people's feelings and judgments are different, related to the way the story is told. Justice cannot be generalized, and we can only achieve justice in individual cases."

• • •

At noon on June 7, 2011, I heard on the news that Yao Jiaxin was executed.

When I turned to watch the TV, a clip played of his final sentencing. He was wearing a horizontal-striped T-shirt. He had a flat shaved head, narrow face, and low-hanging eyebrows. He signed the execution papers and left with his head bowed under the escort of two bailiffs wearing helmet guards.

A lethal injection had been carried out. I watched the rest of the news report, my heart empty. The TV host was reading out the verdict: *"The criminal's motive for committing the crime was extremely despicable, the means particularly cruel, the circumstances particularly bad, and the consequences particularly serious, and he was sentenced to death according to the law."*

I had summoned some of these very words when I was arguing with He Fan. I had marshaled the same logic to support depriving the defendant of his life—so why did I have an annoying feeling of emptiness in my chest? I opened my computer and sought out the face I had never seriously looked at before—the face of Yao Jiaxin. To me he was just a name and a paragraph of two dozen words of fact. I only felt the same shock and disgust toward him as I had felt initially.

I sent a text message to Lao Fan: *Have you seen the news?*

She sent back one word: *Ugh.*

I wrote in my notes that day, "Why is it that people talk about justice and demand death, but when death comes to this moment, instead of feeling satisfaction or fear at its cruelty, I feel a kind of emptiness? It makes me realize what it means to be deprived of life, that all developments, all possibilities, are over, that Zhang Miao is dead, and now Yao Jiaxin is dead, but if everything is just death, over and done with, it is death for nothing."

The drama was past, the reporting ban had been lifted, but the hole the news left in people's hearts was still there. So we sent greetings to the family of the victim and the family of her killer until they agreed to see us two months later.

We visited Zhang Miao's parents first. Her father, Zhang Pingxuan, was outside in his mud pants mixing sand and cement to make concrete. This was his part-time job in addition to farming.

Zhang Miao's marriage had not gone well, so she'd moved back to her parents' house a few months before the accident. There were no souvenirs for the dead in her small barren room; there were only light bulbs. Her clothes had been burned. Two group photos remained of her—in one, she stood in the last row among her classmates, wearing a black dress and white shirt, her hair tied in a ponytail. She was not giggling like the other girls. She stood alone, her back slightly hunched, looking timid and shy, her lips obediently curled up in the smile the photographer demanded.

"When she was a child, she was not well and spent several months in the hospital," Zhang Pingxuan said. What he remembered most about her was "the milk powder we fed her." To him, this expressed the poor family's love for their child. Zhang Miao ended up dropping out of junior high school, and before the accident, she sold spicy hot pot to feed and clothe her son.

The child she'd left behind was only two years old. He played with toys in my arms, and I touched his round head; his soft hair was wet with sweat. Zhang Miao's father gazed at the child, then turned his head and sighed, almost inaudibly. I heard Zhang Miao's mother crying in the other room.

I asked her father, "Do you need to soothe her?"

His dark face was as thin as if it had been carved with a knife. He said, "No, it's impossible to calm her down."

I couldn't sit through the sobs, so I turned back to the camera and said, "I'll go check." I went to the room and sat down next to her. She was lying on the mat crying and said, "Mommy made you dinner. Why don't you come back and eat . . ." I couldn't say anything to comfort her. I just stroked her arm and waved to the cameraman outside the curtain to stay out.

It was not until the day of Yao's execution that the family cremated Zhang Miao. Someone set off firecrackers as a celebration. I asked Zhang Pingxuan how he felt, and he said, "I'm also happy, but I pity his mother and father."

"Even though you lost your child, too?"

The old man took a deep breath from his chest and said, "To be honest, I still have two children to rely on. The Yao family only had one child. I don't know how they feel or what they think. And I still have doubts. Are they actually rich people who look down on the poor?"

He sighed again and said, "My heart is not easy."

Yao's family lived in the dormitory of Xi'an Huashan Machinery Factory, an old Soviet-style building from the 1990s that had once been a state-owned enterprise. It had since closed down. Yao's father, Yao Qingwei, was standing outside the gate waiting for us. He was wearing a white Dacron shirt with a white undershirt underneath. I rarely saw people dressed like this in town. The fabric had been popular thirty years ago, in the days of material scarcity.

There was no elevator in the old building where they had lived for over twenty years. As we went up the stairs, he told me he was born in rural Shanxi, entered military school, and worked in quality control in a military factory. Eight years ago he had left the army. He'd held no regular job since. He lived on the fifth floor, in a three-room apartment with a clean concrete floor, a hard sofa in the corner, and a replica of a landscape painting hanging on the wall, framed in glass. It looked just like my family's apartment from decades ago. The toilet handle was broken. Next to it was a bucket and a large spoon that was used to flush. While we were there, Yao's mother kept cleaning with a rag and mop, never taking a break. She had been a warehouse worker for this factory before she'd retired. The family now lived on a pension.

Mr. Yao took us to his son's room, which had a table, a bed, and an old piano that his son had played for more than a decade. There were two photos on the wall. The top one was of Mr. Yao's deceased parents, and the bottom one was of his son as a boy of fourteen or fifteen years old, as they did not have a picture of him as an adult. On the table was a pair of glasses, and two albums by the Japanese singer Ayumi Hamasaki, who was his son's favorite.

Mr. Yao said, "Forty-nine days . . . the computer still hasn't stopped." They had been playing his son's favorite songs. Before he died he had said, "Dad, can you play these songs for me so I can go back after listening to them?"

There was a big stuffed toy dog on the bed. The mother replaced a cooler and hung a mosquito net. She said, "Summer is coming and I'm afraid the mosquitoes will bite him." She didn't believe her son was dead.

She said, "I'm still waiting for him."

The young man's father said, "When I was in the countryside, I always heard that people turned into ghosts when they died. I used to be afraid of that. Now I wish it were true. But where is there any sound? There is no sound at all."

As evening approached, the living room was half dark, half bright, and he paused for a moment and said, "No, really, people die the way lights go out."

During his last court hearing, Yao Jiaxin repeatedly mentioned his family when talking about his motive for the murder.

"Growing up, all I had in my life was practicing the piano. My mother would beat me, whip me with a belt. One time, when my father saw I was not studying hard enough, he locked me up in the basement . . . I saw no hope. The pressure was so great that I often wanted to kill myself . . ." He sat in the courtroom in handcuffs, sobbing as he said, "I was so anxious and depressed when I saw how hard it was for others to find jobs. I didn't know what to do in the future. I thought, if I stabbed her to death, she would never see me again. I got scared and ran away."

There was no logic to his words. I didn't understand why his troubles with his family had led him to commit something as serious as murder. It confused his parents as well. After their son's death, the couple couldn't sleep for days, wondering what they had done wrong so that their son would say such things.

His mother's round face was covered with tears when we spoke. "Don't people say that strict discipline is the only way to raise good children? Is it wrong to be strictly disciplined?"

I didn't know how to answer.

Yao Jiaxin had been playing the piano since he was four years old, when his kindergarten teacher told his mother that the child had shown talent in playing the keyboard. The family could not afford a piano, but the boy's grandfather, a retired engineer, gave one to them as a gift. The boy's mother would sit next to her son while he played the piano, slapping his hand with a ruler when he made a mistake. This method of training had been common in China until recently. She said, "You can't get the shape of your hands the slightest bit wrong, or you'll never succeed."

Her son cried as he played, but never resisted, "because he knew how much money would be wasted if he made a mistake." The cost of one lesson was forty yuan, a third of her salary. She would take the child by bicycle to the piano teacher; no matter how windy or rainy it was, she was never late. A teacher in elementary school told her not to put too much pressure on him, because the boy always asked all his teachers for homework for the day, and never left his seat between classes except to go to the bathroom, in order to save two hours to practice piano after school. She said her son was willing to do so. Yao Jiaxin was born in 1989, soon after China had implemented its one-child policy in the 1980s to limit population, and the meaning of his name reflected the high expectations his parents had for him.

"As the only child in the family, my father was very strict with me and he did not allow me to make any mistakes," he said at his trial. "He always demanded that I do things perfectly and go above and beyond."

"Ever since he was little, whenever he argued with someone," his mother said, "I would teach him a lesson, no matter who was right or wrong." That was the couple's way of trying to keep their son out of trouble. In the first grade, a classmate told Yao Jiaxin to carry him, or to pay him if he wouldn't. The teacher got his father to deal with it. Mr. Yao made his son carry that child. Later, he told me, "I thought it was just a kid's game. It was no big deal. Just carry him, I said. I did not help him."

After that, Yao Jiaxin never sought help from his parents. When a boy bullied him in middle school, holding his head against the wall, he didn't dare to resist or tell his family, and he skipped school instead. Mr. Yao said, "I told him even if someone beats you, just bear it."

When I looked through the family photos, Yao Jiaxin was always timidly averting his eyes from the camera. He avoided anything that involved confrontation: soccer, fights, even intense piano music. "He was afraid of men, especially his father," his mother said. "He was afraid to refuse what his father told him to do."

Mr. Yao said, "I didn't really hit him, but I'm a soldier and I believe in a command-and-control model. I just told him what to do without giving him a reason."

I said, "There are many ways to criticize, don't you think?"

"I have a sharp tongue, but not toward others, only toward my son. I wanted him to be good and hit the nail on the head. He can be very prickly." He then added, "But in hindsight, I was right about everything."

"What was your son's attitude?"

"My boy never resisted. He just smiled and said, 'Well, I just do nothing right.'"

The mantra of this family was "You can never succeed if you make the slightest mistake." Mr. Yao added, "Boys can't be spoiled. I was afraid he would get me into trouble later."

There were no photos of Yao Jiaxin's adolescence for us to shoot. His mother said that he refused to take pictures after he gained weight in his first year of middle school. He was less than six meters tall and weighed 168 kilograms. His father said, "He was so fat that people couldn't see his eyes when he smiled. Everyone laughed at him, and he told me he wanted double-eyelid surgery."

"What did you say?" I asked.

"I hit him with words," he said. "'Your eyes were given by your parents, and if you change them, it's disrespectful to me.' My words might have been a little . . . like his Mom said, a little hard to take."

Then he added, "But what I said was right."

Yao Jiaxin satisfied his repressed desires through extreme means. To make his eyes look bigger, he threw up everything he ate and lost thirty kilograms in four months, at the cost of a stomach bug. Once he wanted something, he became fanatical, even paranoid. When he became a fan of the Japanese singer Ayumi Hamasaki, his passion overrode even his fear of his parents and he skipped school to go to Internet cafés and download all her songs and games related to her. Once, when someone shouted "earthquake" in one of these Internet cafés and everyone ran outside, he was the only one who stayed sitting still. He said, "If I ran out, I'd have to start all over again."

When Mr. Yao found out his son was off-track, he was so angry that he beat him severely, threw all his records and games in the trash, and then locked him in the basement of a residential building with groceries and only a small electric bulb for light. He locked the door from the outside and kept him there for over a month, letting him out only to attend school. When I asked his mother about a suicide attempt he'd claimed to have made in that basement, she was startled. "I know nothing about it at all. He never talked about his feelings."

Confused, his father said, "I don't know why he said that. He got in there voluntarily and did not resist. All we know is, after that, he was back to normal."

The couple continued to devote almost all of their energy to their only child. Mr. Yao gave up his job to educate his son, studying all the boy's textbooks to tutor him and creating extra homework exercises for him. All the while, he supervised his son practicing the piano every day. In this way, the couple kept their son in what they considered a safe zone. They did not allow him to socialize or have pocket money. His father didn't think any of this was a problem: "I bought him popsicles all the time." Knowing that his son was unhappy, he would say to him, "The Chinese say that a happy childhood means an unhappy future! If I am not strict, how will you survive in the future? Are double eyelids a meal?"

At one point, the boy told a friend that he couldn't stand his father's sarcasm anymore. "My mind is so twisted, I want to stab him to death."

His parents knew nothing about this. As far back as his father could remember, Yao Jiaxin had always been obedient and reverent toward him, showing rebellion only once, when he took his middle school law class book and used it to claim his father was oppressing and controlling him. Mr. Yao turned the book over and said to him, "I am your guardian, so of course I have to control you, because I am responsible for any mistakes you make."

In 2009, Yao Jiaxin was admitted to Xi'an Conservatory of Music. He had gotten first place in the highly competitive college entrance examination. Instead of feeling joyful, he cried out loud. It was the first time he had achieved his goal against his father's wishes.

For many Chinese families, learning piano is just a way to get extra points for college entrance exams. This was the motivation for the Yaos to provide their son with lessons in the first place. But when it came time for higher education, Mr. Yao desperately wanted his son to move on and study science or technology. Piano costed a lot of money to learn as a profession, and promised little financial reward. But instead of being honest with his son, Mr. Yao asked his son's piano teacher to belittle the boy's ability, in turn forcing the boy to, hopefully, give up on his own. He was happy to hear his son say that "the more he learns, the less confidence he has."

Yet Yao Jiaxin persevered to the end and got into the piano program he wanted. Then he had to prove that it was worth it. The tuition fee for one year was twenty thousand yuan. So, starting his freshman year, he worked part-time to earn money. He played piano in hotel lobbies and then worked as a tutor for students until his monthly income was higher than the average civil servant in the city. Mr. Yao was so proud that he praised his son to his relatives, but never encouraged him to his face, showing only contempt. "There are plenty of people better than you. They sit in an office to earn money, you still have to run around on the road."

He said to me, "I would beat him up for anything he did. I didn't want him to overheat, I didn't want him to go that far. What I did was pour cool water on his disposition."

"Why was that?" I asked.

"I didn't want him to be too proud to make mistakes," he said.

Yao Jiaxin promised his parents he would get an office job soon, by setting up a music school to do "big business." To save money, he taught more and more students in his second year of college, so many that it affected his grades. The school warned him about his academic decline. His mania for success even worried his mother. She said, "I'd been saying the whole time, You can't do that, boy, don't go too far."

I asked her, "Why did you worry about that?"

She looked confused. "He hates himself if he can't be the best."

"But weren't you asking him to be the best?"

She hesitated for a moment and said, "Maybe we asked for it."

When I first watched the video of the trial, I thought Yao Jiaxin's complaint against his parents was an attempt to shirk responsibility. As a twenty-one-year-old adult living independently with his peers in college, he was responsible for his own life. But then I learned during the interviews I conducted that he had never actually left home.

As it turned out, he'd returned to his parents' apartment after a week in the dorm because he couldn't live with others. He had obvious obsessive-compulsive symptoms—repeatedly washing his hands, checking things over and over, worrying about this and that, and he had to go home every day to hug his big stuffed dog before going to bed. He was a twenty-one-year-old boy, but he was still a child emotionally, and heavily dependent on his parents. When he first entered prison, he cried for "Daddy and Mommy" every day because he didn't know how to take care of himself, and prison guards had to give him some basic life knowledge about how to get along with other inmates. Before his sentence, Yao Jiaxin said, "It was in prison that I learned how to take responsibility for the first time."

In the past, he would ask his college classmates to help him cut an orange, since this was what his parents always did for him, to protect his piano-playing hands. He only needed to take good care of his hands. He was always rubbing hand cream on them and laying them flat on whatever table he was seated at.

The city of Xi'an has a population of over ten million people and covers an area of over ten thousand square kilometers. The students he taught lived in different areas, and Yao Jiaxin couldn't go home before eleven P.M. For his safety, his mother offered to buy him a car, but his father, being frugal, objected at first. But then a pragmatic viewpoint convinced him. "People often say time is money, and a car can save time."

The family took out one hundred thousand yuan in savings and borrowed another forty thousand to buy a red Chevrolet, the family's first car. Mr. Yao asked Yao Jiaxin to pay for gas and maintenance, as well as give his parents one thousand yuan a month as repayment.

Yao Jiaxin talked about his extreme financial anxiety during the trial, but what he showed to his parents was a different side. His father said, "He seemed to be addicted to earning money. Four thousand one month, and five thousand the next month." He said "addicted" as if he were describing a sick person, but he saw it as a good thing. His generation had experienced abject poverty and famine, and had deep existential anxiety about money.

"I want to force my child to save money for a disaster that could come in the future," he said. "It's good for him to have the motivation to make money. That way, he'll never starve like I did when I was a kid."

Mr. Yao motivated his son by applying constant pressure. When Yao Jiaxin bought an electric massage chair for his father's birthday, his father's face turned grim. "I don't want this," he said. "I only want one thing. If you need money in the future, don't ask me for it."

On the day of the incident, around eleven P.M., Yao Jiaxin was driving home. Later, when a judge asked him which direction he'd been driving in, he'd said, "Sorry, I didn't recognize the direction." He only had four months of driving experience.

There were few people on the suburban road late that night. So he'd turned on his video player and watched Ayumi Hamasaki's concert. Still driving, he looked down to change the DVD at one point. That was when he heard a "tom-tom" sound. He had hit something. He stopped the car, got out, and took the bag on the passenger seat with him. "My parents instructed me to always carry my belongings with me."

But the family had never told him how to handle an accident; the couple, who could not drive, had thought that their son, given his obedience and caution, would never get into trouble. The only thing they'd taught him was to always roll up the windows to prevent robbery.

There was a large knife in the bag. Yao Jiaxin said he had bought it that morning for self-defense while driving on an unfamiliar road that night. His parents did not know about it. His mother said, "He never told us about the things he encountered out there."

The streetlights on the road were dim, and there were no cameras. In the headlights, he saw a woman lying on the ground, facing the direction of his car. Moaning in pain. According to the autopsy report, the collision had only injured her leg and left a bruise on her head. At the trial, Yao recalled having jumbled thoughts for two or three seconds about helping her or running away. And then he thought she was looking at his license plate number, trying to memorize it. He pulled out his knife. Zhang Miao reached out in pain to block the knife. He must have heard her screams or felt her resistance, but he stabbed her eight times indiscriminately until she stopped moving. Her thoracic aorta and superior vena cava were punctured, after which she hemorrhaged and died.

He drove away, leaving the bloody knife in the passenger seat, not daring to look at it. He said at the inquest that all he saw was darkness ahead and "for a moment, it was like all the streetlights had gone out."

• • •

Yao Jiaxin didn't tell his parents the truth until the third morning after the murder. He waited until after his father had gone out, then woke his mother up and said he was scared because he had run over a person with his car. He didn't mention the murder. He told her not to call his father. "I'm afraid of him, I'm afraid to see him."

But she called his father anyway. Mr. Yao took a taxi home and took his son straight to the police station. Yao Jiaxin had wanted to eat the last dumpling his mother had cooked for him, but his father refused to wait. He pulled him out of the house and said in a stern voice, "Go! Before it's too late!" During the dragging, Yao Jiaxin kept crying out, "Why don't I have love?"

Without asking what exactly had happened, his parents sent him to the police station to turn himself in. They believed it was just an accident because they were confident that their son would not dare lie to them. Mr. Yao left his son in front of the police station and let him go in by himself. Later, they learned the truth from the media. His mother said, "I watched the news and heard that he used a knife, a knife, ah . . ."

Her entire face was trembling with pain, and bruises appeared on her forehead. "I just want to ask him why he brought a knife. Why did he do that? You can call the police if you hit someone, the car is fully insured, ah, why do you need a knife?"

Every time she said the word *knife*, her voice trembled heavily.

Mr. Yao said he didn't regret turning his son over to the police—he only regretted not asking him why he had felt driven to murder. "This is my absolute regret, the regret of my life."

There was no answer during the interrogation either. Yao Jiaxin told the prosecutor that he looked at his hands every day and cried. "These used to be piano-playing hands, and now they're murderous hands."

The prosecutor asked him, "What kind of music do you like to play?"

He said, "'My Heart Will Go On,' the theme music from the *Titanic* movie." He said he was moved by the character Jack, who gave his life to save others.

The prosecutor asked, "If you wanted to save people, why did you do this?"

He said, "At that moment, something took over me."

The prosecutor did not ask what it was, and the conversation ended there.

After the episode aired, I received a text message: *I watched your episode about Yao.* It was from a boy named Song, who I'd interviewed seven years ago.

Song was sixteen years old back then. His parents had sent him to a psychiatrist because of Internet addiction. The boy weighed 180 kilograms, and he consoled himself by writing *I'm handsome* on the mirror with a pen and then splashing it with water. The psychiatrist said: "Why is he fat? Because he has to eat to suppress his anger." His anger came from the fact that his father never helped him. His father told me that he walked past his son as if he were just passing by a lifeless stool. "I just ignored him, hoping to see him in trouble as soon as possible to prove I was right to be suspicious of him."

Song said, "He never once encouraged me. I didn't even like the Internet that much. I was addicted to it just because I had no happiness in my life, no sense of belonging." Song took part in a psychotherapy event where each person read a line of poetry. The line he was handed was short: "This is love." But he couldn't open his mouth to say it. He said, "I don't know what love is."

Seven years after that interview, he had just returned from the Navy, had a girlfriend, and always talked to me about everything, like a brother to a sister. But this time he'd only written one sentence after watching the show, with no comment or emotion. I wrote back to him, *So what do you feel?*

He replied, *He's not a bad person.*

I was a little confused. *How do you know?* I covered his story for a long time and couldn't come to any conclusion.

Sister, Song wrote, *let me ask you, when you interviewed him, did you find out that he had ever hurt someone or an animal?*

No. *His mother said he loved animals and forbade her to teach the family dog a lesson. He also refused to eat fish if he saw them being killed. But we didn't use any of this information because I wasn't sure if it was true.*

Song didn't say whether he believed it himself. But he was resolute: *He would feel sorry for the animals because they wouldn't hurt him.*

I said, *Would a compassionate person kill someone?*

After a while, I received a text message from Song. *He was running from responsibility. Scared, immature, didn't know how to explain a mistake to his family, and didn't know how much of a burden he'd have to bear in the future because of it.*

His words reminded me of something Mr. Yao had said. I'd asked him why he thought his son had killed someone. He'd paused for a moment and then said, "Maybe he was afraid of burdening me."

I reviewed the full interview with Yao Jiaxin after he was arrested. When he'd told a reporter that his motive for murder was because of how "difficult" a rural woman might be, the words that followed were not aired. "I'm afraid she will pester my parents endlessly." In another interview, he repeated this statement. "I'm afraid she'll ask my parents for money, and I just wanted to end it myself."

But money was not enough to explain it all. I went back to Song: *Even if Yao Jiaxin was being selfish, his reaction was too extreme, don't you think?*

He paused again for a long time before writing one word—a correction: *Helpless.*

This simple word hit me over and over again, falling harder and harder each time. But it was like rain on a tarp just above me: as I stood underneath, I could feel the vibration, but it didn't touch me. All I could do was ask him, *What do you mean?*

He called me. "It was too cold for texting. Ask whatever you want."

"What do you think of the fact that he slaughtered someone who was already injured?"

"He didn't pull out a knife when he got out of the car, did he? He saw her looking at his license plate . . ."

"So what?"

"The action would appear to him to have bad intention behind it." He heard me try to interrupt him and said, "I know. Of course she's innocent. But you're asking me now what Yao would think, and I'm trying to tell you."

I closed my mouth. "Go on."

He didn't use inferential words like *maybe* or *perhaps*. He spoke directly: "He thought it would be a big deal for him if she remembered the license plate number, and his parents wouldn't spare him if they found out what he'd done."

I couldn't hold back: "How is having a car accident that big a deal?"

"Maybe it's not to you," he said. "But it was to him."

After the killing, when Yao Jiaxin was in jail awaiting trial, his only hope was the forgiveness of his victim's family, and the only people who could help him with this were his parents. But his letters to them went unanswered. Instead of going to the victim's family to communicate their feelings, Yao Jiaxin's parents left their home, avoided the media, and did not clear up rumors about the family's wealth or interference with justice. They pinned everything on the judicial decision. Which was what they had taught their son for years: avoid direct conflict, run away from trouble, and put up with humiliation. And so they left their son alone to suffer the consequences of his actions. With pain and anger, Mr. Yao once said, "His life is his, his crime is his, and I can't influence that."

On the phone with Song, I still wasn't convinced by his argument. "Maybe his sense of helplessness and fear was bigger than I can understand," I said. "But how dare he kill for it?"

Song walked in the chilly wind, panting as he spoke. "There's something I didn't tell you when you interviewed me back then. I once hacked my sister with a kitchen knife. If an adult hadn't stopped me, I don't know what would have happened."

"You?" I couldn't believe it. He had seemed so timid. The first time we met, he couldn't even look me in the eye. He said, "I had hate in my heart because adults were always telling me off, always saying my sister was good, always comparing the two of us, so I thought: I'm going to stab her."

"If the bullies were the adults, why didn't you hurt them instead of your sister?"

"Because I couldn't beat the older ones, but she was weaker than me."

"But she didn't hurt you."

"She snitched on me to our parents."

A sudden chill ran through my chest, and we both didn't speak for a moment. He continued, "Since then, adults have been kind to me—I got a chance to lash out in anger. But Yao Jiaxin didn't have that chance."

I hung up, and a few minutes later, I got another text from him. *I know what you're going to ask me. That was why I didn't text you back for a long time. I was writing: "If it was the same situation when I was younger, I would probably be like him." And then I deleted it again and again.*

I asked why. He said, *I really don't want to blame my dad anymore for what I went through or how I acted. I feel bad now. I see it's not easy to be an adult, not to mention that they all just don't know how to bring up a child. Yao Jiaxin was not as lucky as I am. He just didn't carry on through the years.*

On May 20, 2009, Yao Jiaxin appeared in court for his final hearing and requested an appeal. He cried and got on his knees, apologizing to the victim's family, asking for forgiveness—his last possibility to avoid the death penalty. But the victim's family refused to grant his request. One reason they gave was that his parents had never shown up for him, not even for this appeal. They believed this meant his own parents had contempt for the poor.

But at that time, Mr. Yao and his wife were hiding somewhere near the courthouse, avoiding public appearances, while trying to be as close to their son as possible. Mr. Yao said, "Before the trial ended, we heard firecrackers going off and my wife asked, 'Who's getting married?' And I knew it was over."

On June 7, 2011, Mr. and Mrs. Yao received notice to visit their son in prison. The Supreme People's Court had approved Yao Jiaxin's death penalty.

"When we got there, Yao Jiaxin was already sitting behind bars." Mr. Yao cried as he recalled the moment. "As soon as I walked in, he shouted, 'Daddy, I love you,' and repeated it several times. I said, 'I know, I love you too, don't you say that, I know, I love you too.' That was the first time in my life that I said I love you. He said, 'You live well with my mother, and I will go and be reincarnated first. In the future, when you go, be my children in the next life and I will take care of you.'"

The couple did not know when their son would die, but in their hearts they knew it was the last time they would see him.

Mr. Yao said, "I never believed that people have souls. I would really want people to have souls. I said, 'Give Daddy a dream.' He said, 'I'll give you a pleasant dream, nightmares don't count.' He usually spoke in a very thin voice, but when he said these words, his voice was very, very loud."

Yao Jiaxin told his parents not to blame anyone, that everything was his fault, that he was guilty and willing to atone for his sins. This statement suddenly raised questions in his father's mind. By the time of our interview, he still believed that someone had forced his son to say this. "His words were too mature for me to believe that they were his own thoughts. How could he be more mature than his father?"

In this state of mind, when he heard Yao Jiaxin say he wanted to donate his corneas after he died, he thought it was possible that someone else had authorized and requested it. He angrily said to his son, "I won't allow you to donate. Your parents gave you every part of your body. You brought it into this world intact and you will give it to us intact."

His son mentioned his wish several times, and each time Mr. Yao immediately rebuffed it.

Some people on the Internet had spread rumors that he was a high-ranking military official interfering with justice, calling him "Yao dog" and "Yao slag"—people called his home to scold him and blocked him at the entrance of his building. But he took out all his anger on his son. "You donate your organs, people will use them, and when something goes wrong, I'll be responsible, I've had enough! I hope you take all your sins with you and don't drag others down with you!"

At this point in the recollection, he suddenly stopped talking. I also froze. Yao Jiaxin was dead, and all the assumptions about his relationship with his family were just speculation, conjecture—but when I heard these words and saw his father's irritated expression, any doubt I'd had about it was pierced as if with a knife.

At his father's words, Yao Jiaxin had stopped pleading and said, "Okay, I'll do as you say." It was the last time he listened to his father, against his own will.

By now Mr. Yao was clenching his hands tightly and blinked hard to keep the tears from flowing. His eyes were red. "I was too paranoid. I should have granted his wish that he might want to see us again through the eyes of others. One should not be too impulsive. Impulsiveness is the devil."

When the Yaos returned home, they learned their son had already been executed. Mr. Yao rushed to claim his son's body to donate his corneas, but it had already been cremated. He was given only the ashes. "The greatest mercy is to give life a chance to redeem itself," he said. But all his opportunities were lost.

After the episode aired, the audience's reaction was like a boulder slowly sinking into deep water. There was no big noise or ripple, but a huge, silent vibration when it hit the bottom.

People's comments on my blog were very brief. One read, "He's a man, not a demon." Another read, "After watching it, my father and I both went to our rooms without saying a word."

The Yao family had aroused the suspicion and anger of countless people by hiding from the public eye. Everyone assumed Yao Jiaxin could only have come from a dysfunctional and perverted family. But from the reactions to his story, I knew there was now shock: he had come from a family we all knew. Their love, pain, and long struggle was familiar, though it had led to such an unexpected end.

On June 7, 2011, after seeing his son for the last time, Yao Qingwei was walking home and saw his son on television, walking to the execution chamber for lethal injection.

Speaking of that moment, he stared unblinkingly into the void behind me. "The last time I saw him, I said, 'Son, when you go, put on all the clothes we bought you, it'll be freezing over there.' He said, 'I know.' That day I also made some dumplings for him and brought some dragon fruit he loved. He was already gone by the time I got home. I wondered if he had eaten anything and if he had put on enough clothes."

Around six P.M. that day, he wrote on Weibo, "So helpless, please say something, even if it's just yelling at me. Any sound is comforting." The sobs clogged his chest and forced his body to shake. "This house is dark. There is no movement, no sound. Isn't a curse a sound? When one walks deep in the mountains and doesn't hear even a single bird call, one can get very scared."

He'd been silent for over eight months; only on that day did he reveal his genuine feelings. The next day he continued: "I have an unshirkable responsibility for what happened to Yao Jiaxin. I disciplined my child too harshly, so that he was afraid to face the consequences of his mistakes and did not know how to deal with them, which eventually led to this disaster."

He told me he had been pondering these words over and over again, but he was "afraid to take responsibility." Only after his son's death did he write it down publicly. When I asked him why he broke the long silence, he said, "Because I just want to say to all parents: talk to your children and don't hold back a few kind words. People should learn from death, because it is a lesson I paid for in blood."

There were repeated comments on my blog crying "Hypocrisy!"

"How dare you let a murderous maniac be portrayed as a piano player! How dare you let his parents talk!"

Before the execution, Gao Xiaosong, a famous musician, wrote: "Yao Jiaxin should be run over by a car if he gets out of jail alive, or chopped to death by a knife if he doesn't . . . How can a person love music if they don't respect life?" Tens of thousands of people retweeted his words.

A month later, he hit four cars and injured one person while driving drunk. I interviewed him when he was released from jail six months later.

"If someone asks you how a man who loves music can . . ."

He interrupted me: "I deserved it. I was too arrogant and lacked respect for life. Then I learned that a man known as the devil could be me."

One of my superiors stopped the interview from being aired, and asked me, "Why do you always want to put scum on TV?"

It made me think back to seven years earlier, when I had failed in my first interview with Song. I'd put a lot of effort into preparing, but he wouldn't talk. With a fake smile on my face, I'd nudged him. Two cameramen, having trouble with angles and lighting, were equally flustered.

Eventually, frustration pricked my heart like a needle. I sulked and said to Old Fan, "Since everyone is dissatisfied, let's not shoot anymore." I turned around and walked out the door.

Old Fan, the director, was nervous about what seemed like an imminent failure. When we got back to the hotel, she said, "It's not your words, it's your face."

"What's wrong with my face?"

She was put off by my tone. "You know, you're nice to others, but you're harsh to me . . ."

I never thought I would be perceived that way. I had always thought others saw me as vulnerable. My mother, a tough woman who scorned the weak and believed that cruel experiences could make a child stronger, sent me to first grade when I was four. For years I was the weakest person in the class, rarely attacking others or fighting back.

I thought Old Fan's complaints were unfair. I said, "You need to stop thinking of yourself as a victim every time."

Her tension turned to anger and she shouted, "I've had enough of you." She slammed the door and left.

When I calmed down, I sent her a text message. *If you can't win the argument, just hit me. Why put yourself out in the cold?* A few minutes later, I got a text saying, *I'm outside. Forgot my keys.* I opened the door to find her dripping wet, with strands of curly hair stuck to her face. I went into the bathroom, grabbed a towel to dry her hair, and said, "Okay, okay, I was wrong. Okay?"

She broke into tears and hugged me. I patted her back awkwardly.

When I was covering Song's case, I had written a note: *Authoritarianism means that a person is convinced that he himself is never wrong.* I didn't realize that I was the very personification of that definition. I thought I was a forgiving person, but forgiveness for me was just swallowing all the unpleasant feelings until they turned into a little fist in my heart that I would later use to hit the people closest to me.

I had never said "I was wrong" before I'd met Old Fan; now those words turned out to be the three most beautiful words in the world.

I asked her, "Why do you have to be so vulnerable? It's just work."

She said, "Because it matters to me. You matter to me."

No one had ever educated me in this way before.

We tried interviewing Song once more. Strangely enough, he wasn't angry with me for the previous ruined interview. He actually sympathized with my weaknesses and said, "If you had kept acting like a journalist instead of a human being, I wouldn't be saying anything to you."

When I asked how he had felt when his father apologized to him and took his hand in public during group therapy, he laughed. "Gosh, that's so fake, let me tell you."

"Do you feel anything special, like your father said?"

"No, not at all." He avoided eye contact.

"Are you telling me the truth, or do you not want to admit it?" I smiled.

"When I look you in the eye, I'm telling the truth. When I'm not looking, then I'm not." He laughed.

"Everyone lacks the courage to say what they feel sometimes," I said. "But at that moment, did you feel you forgave him a little?"

He looked me in the eye and said, "Maybe . . . a little."

The interview was over. When the camera clicked off, Song and I looked at each other and smiled. He said, "I conquered myself." I said, "Me too." He gave me a big hug and said, "Comrades in arms."

I felt a warmth I had never imagined. When the gentle, silky emotion penetrated my heart, that tightly clenched little fist, whose rusty joints creaked open and closed, open and closed, slowly but surely unclenched. As my colleague Kai Ling said: "To do journalism is to deal with the disease of the era. We are all its patients, and the interview is a mutual inquiry between patients."

When the interview at the Yao family's apartment was over, we packed up our gear and prepared to leave. Mr. Yao invited us to stay for dinner. We rarely ate at the homes of our interviewees, but that time we all stayed, so that he could put aside what was on his mind while he was busy. He pulled out stacked plastic stools for us to sit at the brown table, saying he would make a bowl of tomato noodles for each of us. While cooking on the stove, he muttered to himself, "Not good, I have cooked so little in the past two months, the noodles are all sticky."

The fridge was empty, so he fried a small bowl of spring onions for us as a dish. After being left on the balcony for a long time, they had already withered.

I said, "Let your wife come and eat too."

He said there was no need to call her, with the same wooden expression on his face as I'd seen on Zhang Miao's father's. His wife was lying on their son's bed inside the mosquito net, cuddling the big plush dog. It was dark when we left, and Mr. Yao sat at the table, frozen, eyes unblinking, face crumpled. He didn't turn the lights on. Music was still playing in the room, a Japanese song he didn't know the words to. It was "Dearest" by Ayumi Hamasaki.

"Ah, thinking back to the first day when we met
I was always at a loss
We took a long way around
And hurt each other so much
Ah, I only wish that before I fall into the eternal sleep
May your smile
Be with me forever."

Chen Meng (August 30, 1961–December 24, 2008).

Eleven
Chen Meng Never Dies
2007-2014

On July 16, 2007, Chen Meng called me in and said, "You are in real trouble now."

He had just come from a meeting in which the station manager called me a "constant troublemaker" and said, "We should get to the root of the problem this time."

I heard concern in Chen's voice, something he rarely showed. He was never caring or gentle toward me. He preferred to keep constant watch, so as to prevent me from wasting my life making mistakes. For years I had fought against him and ignored his admonitions. Now he said, "You're not someone I can teach with words. You won't turn around until you hit a wall."

He thought I had hit it.

The trouble was from a quote I'd gotten from Hao Jinsong, a Beijing lawyer who worked to ensure that the rule of law was upheld—no matter how minor the situation—through citizen lawsuits. "If you don't exercise your rights," he'd said, "they are just words written on paper."

I'd felt moved to quote him when I was doing an investigative report for *News Probe* on the government's construction of over-standard luxury office buildings. In the episode, which aired on June 22, I urged readers of my blog to document the buildings through photos. "The Chinese Constitution guarantees citizens the right to criticize, suggest, complain, sue, and prosecute state organs and staff, and people can exercise this right through the press, letters, and petitions. They are just words written on paper if you don't exercise them." Then, quoting Hao Jinsong, I encouraged them to exercise this right. "You are citizens, and now you can be journalists, too."

When I returned to Beijing from my work, I found that my challenge on the episode had made the news. In only a week, over fifteen hundred photos and tips had poured in, spotlighting government buildings across the country. As a result, many local governments were complaining to the propaganda department, as they were in charge of us.

Without a word of either comfort or criticism, Chen Meng asked me how I wanted to deal with the trouble I'd caused.

I said, "I don't care, I can leave."

"I was the one who brought you on board. I'm responsible for you." I could tell he wanted to offer his advice.

But it was just a job for me, so I interrupted him. "No need, I can always do something else, like what I did before I met you."

I didn't intend to hurt him, but he was silent. Later, after his death, it was the moment I regretted most.

The next afternoon, I was called into a big meeting with all the key leaders and colleagues of the news center. There would be a public reprimand before my fate was decided.

I didn't care at all. In my mind, I didn't think I had done anything wrong. I wouldn't be ashamed if they removed me from CCTV.

All the leaders at the meeting had to say something, one at a time. But all their criticisms avoided the core issue. They said, "You earn money here and don't do what you're told, you have no work ethic."

I thought, "Oh, we have different definitions of work ethic."

They said, "We're all the beneficiaries of stability, and society can't be chaotic."

I thought, "That's exactly why I did what I did, for a stable society."

Finally, they said, "How can a normal person be a journalist without a press pass?"

I almost laughed out loud.

At the end of the meeting, my producer, Zhang Jie, called my name: "Chai Jing, reflect on your mistakes."

I said, "I take full responsibility, and I apologize for dragging my producer down by writing this blog post without his permission. But for me, the vocation of a journalist is to express." Then I pulled out a piece of paper. "I will read out this blog entry that brought trouble, and I hope you will learn from it."

One passage in the entry said, "In July 1945, an intellectual, Mr. Huang Yanpei, asked Mao Zedong how to break the cyclical pattern of 'rise and fall and success and failure' of successive dynasties in Chinese history. Mao said, 'We have found a new way out, and that is democracy. Only by letting the people supervise the government will the government dare not slack off. Only if everyone stands up and takes responsibility will all political standards not easily change with the change of power.'"

There was only silence, and the meeting was over.

The next day, Zhang Jie and I sat in the office waiting for the results. The wait was much longer than we expected. At last, the boss called him into the office. We'd thought there were only two possibilities: either they would fire us immediately, or the trouble was somehow over.

Three hours later, Zhang sent me a text message: *The second one.*

We later learned the reason we were spared. Several people had taken CCTV to court that day because the network had tried to clean up many of the "illegal workers" who had been employed without formal contracts, and leadership had feared that firing us would add fuel to the fire. The boss even said a lot of heartfelt words to Zhang Jie to reassure him that the trouble was forgiven.

It reminded me again of something Hao Jinsong had said during one of his trials: "No matter what agency you are, standing in court, I am equal to you, and you must argue with me by legal means."

Afterward, Chen Meng asked me to have dinner with him. He didn't talk about my blog. He just asked, "What did you learn from your investigation of this topic?"

I spoke about the number of luxury government buildings and the waste of financial resources.

He interrupted me and shook his head. "You're drawing simple conclusions about a complex matter and arguing for the sake of arguing."

It shocked me that he wasn't taking my side. For years, he'd been steadily marginalized at the news center, until the only program under his management was *Social Record*. His superiors often criticized him for allowing risky programs to air. He'd been pushed so far from the inner circle of power that he couldn't even attend the meetings where my future was debated. And now he was defending them?

He said, "There are at least several dimensions to this subject—motives, design ideas, land, funding, the decision-making process, the relationship between the central and local governments . . . Do you have a coordinate system for looking at it? How many coordinates are there?"

Seeing the irritated look on my face, he pointed at me with a cigarette in his fingers. "Wow, you think that's easy? The responsibility of a journalist is to describe complexity. It's a lot harder than expressing simplicity."

I said, "At least I didn't express it incorrectly."

His brow furrowed. "That's exactly why you're wrong. Journalists don't express their personal opinions and ideas, but provide facts and information to their audience. Do you feel like a badass when you say something sharp? After those words are taken away, what's left?"

Watching me duck my head, he eased his tone. "Your themes have to be embedded in the structure of your entire episode, the overall narrative, until no one can pick any of it apart."

Before the dinner ended, he said, "CCTV is a public platform. Your job is to serve the public, not to express yourself."

After that, I stopped writing on my blog for a year. I never commented publicly on any news again; my job was to report complex facts without direct commentary in my own words, and it was Chen Meng who'd convinced me that this approach was the foundation of a journalist's principles. It gave me my sense of responsibility.

It was also the last lesson he taught me. On January 22, 2008, the news commentary department was abolished. The sign outside our department door, which had read "To be truthful, fair, balanced, and avant-garde," was removed. CCTV cut off the last program managed by Chen Meng. Two months later, he was diagnosed with terminal stomach cancer and died in December of the same year at the age of forty-seven.

I was with him in the hospital during his last moments. He couldn't speak. I held his hand for the first time; the heat stayed in my palm. My regret was that I had rashly said that I didn't care about the job he'd given me. It was more than a job. He had given his life to his work, and now he had left that work in my hands.

At the end of September 2009, I was transferred out of investigative journalism with no reason or documented notice. It surprised the head of the news center because he hadn't gotten any signs either. What's more, as a symbol of trust, CCTV had recently assigned me to cover special reports on the Beijing Olympics and the National People's Congress, even allowing me to restart my blog for the sake of the program's promotion on the web. Then my boss had gotten a verbal notice: Let her leave, immediately.

I didn't ask questions because I knew why.

Five months prior, I had interviewed a man named Wu Baoquan. He was in prison for posting information online accusing government officials in Ordos of forcing farmers off their land, paying them hardly anything for it, then making large profits by selling the land off to developers. In particular, he'd criticized the head of the local government, calling him "the king of hell." The police detained him for ten days. But he wasn't cowed. After being released from jail, he continued to post his criticism online, and even spoke to a journalist investigating the suspicious land deals. He was sentenced to one year in prison for "defamation." When he appealed, the result was an additional year in prison. When I met him, he had already served the first year.

I asked, "Why did you do this?" He was not a resident of the city, and the matter had nothing to do with his personal interests.

He said, "I once read an article about a man named Hao Jinsong. He said that if you don't exercise your rights, then they are just words written on paper. The article was called . . . called . . ."

"'I'm Just Tired of Giving In,'" I said.

He looked surprised. "That's right."

I was the one who'd written the article. Mr. Wu believed in these words and the result was that he sat before me in a blue-and-white-striped prison uniform. After his incarceration, his factory had closed down and he'd gotten divorced. The prison was more than a thousand kilometers away from his hometown, and only the local villagers visited him. An old man wearing a tattered blue hat and collecting garbage for a living gave him fifty yuan and said to me, "Let him out, I'll go to jail for him, I'm old anyway."

During the interview, Mr. Wu wanted to say something to his sixteen-year-old daughter. I agreed. He said, "Give me some time." He lowered his head for a moment. Jaw clenched, he looked up again and smiled for the camera. "Son . . ." He turned to me and explained, "I call my daughter 'son.'"

He went on: "Son, don't worry about your dad. Help your mom with her chores . . ." His lips quivered, but he maintained his smile. "Remember what Daddy told you. Daddy is not a bad man."

The warden reminded me it was time. I said, "Take care of yourself, there's a long road ahead."

His face twitched, but he kept his smile even then. "Okay."

A prison guard handcuffed him and took him away. Ten meters later, I heard piercing cries. The sound was like an explosion coming from his chest. With his hands cuffed, he couldn't wipe his tears. All he could do was turn his face to the sky and let out a wail of pain. He disappeared around the corner, but the cries still echoed in the empty hallway. I gripped the wooden chair tightly. I had conducted the interview under the supervision of local officials, and at that moment a female official turned to me. "This man is so cunning that I have to tell the mayor to take immediate action," she said.

After listening to this woman's report, the mayor, who was wearing a Longines watch, said to my face with an irritated look, "When he gets out, we'll find another charge to put him back in."

When I went back to Beijing on April 24, officials from Ordos were on the same plane with us. They flew first class. Ordos was the richest city in mainland China, thanks to its coal resources. In 2009, its economy exceeded the two-hundred-billion-yuan mark, and with such great wealth and political resources, they could easily stop the broadcast of this episode.

Our hope was to beat them to the punch. The soonest we could air was the next day—Saturday night—and all government departments were closed on Saturday. If we could work quickly, we had a chance.

Old Hao and I spent Friday night and all morning Saturday editing. At three P.M., the rough edits were done, and we waited for the composite review.

As we waited, Old Hao said, "Take a nap." I said I was not sleepy. She lay on the sofa and I stood in front of the window. The sky became dark; a sandstorm was coming. Outside was a cage-like dormitory building full of anti-theft bars. A pot of bright red flowers bloomed on the iron railing of the fourth-floor balcony. I took a dusty old book, put it under my arm like a cushion, and looked at it.

As soon as we entered Editor-in-Chief Yuan's office, he said, "It turns out you're a step behind them."

On Saturday afternoon, all state-controlled news organizations had received an urgent notice that no negative coverage of the judiciary would be allowed.

There was no longer any need to review the episode, but Yuan decided to take a look anyway. It was his way of reassuring us that there was still one audience in the world. The show had not yet added a dubbing track. Old Hao read out the script as the footage played. During the prison interview, I'd asked Mr. Wu, "Do you regret it?"

"I don't regret it," he said. "Because I tried, as a citizen."

"Do you still trust the law?"

"No," he said, "I believe in it."

A voice-over narration should have followed, but there was silence. I looked over at Old Hao, who was covering her face with the paper in her hands to hide her tears. The producer, Zhang Jie, and I were also crying. Yuan looked at the three of us and said to Zhang Jie, "After so many years of journalism, still so emotional, huh?" He turned back to the screen and said, "Let's keep watching."

The video got to where the farmers described what had happened when they tried to demonstrate against the expropriation of thirty-two kilometers of their land. More than a dozen people had been arrested just for the sit-in demonstration, and the petitioners who went to Beijing had been stopped at the station. That was when they had reached out for help, and one of them had asked his old friend Wu Baoquan to make the matter public.

I asked the police chief, "Why did you arrest people when there was no evidence that they had endangered public order?"

He said, "We knew it would happen, so we prevented it."

"But if you prevented it, then why did you still arrest people?"

He said, "For the sake of social stability."

"But isn't due process of law what ensures stability?"

He was silent.

Yuan said, "Stop."

He turned to me and said, "You should've pursued the other question: Did your action bring about social stability?"

After reviewing the film, I dragged my suitcase home. The dust storm had come. I walked hard against the wind, my suitcase stumbling on the potholed tiles, my head down and my mouth tightly shut. But the sand still hit my eyes and made its way between my teeth. The wind blew over parked bicycles, one pushing over another, sending them all crashing to the ground on both sides of the street with a loud noise. This was the first time I wanted to quit my job at CCTV. Enough was enough.

I went home and asked a few friends who worked for the local newspapers to follow up on the Wu Baoquan case. Then I went to bed. But I couldn't sleep that night, so I got up and wrote a post about Chen Meng on my reopened blog. It was the first time I'd mentioned him after his death.

"Chen Meng was not hostile to anyone, he just insisted on logic and exhausted all possibilities to pursue the truth. To him, the only great enemies were truth and falsehood. He once told me that true death is when people are alive but ignorant and senseless. As long as fear does not drive us to become the person we oppose, Chen does not die. As long as we respect and uphold the standards of the profession, Chen does not die. As long as we can say, 'No, it's not true,' when people are submitting to errors and lies, Chen will never die."

After venting all the feelings in my chest, I gave up on the idea of quitting. It wasn't time to leave yet; I hadn't exhausted all the possibilities.

I have been waiting for Wu Baoquan's case to be retried, as the president of Ordos Intermediate People's Court had promised me in an interview on April 22. I had asked him, "Is it a crime to 'defame the government' according to Chinese law?"

He said no.

"So what do you mean by 'defaming the government'?"

"I'm not sure, exactly, what it means."

He was not illiterate when it came to the law; he was a president of the Central Court. Yet he was not willing to defend his own verdict, and he was giving extremely absurd answers in front of all the government officials around us. There was only one explanation for this: it had been a verdict made under great pressure, and now only another pressure could make him reopen the case. He said to me, and to them, "Since reporters like you keep asking these questions in hot pursuit, we will have to re-examine the case."

I waited until September, but there was no news. So we sent our report to "Inside Reference," a channel of information to the highest levels of power. We expected that political pressure from the top would get the case going again.

And we were right. Several days later, the case was retried. On September 16, Wu was convicted yet again for the same crime, but his sentence was reduced by six months. At least he would be out soon, I thought. But Wu's lawyer received a letter from him containing his will. He was convinced it would be impossible for him to leave prison. He didn't say what he had gone through, he just wrote, "If I die in prison, please let my daughter know her father would never die by suicide."

There was one last hope for Wu—only the Supreme People's Court could turn the situation around. On September 17, I sent an official letter to the court: "The Chinese Constitution guarantees citizens the right to criticize, suggest, complain, accuse, and prosecute state organs and staff. In at least three cases in China this year, the police have arrested people for 'defaming the government,' and these people have received different verdicts. How do you respond to the public's call for the Supreme Court to adopt a more uniform standard of application of the law?" Whether or not any of my interviews on the matter would air, I wanted to let them know what the public expected, and attention from the highest level of the court would at least keep Wu safe.

Early in the morning on September 18, on our way to an interview at the Supreme People's Court, our car turned onto Chang'an Avenue. It was about to be temporarily closed for the National Day ceremony drills, and one section after another was fenced off behind us, leaving no one in front of the road, and no one behind it.

Old Hao and I were silent. We felt uneasy about what we were about to do. Our previous interviews in Ordos were just work, but everything we did now, after the reporting ban, would be considered personal. I didn't want her to get in trouble, so I took charge of all communications.

"Is it because you wrote the article that you feel you are responsible for him?" she asked me.

It was. But not only that: I had built my entire career on the same belief as Wu's. If I only expected others to practice it and pay the price of losing freedom and more while I continued to enjoy my work, then my own pursuits would be nonsense.

And in fact this turned out to be my last interview for *News Probe*. I was told to leave a few days later and could no longer take part in any investigative reporting. When I went home late that night, the elevator had stopped. I went to the stairwell and climbed up to the eighteenth floor. The walls were cold, reminding me of an interview I had done once on a snow-covered mountain. I remembered stomping my frozen feet in the dirty snow, and standing on tiptoe to pick a small orange from a tree—so sweet was the orange quenched by ice. My colleagues were cooking noodles on a farmer's stove, putting sausages and peppers in the steaming pot. They called me to eat and I shouted loudly, "Coming!" Then I took one last deep breath of the bitter wind and snow and said in my heart, *Damn, I fucking love this job. I will grow old here and die here with my people.*

Now it was time to leave.

In my diary that night, I wrote what Wu had said to me: "Do I regret it? No, I don't, because I tried."

A month later Wu was released ten days early from his sentence, without a reason. I was relieved to see him in the newspaper with a shaved beard and a childish smile.

CCTV placed me at *Face to Face*, a program known for interviewing officials in the studio. It had a clean reputation and hadn't gotten into trouble in years.

The first person I wanted to interview was Hao Jinsong. A few months back, when I'd called him for some legal advice, he'd been in a bad place and sounded depressed. I'd told him Wu Baoquan's story. "You are this man's role model."

Not long after, in October, he represented a famous case in Shanghai. Some undercover agents posing as hitchhiking passengers had lured a number of private car drivers into an ambush, throwing money at them so as to allow law enforcement officers of the Minhang District Traffic Team to fine the drivers over ten thousand yuan for "illegal operation" (only cab drivers could take paid services). One driver, who'd cut off his little finger with a knife because he was so deeply aggrieved, approached Hao Jinsong as a citizen's representative to sue the traffic team.

On November 19, 2009, Shanghai Minhang Court heard the case in public. The trial lasted only one hour. When Hao Jinsong argued that the defendant had designed a trap and took illegal means to punish citizens, which seriously hurt the plaintiff—and damaged the credibility of the government, the public order, and the morality of society—the head of the traffic team was red-faced, but didn't say a word. His lawyer did not put up any resistance either, only repeatedly saying that the penalty decision had been withdrawn. The court ruled that the Minhang traffic team had used improper means to get evidence in violation of the law.

"This is a benchmark win," Hao Jinsong said. The media surrounded him at the court's entrance. "It ends years of history in which no plaintiff in such cases in Shanghai has ever won, and we need it to build people's confidence in the law."

My interview with him aired three days later, as my first episode of *Face to Face*. Such a character was not the usual choice for this program, but my application was approved by Editor-in-Chief Yuan, who said, "No matter what kind of court you play on, keep playing, and keep your muscles from atrophying."

In the interview, I asked Hao Jinsong, "You said you don't even have a car, so why do you care about this case?"

He said, "If the law is being trampled on, and you don't speak up—if other people's rights are violated, and you don't speak up—one day, when you encounter injustice, no one will speak up for you."

Before the conversation ended, I asked, "Have you ever had a moment of frustration?"

He looked at me, paused for a moment, and said, "Yes. But the people who have faith in me give me the strength to keep going."

Over the next year, I interviewed many officials in the studio. In the traditional media model, officials simply act like authority figures in this setting, releasing information without being questioned or challenged. One viewer thought my move to the show meant that I had lost my critical stance and left a sarcastic comment to that effect on my blog: "Since you're no longer going out to do real reporting, what do we call you? A potted plant in a greenhouse?"

I replied, "If I'm a journalist, I'm everywhere—otherwise my title is irrelevant."

Seeking the truth was not just the mantra of *News Probe*; it is the guiding principle of journalism. A forty-five-minute one-on-one interview can also be an investigative piece, if the interviewer wants to seek the truth. And so, from the consequences of development relying on coal resources to the desertification caused by large-scale land acquisition, to the hidden danger caused by unreasonable urban planning and the harm of a single-GDP index system, I took Chen Meng's advice and created a coordinate system on which to plot the dimensions of the Ordos story through interviews with different officials.

In 2010, when I interviewed Chen Xiwen, the director of the Central Agricultural Office, I asked, "What if the local government forcibly expropriates farmers' land through the police?"

He said, "The consequence of forcible land expropriation would be the accumulation of social conflicts."

"Yet the government says the farmers are willing to accept this as long as they get compensation."

He was a little annoyed. "The farmers are willing? Would you dare to tell them how much their land sold for when it went to developers?"

He told me that, nationwide, farmers got only 5 percent of all the proceeds from land sales; the rest went to the local government. The root of this problem was a phrase in the 1982 constitutional amendment: "Nationalize urban land." It allowed the government to expropriate farmers' land for construction at planned-economy prices and then sell it at market-economy rates. Which meant that the issue we were discussing went well beyond exposing a single case of farmers being shortchanged; the law needed to be reformed.

After the interview aired, Chen Xiwen sent me a text message saying the same thing that Wu Baoquan had said to me: *There's not much one can do, but we have to give people hope for tomorrow.*

Of course, not everyone I interviewed was like him. The bureaucracy of any country is complex, run by all kinds of people—one force destroying, another building—and my profession required me to present this complexity.

A friend of mine once told me that he was at a bar when one of my interviews came on TV—it was an interview I'd done with an official who had a bad reputation, and the people my friend was with had mocked me for talking to such a person. My friend defended me, saying that I was in a difficult situation, and I was only doing this to survive. I said I did it because the information provided by that person was relevant to the public, and they had the right to know and question what the official had to say.

He said, "Then you're a f—"

He held back the hard word and laughed. "Are you really naïve enough to think you are equal to those in power?"

I laughed too. "Many things can only come true when someone believes in them."

On the afternoon of the sandstorm, while I'd been waiting for Wu Baoquan's film to be reviewed, the old book I had propped under my arm was written by the Chinese scholar Hu Shi in the 1940s. It was open to a page that read, "A member of the media in an era of substantial change should be fair and sincere, honest and responsible, for they hold significant power in their hands."

What impressed me most about Wu Baoquan was that he was neither angry nor self-pitying after being released from prison. He said that if he had the chance to do it all over again, he would've posted more evidence and procedural issues, rather than emotional rhetoric. At first I thought the government had pressured him to say that, but then he explained that in getting to read so much more in prison, he had learned how to better use the language of the law to defend his rights. He said, "In the unprecedented new age of the Internet, I hope the government will also learn their lessons and learn how to govern an increasingly strong civil society—a rational and sound society that needs to be built by both sides."

Anger is just the pain of incompetence. A persecuted innocent person who can still keep improving himself and appeal to the other side to reach a consensus is truly powerful, truly free.

At the end of 2010, the Information Office of the State Council organized a training for twenty spokespersons. I was invited to facilitate. At the beginning of the training, I asked the officials to talk about their views on the media. One of them was tough, talking about why he tended to block media coverage of him: "They won't say anything good about me whether I'm open to them or not." The others nodded.

When the training started, I turned the podium into the site of an imaginary press conference. "Suppose a rare snowstorm causes many railroads, roads, and airlines in the country to be disrupted," I said. "Many passengers are stranded and there is even a food shortage. You are now the spokesperson of the National Development and Reform Commission. How would you host this conference?"

Each person took turns on stage, and the other nineteen people played reporters. Whenever someone got stuck on stage, a challenger would come up to replace him. Anyone who had the courage to go back on stage would get the most applause. The atmosphere in this small classroom, full of childish games, became more and more active. When the training ended, I praised the tough officer for playing the best reporter. I asked him about his experience being the one asking the questions. "Did you feel hostility toward the people on stage?"

He froze, then said, "No, I just wanted to play my role well."

This press conference had actually happened in January 2008, after a snowstorm that affected over seventy million people. But all the questions that had been asked were written and reviewed in advance. Later, when I interviewed an official from the NDRC and asked him about the management loopholes in disaster relief, the official took a long breath and said, "Finally, someone is asking me about this."

I told these spokespeople the story. "When you shut out the media," I concluded, "the result is that everyone believes the rumors and no one will come to you to ask the questions you want to answer."

I ended the session with one last story. In Ordos, when I asked a police officer why he didn't verify the information cited by a citizen objecting to the legal aspects of the land-acquisition process, he was a little puzzled. "How can the government be wrong?"

Then I said to all the spokespersons, "You think the media is biased. Yes, maybe some in the media are biased, as in every country. But the best way to fight bias is to let ideas compete with ideas. Let reason beget reason. It's also for your own good, because when you're in power, the people around you might say in good faith, How can you be wrong? They will keep saying that until one day you might make an irreparable mistake."

So far, twelve officials in Ordos have been jailed for corruption, including the police chief I interviewed and the mayor who wore the Longines watch.

In February 2011, I left *Face to Face* and the news center altogether.

The boss of the news center wasn't surprised that I quit and didn't even ask why. He knew I was leaving not to go off and do what I wanted to do, but because I knew what I didn't want to do. He just asked, "What are you going to do after you stop covering the news?"

I said, "I'm going to tell the story of ordinary people." This was what Chen Meng had done in 1993.

I went to Li Lun, the former producer of *Social Record*, the program that had run for a long time under Chen Meng's direction. I asked to join his show, a documentary program in a poorly rated slot on another CCTV channel. Li was surprised and asked me why I would leave mainstream news for a program on the sidelines that didn't even have a reporter appearing on camera.

I said, "Because I watched the episode that aired last month."

The story was about a man who was in the countryside helping 124 miners with silicosis. When he returned to the hotel, he lay on his bed under the dim light and talked to the reporter about it in a way I'd rarely seen on television. He opened right up. The reporter must have spent a lot of time with him in that poor, remote place, eating together, living together, freezing together, to gain trust. And behind that footage was a team—the filmmakers, the editors, the reviewers—who shared common values on how to understand people and how to present them. I didn't care about the size of the platform, or showing my face or not; I wanted to work on a team like that.

In August 2011, we started *Seeing* together, interviewing people like Yao Jiaxin's parents—people who are no longer in the news or who have not yet been noticed. At the beginning of the show, I would say, "There are endless events that happen every day—we only know them. Now we see, we feel."

The next two years were a struggle, but we had never expected it to be an easy road. Searching for the truth about human nature was a principle that Chen Meng had instilled in me eighteen years ago, and while it was simple, it was also difficult, because focusing on individual human beings was considered bourgeois and had been rejected by Chinese society for a long time. History may repeat itself, but what we could do was hold fast to it until the inevitable end comes. I always remembered a quote from the record left by Chen Meng after his death: "When you have to get an inch, then you get an inch. But when you find an opportunity to push in, then you have to push in. Be completely clear and awake to your end goal, and completely clear and awake to the ideas that lead to that end goal. When you know exactly where your target is, you can miss it when the situation calls for it, as a tactical maneuver. But you can never lose focus on it. That's called deviating."

"Don't deviate," he said.

In 2014, the end came. I resigned from CCTV, the place where I had worked for fourteen years, and for which I had nothing but gratitude. On the first day we met in 2000, Chen Meng had asked me, "If you did news with us, what would you care about?"

I had said, "I care about the people I report on in the news."

These words had taken me on a long journey. What Chen offered me back then was not just a job, but a way to live, to throw myself into this thorny world, to open my eyes from ignorance and obscurity, to experience the principles of journalism with flesh and blood until I was intertwined with people's destinies like water in water. When the moment of departure came, it was so calm that only an old saying came to my mind: When the fruit is ripe, it falls.

Li Lun asked me about my plans. I said I wanted to cover the air pollution issue.

"On which platform?"

I was open to anything—in 2014, there were 670 million Internet users in China. That's where the news was, I thought, where the people were.

"Will you be able to broadcast it?" Li Lun asked.

"I don't know."

"Where does the money come from?"

"From me."

Twenty years ago, when I was a young radio host, a listener wrote to me and said, "One day, the public will be your best employer." They made it happen by buying this book, *Seeing*, when it came out in China. The royalties I earned gave me the freedom to cover the subject of air pollution without time constraints, platform constraints, or subject-selection constraints.

But Li Lun was still confused. "You've left CCTV, why would you continue to cover the news?"

I said, "Because it's not just news."

Air pollution in China was at its worst level in fifty-three years, with massive, prolonged periods of pollution causing schools to close and flights to be grounded in many places. What I saw in Shanxi eight years ago was happening in Beijing. I often had to keep my newborn daughter at home for an entire week. She would press her little hands against the glass window to see the outside world, only to find a dark world with no color. If this continued, she would grow up like Wang Huiqin, without seeing the stars, the moon, or the white clouds. This was not news, this was our life. I couldn't do anything else until I fought for her future.

I handed back all my papers, including my press pass. I was no longer a journalist, but I was still a citizen.

After resigning, I went to the park near CCTV for the last time. As usual, I climbed a hill and sat on a wooden bench, looking up at the sky behind the branches of the trees, immersed in the endless chatter of birds and insects.

It was a rare nice day, as it had just rained heavily. Clouds rolled in, and in the distance were cobalt-green mountains. Not far ahead of me was a lake formed by a spring that had been gushing for centuries, and the wind blew from above the lake, carrying the fresh smell of earth and grass.

I sat for a long time until I heard the sound of water under the dense vegetation. The spring broke through the ground under pressure after the rain. Water flows without purpose; it just has to flow. When it is in tiny quantities, it drips from the top of the hill—when it is huge, it strikes the rocks and rebounds into the sky. When it meets mountains and valleys, it becomes rivers and lakes. With its tense energy, no matter what obstacles it finds or where it ends up, it flows, and it is always flowing.

About the Author

PHOTO BY ZHAO JIA

Born in 1976, Chai Jing is an award-winning reporter and television host in China. While working at CCTV from 2001 to 2014, she gained recognition covering the SARS epidemic in 2003. Her reporting on domestic violence in China contributed to the enactment of groundbreaking anti–domestic violence legislation in 2005. In the same year, Chai released "In the Name of Life," an interview with members of China's LGBTQ+ population that marked the first open appearance of queer people on CCTV. In 2007, she won the National Green People Award for her coverage of pollution in her hometown. *Seeing* has sold more than five million copies worldwide since its Chinese publication in 2012. In 2015, Chai Jing was named one of *TIME* magazine's 100 most influential people, and one of the top 100 global thinkers by *Foreign Policy.*

About the Translators

Yan Yan graduated from Columbia University in 2008 with degrees in English and religious studies. After working at the Alibaba Group in Hangzhou, China, his hometown, he backpacked around the world and eventually settled down in Brooklyn, then the Hudson Valley. As a freelance translator, he translated works by Hans Christian Andersen Award–winner Cao Wenxuan, including the Dingding and Dangdang series, *XiMi*, and *Mountain Goats Don't Eat Heaven's Grass*, as well as updated editions of *The Grass House* and *Bronze and Sunflower*, for China Children's Press & Publication Group. More recently, he has been translating works with the Chinese literary icon Wang Xiaobo, which include a novella collection titled *Golden Age* and an essay collection titled *The Pleasure of Thinking*.

Jack Hargreaves is a translator from East Yorkshire who is currently based in London. His literary work has appeared on *Words Without Borders, LitHub, adda, Arts of the Working Class, Samovar, The Southern Review*, and elsewhere. Published full-length works include *Winter Pasture* by Li Juan (with Yan Yan) as well as Shen Dacheng's short story "Novelist in the Attic" and Wen Zhen's "Date at the Art Gallery" for Comma Press' *The Book of Shanghai and The Book of Beijing*, respectively. He was ALTA's 2021 Emerging Translator Mentee for Literature from Singapore, volunteers as a member of the Paper Republic management team, and is currently on a three-year virtual residency for young artists in Nanjing, in association with the city's UNESCO City of Literature program.